Race

Against

Time

A REPORTER REOPENS
THE UNSOLVED MURDER CASES OF
THE CIVIL RIGHTS ERA

JERRY MITCHELL

SIMON & SCHUSTER

NEW YORK   LONDON   TORONTO   SYDNEY   NEW DELHI

Simon & Schuster
1230 Avenue of the Americas
New York, NY 10020

First Simon & Schuster hardcover edition February 2020

SIMON & SCHUSTER and colophon are
registered trademarks of Simon & Schuster, Inc.

For information about special discounts for bulk purchases,
please contact Simon & Schuster Special Sales
at 1-866-506-1949 or business@simonandschuster.com.

The Simon & Schuster Speakers Bureau can bring authors to your live event. For
more information or to book an event contact the Simon & Schuster Speakers
Bureau at 1-866-248-3049 or visit our website at www.simonspeakers.com.

Interior design by Ruth Lee-Mui

Manufactured in the United States of America

1   3   5   7   9   10   8   6   4   2

Library of Congress Cataloging-in-Publication Data is available.

ISBN 978-1-4516-4513-2
ISBN 978-1-4516-4515-6 (ebook)

To the One who loves justice

Contents

PART I

JAMES CHANEY

ANDREW GOODMAN

MICHAEL SCHWERNER

1

The Ford station wagon topped a hill before disappearing into the darkness. Mickey Schwerner drove, deep in thought. Fellow New Yorker Andy Goodman propped his body against the passenger door, drifting off to sleep. Mississippi native James Chaney, the lone African-American, swallowed hard, shifting in the backseat.

Two cars and a pickup truck raced to catch up. Schwerner spotted them in his rearview mirror. "Uh-oh."

The noise woke Goodman. "What is it? What do they want?"

Schwerner rolled down the window and stuck out his arm, motioning for the car to pass. "Is it a cop?"

Goodman gazed back. "I can't see."

The car crunched into the wagon, and Schwerner wondered aloud if their pursuers were playing a joke.

"They ain't playin'," Chaney said. "You better believe it."

Metal and glass smashed again. "What are we going to do?" Goodman asked.

Schwerner told his fellow civil rights workers to hold on. He jerked the wagon off the blacktop onto a dirt road, sending up a swirl of dust. His pursuers weren't shaken. Instead, they flipped on police lights and began to close the distance again.

Schwerner spotted the crimson glow in his rearview mirror and cursed. "It *is* a cop."

Goodman advised, "Better stop."

"Okay, sit tight, you guys. Don't say anything. Let me talk."

Schwerner turned to Chaney. "We'll be all right. Just relax."

The wagon squeaked to a stop. Doors opened and slammed shut, interrupting a chorus of frogs.

Flashlights bathed them in light. A Klansman with a crew cut told Schwerner, "Y'all think you can drive any speed you want around here?"

"You had us scared to death, man," Schwerner replied.

"Don't you call me 'man,' Jew-boy."

"No, sir, what should I call you?"

"Don't call me nothing, nigger-lovin' Jew-boy. You just listen."

"Yes, sir."

The crew cut moved closer to the driver and sniffed. "Hell, you're even startin' to smell like a nigger, Jew-boy."

Schwerner reassured Goodman, "We'll be all right."

"Sure you will, nigger lover."

"He seen your face," a fellow Klansman advised. "That ain't good. You don't want him seein' your face."

"Oh," the crew cut replied, "it don't make no difference no more."

He pressed his pistol against Schwerner's temple and pulled the trigger. Blood spattered against Goodman. "Oh, shit, we're into it now, boys," one Klansman said.

Three shots echoed in the night air.

"You only left me a nigger, but at least I shot me a nigger," another Klansman said with a chuckle, joining a choir of laughter.

Everything went dark. White letters spelled out on a black screen: "Mississippi, 1964."

I was one of several dozen people watching the film *Mississippi Burning* tonight, squeezed inside a theater where coarse blue fabric covered metal chairs. Nothing distinguished this movie house from thousands of other multiplexes across America. Except, of course, that this was not just any place.

This was Mississippi—a place where some of the nation's poorest people live on some of the world's richest soil, a place with the nation's highest illiteracy rate and some of the world's greatest writers. Decades earlier, Mississippi had bragged in tourist brochures about being "The Hospitality State." What it failed to mention was it led the nation in the lynchings of African-Americans between the Civil War and the civil rights movement.

Through newspaper photographs and television news, Americans had witnessed the brutality in Mississippi for themselves. In spring 1963, they saw police dogs attack civil rights workers in Greenwood. Months later, they observed the trail of blood left by NAACP leader Medgar Evers when he was assassinated in the driveway of his Jackson home. During the summer of 1964, Americans watched sailors tromp through swamps in search of the three missing civil rights workers, Chaney, Goodman, and Schwerner, who were last seen leaving the small town of Philadelphia, Mississippi.

For forty-four days, the drama unfolded before the nation. Mississippi's US senator Jim Eastland told President Lyndon B. Johnson that he believed the missing trio were part of a "publicity stunt," and Mississippi governor Paul Johnson Jr. suggested they "could be in Cuba." Days before the FBI unearthed their bodies on August 4, 1964, the governor spoke at the Neshoba County Fair, just two miles from that grisly discovery. He told the cheering crowd there were hundreds of people missing in Harlem, and "somebody ought to find them."

The killings came to define what the world thought of Mississippi, and no subsequent events had dislodged it by the time I came here in 1986 as the lowliest of reporters for the Pulitzer Prize–winning newspaper *The Clarion-Ledger*. I arrived the day before my twenty-seventh birthday, the same day the paper carried a story about the burial of Senator Eastland, the longtime chairman of the Senate Judiciary Committee who had bragged about having extra pockets sewn into his jacket to kill all those civil rights bills.

The days of Jim Crow had long passed when I drove into this capital city of nearly 200,000 with my wife and our baby daughter. Jackson was bursting with New South pride and Old South prejudice, but doing its best to conceal the latter. I had been here three years now, from 1986 to 1989, and put thousands of miles on my Honda hatchback in that time, trying to find my feet as a reporter while trying to understand this beautiful and haunted state. When I first heard Mississippians refer to "the War," I thought they were talking about Vietnam—only to discover they meant their great-grandfathers' Civil War, which their descendants, it seemed, had never stopped fighting.

At my desk, I had read the January 9, 1989, issue of *Time* magazine, which featured the *Mississippi Burning* movie on the cover. Jackson had been abuzz about the film since last spring, when some residents complained about "Hollywood liberals" invading their town. Disdain turned to curiosity when word spread that actor Gene Hackman had been spotted at Hal and Mal's, a popular pub and eatery. Lunch crowds doubled.

I was curious, too, about this movie and how it would impact Mississippi. I had volunteered to cover its state premiere at a January 10 press screening. At *The Clarion-Ledger*, the statewide medium-sized newspaper, I felt like little more than a rookie. And tonight's assignment seemed like a welcome break from the court beat, where I faced the daily battle of getting scooped by my more talented rival at the *Jackson Daily News*, Beverly Pettigrew Kraft. I could hardly count it as a victory that she wasn't in attendance. This was, after all, a minor story.

But I hadn't counted on the attendance of the man sitting next to me at the screening. After the opening scene, his voice startled me, deep and resonant. "That's not accurate," he said, gesturing up at the title card. He leaned over and explained that it was Chaney, not Schwerner, who was the driver that night.

As the night wore on, I learned just how much he knew. His voice blended with the images on-screen. After a young African-American witnessed KKK violence, FBI agents in the film concealed his identity with a cardboard box, driving him around Neshoba County to look for his attackers. The man next to me leaned my way and said, "That really happened."

When the house lights came on, I asked what he thought of the movie.

"It's fiction, all right," the white-haired man replied, explaining that the movie had fictionalized how the FBI had solved the case.

I jotted down his words on a legal pad I was carrying, and I began to chat with the man, who had firsthand knowledge of the case. Roy K. Moore was the retired special agent in charge of the FBI in Mississippi, which investigated the June 21, 1964, killings we had just seen reenacted on-screen. I was grateful he had come, allowing me to tie Hollywood to the real history in tomorrow's newspaper.

Moore turned to speak to the two men behind us. They included Jim Ingram, a six-foot-four Oklahoma native who had been involved in the investigation and headed the FBI's civil rights desk in Mississippi, and veteran journalist Bill Minor, who had covered the killings and invited the pair here.

While the rest of the press left, I lingered and listened to these old men, wondering why my history teachers had failed to mention these events in class. I peppered the men with questions about the case. They told me that more than twenty Klansmen had taken these three young men out to a dark, remote road and executed them. They said locals knew these suspects, yet no one turned them in. The perpetrators kept working and walking the streets as if they had been caught speeding, rather than carrying out a triple murder.

"No one was ever prosecuted for murder?" I asked.

"Nobody," Moore replied.

I had heard of people getting away with murder before, but I had never heard of twenty people getting away with murder at the same time—no less, in a case that made headlines around the globe. They had shot to death these three young men, and the state of Mississippi had done nothing about it. How was that possible?

Even now, the former investigators seemed at a loss to explain it.

Mississippi Burning became one of the nation's most controversial films. Critic Roger Ebert called it "the best film of 1988," saying it makes "an important statement about a time and a condition that should not be forgotten." But veterans of the civil rights movement bashed the movie for turning agents from J. Edgar Hoover's FBI into heroes while portraying activists as cowards.

The bickering blazed hotter in Mississippi than anywhere else. Crowds flocked to the film, some to be entertained and some to be outraged. Mississippi governor Ray Mabus, who had Hollywood good looks to go with his Harvard University education, appeared on the *Today* show and spoke to the National Press Club. "The message I don't want people thinking is, 'That's Mississippi today.' The message I do want them coming out with is how far Mississippi has come. I know that there are things in our past that everybody would like to change—in all of our pasts—but we can't affect that. What we can affect is the future."

As I wrapped up my story on the film premiere, I sought a comment from Mabus's office, telephoning his press secretary, Kevin Vandenbroek. He echoed the party line about the film: "A mixed blessing. If there's a silver lining, it gives Mississippi a chance to say, 'That was then' and, 'This is what's going on now.'"

But there was something else he wanted to say. He asked to go off the record, and I agreed. An award-winning radio and TV reporter before taking his current job, Vandenbroek couldn't resist sharing a little advice. "Have you ever thought about the case, the real murders being revisited?"

"No," I said.

"You know it's not too late. Bill Baxley, the attorney general over in Alabama, prosecuted some Klan cases back in the seventies. Went after those bastards that blew up those four girls in the Birmingham church."

"I didn't know that. How can you—?"

"I thought you were a court reporter."

"I am."

"Aren't you forgetting something?"

"What's that?"

"There is no statute of limitations for murder."

2

The next day, I telephoned Roy K. Moore, the retired FBI agent. I told him I was interested in writing a follow-up story that separated fact from fiction in the movie. He welcomed me to stop by his lakefront house for an interview.

On the drive over, I ticked through my questions for him, and I realized they all boiled down to the same central concern: "How could these Klansmen get away with murder?"

Moore had fought the KKK throughout the civil rights movement. When we sat down and began talking, I could see that my own question was one that he had been asking himself for many years.

The simple fact of it, he explained, was that white men could kill African-Americans with impunity back then. The law enforcement officials in Mississippi were not only sympathetic to the KKK; the FBI discovered that many belonged to the Klan themselves. And in the few instances where killers actually went on trial, they faced juries made up of nothing but white men. Moore explained that the juries were all white because the names of all potential jurors came from voting rolls, and Mississippi had long done its best to bar African-Americans from voting through its 1890 constitution. The juries were all male because state law barred women from serving on juries until 1968. The rigging of the system stunned me.

Despite the swarms of FBI agents investigating the case, Moore told me that nearly every member of the murderous mob kept his mouth shut. One killer, James Jordan, eventually talked, and in time the Mississippi Burning case came together, giving Moore all the evidence he thought was necessary. He explained to me that at this point, "we did meet with the governor. We told him we had enough evidence to prosecute." If the state wanted to send the murderers to trial, there was enough substance to see it through. But the governor told Moore that the state "couldn't," essentially refusing to uphold its own murder laws.

"He asked us to prosecute instead," Moore said. But that meant bringing the Klansmen in on federal charges, the only jurisdiction FBI agents could have in the case. Moore explained there is no federal charge for murder, so the best the agents could do was to pursue lesser charges, such as civil rights violations, even though this meant much lower penalties.

In 1967, three years after the murders, eighteen Klansmen went on trial in US District Court in Meridian, Mississippi. The federal jury convicted seven of the killers on charges of depriving Chaney, Schwerner, and Goodman of their civil rights. Yet those convicted spent only a few years behind bars before their release, soon joining the eleven other Klansmen who walked free.

That outcome still weighed on Moore. He had closed dozens of major cases, but the "Philadelphia case," as he called it with his flat voice, was still an open sore.

I asked if he knew where the suspects were today. The retired FBI agent told me he believed that Jordan ended up in Florida, and, as far as he knew, the ringleader of the murders still ran a pinball business in Laurel, Mississippi. I had stopped in that small town several times and wondered if I might have stood behind him in line at a convenience store, waiting to pay for gas.

If I wanted to know more details, he said, I should read a book by Don Whitehead on the case, *Attack on Terror: The FBI Versus the White Knights of the Ku Klux Klan in Mississippi.* He handed me his own faded black copy and held my gaze.

"Those guys got away with murder," he said. "It's not too late."

Back home that night, I opened up *Attack on Terror* and found a history I never knew. The Mississippi Burning murders were the crest of a massive wave of Klan activity, one that began after the 1954 US Supreme Court ruling that ordered the desegregation of public schools. In response to the ruling, Mississippi's leaders had formed the white Citizens' Council to fight desegregation by legal means, gathering a team of the best lawyers and judges, while numerous KKK organizations formed at the local level, to fight back extralegally. White Citizens' Councils and Klan chapters would spread throughout the nation in the 1950s and '60s, but nowhere were they more concentrated than in the South. In Mississippi, a chapter of the Klan called the Original Knights of the KKK, headquartered in Louisiana, recruited the first wave of new Klan members. But still, desegregation marched on.

By the 1960s, I learned, white Southerners were growing more desperate. Thousands joined the Invisible Empire, believing that the Klan could better halt integration than the white Citizens' Councils. This pattern stretched all the way back to the Klan's founding, in the aftermath of the Civil War. Whenever the legal framework undergirding white supremacy was shaken, racist rhetoric rose up, and white mobs turned to lynchings and other violence.

Throughout Mississippi, the KKK flexed its political strength. One Mississippi politician recalled of the era: "If you were in politics and associated with the Ku Klux Klan, you would be stout. If you were in business and associated with the Klan, you would be successful."

Yet the civil rights movement kept achieving victories—as James Meredith became the first known black student at Ole Miss in 1962, as millions marched on Washington in 1963—and the swell of anger and extremism in Mississippi kept growing. A man named Samuel Holloway Bowers Jr. was poised to sharpen that anger to a deadly point. By the early

1960s, he had soured on the Original Knights of the KKK, disappointed at their passiveness. He came to believe his state needed its own homegrown Klan chapter.

In the wake of Meredith's admission to Ole Miss, Bowers founded his own branch of the KKK—Mississippi's White Knights of the Ku Klux Klan—with action in mind. I learned from Don Whitehead's book that the White Knights were perhaps unparalleled in their brutality. Soon after its founding, the chapter would be labeled by the FBI as the nation's most violent white supremacist group. Through beatings, bombings, and killings, Samuel Bowers's lieutenants vowed to do all they could to halt desegregation and voting rights for African-Americans.

At the same time that Bowers's White Knights began to spread across the state in early 1964, news came that civil rights workers from the North planned to "invade" Mississippi during the coming summer. The state's battle over civil rights had gone national.

In response, state lawmakers passed new laws to crack down on activists and doubled the number of state troopers in preparation for the summer. Meanwhile, the White Knights expanded dramatically, claiming members in every one of Mississippi's eighty-two counties. Bowers rallied his Klansmen as Freedom Summer loomed. "When the first waves of blacks hit our streets this summer, we must avoid open daylight conflict with them," he told them. "We must absolutely avoid the appearance of a mob going into the streets to fight the blacks."

But he urged his men to get their guns ready. "When the black waves hit our communities, we must remain calm and think in terms of our individual enemies rather than our mass enemy. We must roll with the mass punch which they will deliver in the streets during the day, and we must counterattack the individual leaders at night," he said. "Any personal attacks on the enemy should be carefully planned to include only the leaders and prime white collaborators of the enemy forces."

The Mississippi Burning murders, I now saw, were the result of a months-long battle plan. From the start, the White Knights intended to carry out these killings come summer. The murders were meant to send a message not just to African-Americans and civil rights activists throughout the state but to the nation at large. Bowers meant to tell all of America who held power in Mississippi, who called the shots, who could do as they pleased, and who needed to live in fear.

And it wasn't just the violence that was meant to send a message. The murderers' impunity was just as important, as demonstrative as the killings themselves. With impunity came a reign of terror.

Civil rights leaders understood what the Klan was saying. When two years had passed with no convictions, in 1966, Martin Luther King Jr. marched into the town of Philadelphia and gave a speech addressing the injustice. "I believe in my heart that the murderers are somewhere around me at this moment," he announced, meaning to strike fear and conscience into the hearts of the killers. But the White Knights weren't shaken. Deputy Cecil Price was standing just feet away from King at the time, and he shot back: "You're damn right. They're right behind you."

Deputy Price was a member of the White Knights. He had been a part of the murdering mob that night. And he wanted King to know it. King held his composure in the moment, but he later called the town of Philadelphia "the worst I've ever seen. There is a complete reign of terror here."

As I reviewed the Mississippi Burning case and its aftermath decades later, I found myself wondering what was different now. I thought about the comments by Governor Mabus and his office on *Mississippi Burning*. He wanted the people to see that "That was then. This is Mississippi now." But was he right? The message that Bowers had wanted to send—*We're in power here. Look what we can get away with*—had come across loud and clear in 1964. King had heard it hauntingly two years later. And, decades beyond, the killers were still walking free.

As long as they did, the White Knights' message still resounded over the streets of Philadelphia, over Mississippi, and over the nation.

3

Days after the final credits rolled in *Mississippi Burning*, the film continued to play in my mind. Again and again: the Klansmen fired, the blood spattered, and anger would swell in my soul.

Martin Luther King Jr. had talked about the arc of the moral universe bending toward justice, but I wondered what he would say after a quarter century. Was there still time for the arc to swing around?

I decided to find out.

From my years of covering courts, I knew that any murder prosecution would have to go through the local district attorney, Ken Turner. He was young, smart, and overworked—handling every prosecution, from shoplifting to murder, for four counties in east Mississippi.

I telephoned his office, and a secretary patched me through to the prosecutor. He sounded harried when he answered. When I brought up the Mississippi Burning case, he sounded even more anxious to end the call.

"Have you ever thought about prosecuting the case?" I asked.

He batted away my question like a deft politician. "I'm interested in prosecuting any murder case," he said. "I would have to have enough facts. We can't prosecute on emotion."

It was clear enough that he had little desire to pursue this case, but his words were enough to pique my curiosity and keep me moving. What facts from the case still remained?

Roy K. Moore had told me that the evidence from the 1967 federal trial in Meridian, Mississippi, should still exist in the court's files. But upon reaching out to the court clerk, I learned that the trial exhibits were all gone. Even the burned-out station wagon the trio had been driving had been destroyed.

This was a serious roadblock, before I had even gotten rolling. But the case had already gotten ahold of me. There was an immense amount to read and learn, so many details that had been brushed aside or forgotten over the years. I was already spending fifty hours a week or more covering courts, but now I started adding to my time at the office. Back home, my wife, Karen, was not thrilled. Our daughter, Katherine, was three years old, and we were talking about having our second child. Ideally, I'd be trying to find ways to spend more time with my family rather than adding to my hours at *The Clarion-Ledger*. But Karen also understood where my growing obsession was coming from. She and I had fallen in love while working at our college newspaper, and she knew the electric feeling of discovering a story that needs to be told.

In hindsight, it's also clear to me that I dove so deeply into the case so quickly because my future at the paper was looking increasingly uncertain. I had been losing scoops to my rival, and our newspapers—*The Clarion-Ledger* and *Jackson Daily News*—would soon be merging. The editors had hinted they might take me off the court beat, which I knew meant I could no longer pursue the Chaney, Goodman, and Schwerner killings. If I was going to go out, I might as well go out swinging.

My first lead on the case came a few weeks later, when fellow reporter Joe O'Keefe came by my desk with an intriguing tip he had received. He talked to me about a defunct organization called the Mississippi State Sovereignty Commission, which worked with and even helped fund the white Citizens' Councils, trying to combat desegregation in the state. Between 1956 and 1973, the commission had collected spy files on more than 10,000 people and 250 groups it deemed "subversive, militant or revolutionary." The governor himself had headed the agency, amassing more than 132,000 pages of secret records. But no one could see these files, even now, because the Mississippi Legislature had sealed them for fifty years.

The magnitude of it caught my attention: *132,000 pages, and fifty years? Why would lawmakers seal them for so long—unless they were hiding something?*

Back in 1977, the American Civil Liberties Union of Mississippi had filed a lawsuit to open these sealed records, and the state of Mississippi had been fighting ever since to keep them closed. O'Keefe said he had been told that state officials had just made it possible for us to get a glimpse into this gold mine. They had accidentally filed some of these secret records in an open court file. He knew I covered courts, and he asked if I would get the documents so that we could work together on the story.

"Sure," I replied. I needed every scoop I could get, and if the sealed documents were so extensive, there was a chance they might contain something about the Mississippi Burning case. I grabbed my briefcase and walked across the street to the federal courthouse.

Inside the federal clerk's office, wooden drawers held case numbers on index cards. I thumbed through the cards until I found the case that Joe had mentioned, J77-0047(B), *American Civil Liberties Union of Mississippi v. Governor Ray Mabus.* The (B) meant the case was being heard by US district judge William H. Barbour Jr., whose office was just a few doors down the hall. I asked a clerk for the file, and she returned with a file that was almost a foot thick.

Standing at the counter, I began to flip through the file. I saw the latest request by Mississippi officials, arguing to keep the files sealed until 2027. Attached to the motion, just as Joe had said, were pages of the secret records.

"This Report is Confidential," the first page advised, before detailing a shocking scheme. In early 1964, the year of the Mississippi Burning killings, a Sovereignty Commission spy named "Agent Y" had infiltrated the Jackson headquarters for the Council of Federated Organizations (COFO), an umbrella organization for several civil rights groups. COFO included the National Association for the Advancement of Colored People (NAACP), the Congress of Racial Equality (CORE), the Student Non-violent Coordinating Committee (SNCC), and the Southern Christian Leadership Conference (SCLC), headed by Martin Luther King Jr.

In spring 1964, all these groups were preparing for Freedom Summer, when college students from across the United States would arrive in Mississippi to aid with education and voter registration. Agent Y joined the civil rights activists. He sang with them. He protested with them. And on May 13, 1964, he stole from them—taking about one hundred Freedom Summer applications listing names of workers, along with their hometowns and schools. He swiped pictures so that the commission would know their faces, and he made sure that the records were only missing for a few hours. After midnight, Agent Y replaced the stolen files "in their proper place in the office. No suspicion was apparent."

I felt a chill as I read the names of all the incoming Freedom Summer workers, most of them college students heading to Mississippi for the first time. And I noticed how close this date was to the murders the following month. I had read that Mickey Schwerner and his wife, Rita, had visited the COFO headquarters often while preparing for Freedom Summer. I wondered if Agent Y had run into them.

I imagined someone at the commission labeling spy files with their names and slipping their photographs inside along with a copy of a general report. This report depicted civil rights workers as desperate and starving communists who survived on candy bars, Popsicles, and cigarettes. I knew that Mississippi officials hated the civil rights movement, but this was something else. Now I had proof they broke the law.

I tucked the four-page spy report underneath my arm and hurried down the hall to a small room with a Xerox machine. After removing the staple from the document, I fed the papers into the behemoth.

Just then, an older man, dressed in a gray suit and red tie, poked his head in the door. I froze. The files in my hand were supposed to be secret for fifty years. The judge on the case could jail for contempt of court anyone who shared them. The Xerox machine roared as it began to spit out copies.

"Do you know where the marshal's office is?" the man asked.

My throat tightened. I did my best to swallow, pointing east, trying to speak in a normal voice. "It's at the end of the hall."

He closed the door, and I leaned against the copier, trying to catch my breath. When his steps receded in the distance, I slipped the copies into my briefcase and returned the originals to the file. Then I bolted down the four flights of stairs, feeling I had my first scoop in months.

The pages of the leaked Sovereignty Commission records told the story of a state breaking the law to preserve its way of life. More than that, the records provided a tantalizing lead, hinting at a rich vein of information yet to be uncovered. O'Keefe and I began calling the names on the documents as well as names of those we knew who had been involved in the civil rights movement. He interviewed former Mississippi state senator Henry Kirksey, who said the use of spies might explain how segregationists appeared at marches well in advance of them.

I telephoned a civil rights activist named Ken Lawrence, who had helped bring the ACLU lawsuit. After arriving in Mississippi in 1971, the Chicago native had become a target of surveillance by both the commission and the FBI because of his involvement in the far-left Southern Conference Educational Fund. He chastised Mississippi officials for continuing to keep the spy records closed. "They're trying to protect the politicians who were responsible, most of whom are still alive."

He continued to rail against the Sovereignty Commission, and he urged me to take a deeper look. When I pressed him for details about all the things the spy agency had done, he balked at sharing more information. "Trust me," he said. "It was the absolute worst in the country." That, however, was all I could get out of him.

At about the same time, *The Clarion-Ledger* began working on a project to run in connection with the twenty-fifth anniversary of the Mississippi Burning killings. Much of the package focused on hot spots during the civil rights movement and how much those towns had changed in the quarter century since.

The editors left me out of the project—the day-in, day-out court beat was still my main responsibility—but I kept digging into the case anyway. I used breaks at the court to read books on the case, and one day I walked down Pearl Street to talk about it with Al Binder, one of the state's most prominent lawyers.

Binder cut such an impressive figure as the southern gentleman lawyer that Jason Robards had portrayed him in a TV movie a few years back. But he hadn't always been so august. A onetime segregationist who spoke for the Mississippi Sovereignty Commission, he changed his ways after a wrenching conversation with Martin Luther King Jr. In the mid-1960s, Binder had turned around and helped other Jewish leaders battle the KKK.

He was pleased to hear I was investigating the Mississippi Burning case. "Those sons of bitches got away with murder, Jerry."

I told him about the destroyed evidence, about the prosecutor's seeming indifference, about how I was struggling to find out where to start. He leaned forward, his soft Mississippi Delta accent seeping through his voice.

"Why, every trial has a transcript," he said.

I nodded, not quite following.

"All that sworn testimony from back then could be used in any new trial."

He explained that under Mississippi court rules, as long as cross-examination took place, sworn testimony was admissible. If those who testified are still available, they could be called as live witnesses, but if they were dead or unavailable, their testimony could be read into the record—as if they were still alive.

I marveled at this. It had never dawned on me that the testimony from the 1967 federal trial could become evidence in a new trial.

As soon as I arrived back in the office, I dialed US district court clerk Sue Thompson in Meridian to try to get my hands on the transcript. Instead, I hit another roadblock. A US attorney I knew had already checked out the transcript, their only copy. When I called him up, he wouldn't share it with me or tell me why he wanted it. "I checked it out on behalf of another party," was all he would say.

• • •

I felt frustrated. The secrets were piling up, and the answers were nowhere to be found. The district attorney had been of no help. The evidence was long gone. The 1967 trial testimony seemed like a way to budge Mississippi authorities, but it was out of my grasp as well. Then there were the thousands and thousands of sealed Sovereignty Commission records. What was in those files?

I knew Lawrence knew, but so far, he wasn't saying. I telephoned him anyway.

When I pressed him about sharing the sealed documents, he said he had signed an agreement with Judge Barbour and could be found in contempt of court if he revealed any of the contents. "I regard the state law sealing these files as unconstitutional, but I don't want to go to jail. And that's what Judge Barbour will do if I tell you what's inside these files."

"But don't you think everybody should know what the commission did?"

"Listen, I want these files opened more than you do. Don't you understand? I want everyone to know every despicable thing that this commission did. I want the people responsible to be punished."

"Responsible for what?"

Lawrence chuckled. "Nice try, Jerry."

"I understand you can't give me specific details, but it seems to me you can at least give me some indication of what's in there, some hint of what's contained in the files. You can at least do that."

"What do *you* think is contained in the files?"

"I don't know."

"Take a guess."

"The state committed more theft?"

"No, no, worse than that."

"I don't know."

"C'mon, what's the worst crime imaginable?"

"Murder."

Silence followed, the most deafening I have heard.

Moments later, he spoke. "Now do you understand?"

4

The wall inside Mississippi attorney general Mike Moore's office bore the photographs of many children and the framed "lucky tie" he had worn during his 1987 campaign. The former district attorney from the Gulf Coast reminded me of a southern Bobby Kennedy, making a career out of championing issues for children and others who were vulnerable. Even the way he held his jacket reminded me of a Kennedy, crooking his right index finger to clasp it over his shoulder.

I came here because I knew two retired FBI agents had visited his office recently. They told me he had asked them about the viability of the Mississippi Burning case.

With that new information, the gears clicked into place. He must be the one who borrowed the 1967 federal trial transcript in the Mississippi Burning case.

When Moore strolled into his office, he was smiling. "Jerry Mitchell!"

He seemed happy to see me and was a man who warmed to the sight of most publicity. But Mike Moore shivered a little when I mentioned the Mississippi Burning case. I told him I knew about him talking to the two retired agents about the case. I told him, too, that I knew he had the trial transcript.

This was a bit of a bluff. I didn't know that for a fact, but it made total sense that he had the transcript, given his conversation with the agents. As attorney general, he had the power to pursue these killings.

He exhaled. "Jerry, I don't mind telling you that we're looking at this case right now, but I really don't want you to spread it around. We're trying to quietly check around."

My heart skipped a beat when I realized what he was saying. He was confirming my suspicions. And if the attorney general was investigating the Mississippi Burning case, that was a big story. It was also a story that could spark the momentum I was hoping for.

He seemed eager to go off the record, but I was afraid to let him. "Mike, I'm going to do a story on you having the transcript. Whatever you want to say about it beyond that is up to you."

He clammed up, and within a few minutes I was back on the sidewalk. The more I reflected on his reticence to go public with his investigation, the more it made sense. Over in Alabama, the attorney general had won a KKK cold-case conviction back in the 1970s, but he paid the price when he ran for governor, getting clobbered by a candidate who made barbells. The same case that could bring Moore national attention could doom him politically in Mississippi.

Although the attorney general refused to share his copy of the transcript, former Neshoba County Sheriff Lawrence Rainey made the task easier. After the release of *Mississippi Burning*, Rainey—one of the original suspects in the murders—sued the filmmakers for defamation. He filed an $8 million lawsuit against Orion Pictures. But instead of seeking a settlement, the lawyer for the studio set out to prove Rainey's guilt, collecting copies of thousands of Mississippi Highway Patrol records, FBI documents, and the 2,802-page transcript.

Reporter Leesha Cooper obtained a copy of the transcript and shared it with me. I began poring through the pages. The testimony of several witnesses made up the backbone of the prosecution's case. There was the testimony of police officer Wallace Miller, who turned against the KKK, and Klansman James Jordan, who was part of the killing party. Both were dead.

Then I read the testimony of Delmar Dennis, an FBI informant within the Klan who testified that Klansmen in spring 1964 voted to "eliminate" Mickey Schwerner. The defense in the 1967 trial did its best to cast Dennis as a despicable traitor, questioning him about the $15,000 he received from the FBI over three years for his time, travel, and other expenses.

"You are paid for information?" the defense lawyer asked him during cross-examination.

"I have been paid for the information, yes, sir."

"Information that you are now testifying about."

"Yes, sir, same information."

"And instead of thirty pieces of silver, you get fifteen thousand dollars?"

US district judge Harold Cox interrupted. "Counsel, if we have any [more] quips like that, I'm going to let you sit down."

As a result of his testimony, Dennis had his home shot into.

Soon after, he moved from Mississippi to California. But no one seemed to know where he was these days. Directory assistance in Los Angeles and San Diego yielded no listings, nor did the Mississippi cities I checked.

Roy K. Moore had no clue, but one of his old colleagues shared the name of retired agent John Proctor. When I reached Proctor, he rolled the informant's name off his tongue like a former classmate's. "Delmar Dennis . . . He was working for the John Birch Society for a while. Last I knew he was living up in Knoxville."

Perfect. Now I was getting somewhere.

I dialed directory assistance. "We do not have a listing for a Delmar Dennis in Knoxville, sir," the operator said.

I sighed.

"But there is a Delmar Dennis listed in Pigeon Forge."

"I'll take it."

5

The only photograph I could find of Delmar Dennis showed him with slicked-down blond hair and piercing eyes. He wore a dark suit with a cross pin on his lapel, holding a Bible in his right hand and a Klan hood in his left.

When I reached him by telephone, I heard a nasal monotone dominating his Mississippi drawl. He said he grew up in a small community known as Pea Ridge, not far from Meridian, where many of the Klansmen involved in killing Chaney, Goodman, and Schwerner lived. He was devout from a young age, and when he delivered his first sermon at age fourteen, a black friend named Andy came to listen—only to be turned away by the all-white church. To make sure no other unwanted visitors appeared, a deacon sat in back with an oak club. Dennis would come to believe in segregation as strongly as the church leaders, joining the white Citizens' Council and then the KKK.

When the subject of the Klan came up, Dennis began talking about the White Knights. He explained there had been a klavern—the KKK's word for a group chapter—in each of Mississippi's eighty-two counties. I told him I had read there were 5,000 members then, and he said I was way off. He found an old flier for the White Knights, which put total membership at 91,000. The number stunned me. That was bigger than every city in Mississippi, except Jackson.

"And that doesn't count the sympathizers," he said.

"How powerful were the White Knights?"

"Very powerful. They considered themselves a national organization."

He talked of Klansmen staying in a Mississippi congressman's office when they traveled to testify before the House Un-American Activities Committee in 1965 and 1966. On top of that, he said the White Knights had secret members.

"Secret members?"

"Members nobody else knew about. They were sworn in to the Klan secretly."

"Who were they?"

He said they were businessmen, politicians, lawyers, and others. Only Imperial Wizard Samuel Holloway Bowers Jr., the head of the White Knights, knew their names.

Dennis told me that he first joined the White Knights in early 1964 and served as a chaplain, collecting fines from Klansmen who cursed. He chuckled. "Nobody paid." By fall 1964, he began cooperating with the FBI, becoming a valuable informant inside the White Knights.

I asked him what led the White Knights to kill Chaney, Goodman, and Schwerner. Dennis said several Klansmen were upset in spring 1964 because Schwerner was helping register black voters in Meridian. The KKK already had a derisive nickname for him—"Goatee." His facial hair symbolized everything they hated.

During a meeting, Dennis said Klansmen grumbled to call for a vote on Schwerner's killing, but the leader of the meeting, Edgar Ray Killen, silenced them. "That's already been taken care of," he said. "The approval has been given by the state."

Dennis explained, "Approval by the state meant Imperial Wizard Sam Bowers had already authorized Schwerner's 'elimination.'"

I'd seen a photo of Bowers dressed dapperly in a dark suit accented by a white handkerchief in his left breast pocket, flashing a knowing smile that seemed to say that no jury would ever convict him. His friends described him as a peaceful man who taught Sunday school each week. And yet he was the same man that the book *Attack on Terror* described as ordering fellow Klansmen to target incoming civil rights workers. If Klansmen caught these enemies outside the law, he told them, "you have a right to kill them."

Dennis said the White Knights had four kinds of projects. "A Project 1 was harassment—throwing tacks in someone's driveway or something like that. A Project 2 was a cross burning. A Project 3 was a beating or house burning. A Project 4 meant a killing. A klavern could authorize a 1 or 2, but any Project 3 or 4 had to be approved by Sam Bowers."

In a June 16, 1964, meeting, Dennis said two klaverns—one from nearby Philadelphia and the other from Meridian, less than an hour down the road—gathered at an abandoned gym of the old Bloomo School. Killen was presiding over the gathering of more than seventy-five Klansmen when former sheriff Ethel "Hop" Barnett interrupted, describing guards at the Mount Zion Methodist Church in a nearby African-American community. He said there must be civil rights workers there.

Dennis stayed while Klansmen dashed out. They clutched their guns, piled into vehicles, and peeled down the asphalt road. When they arrived at Mount Zion, two groups of Klansmen blocked the exits, keeping about a dozen church members from leaving and asking about the civil rights workers.

When the churchgoers said they didn't know where the workers were, the Klansmen didn't believe them. They snatched an elderly man named Bud Cole from his car and asked him where the guards protecting the civil rights workers were. When Cole said they didn't have any guards, that this was a church meeting, a Klansman retorted, "You're a damn liar."

Klansmen kicked and beat Cole until he lay unconscious. A man in a police uniform ordered Cole's wife, Beatrice, to walk down the dirt road while the beating went on. She asked if she could pray. A Klansman with a club said, "It's too late to pray."

She fell to her knees and began to pray anyway.

Then one of the Klansmen yelled out, "Leave him living."

The beating stopped. She rushed to her husband, cradling his bloody head in her lap, while Klansmen set the church on fire.

Dennis asked me, "You know why they burned the church, don't you?"

"No."

"To lure the civil rights workers there."

Now I could see how the pieces fit together. From Dennis and other interviews, FBI documents, and books, I came to understand what happened that June when the civil rights workers drove to Neshoba County:

On June 21, 1964, Mickey Schwerner stepped across the ashes of what had been the Mount Zion Methodist Church. He spotted charred hymnals, broken blocks of concrete, and remnants of a tin roof, seemingly twisted by hate. It was the first day of summer, and sweat beaded on his brow.

A few weeks before, the twenty-four-year-old CORE leader from New York City had called his parents, telling them of the immense opposition to registering African-Americans to vote in Mississippi. The fatigue had been getting to him, working as many as twenty hours a day.

What encouraged him was how much enthusiasm and progress he'd already seen. Weeks earlier at this Neshoba County church, members had met with him and fellow civil rights workers James Chaney and Dave Dennis. The congregation had agreed to let them set up a Freedom School, aimed at improving the education of African-American teens and children. Now Mount Zion had burned down, and Schwerner knew it was no coincidence.

Wearing a blue baseball cap, faded Wrangler jeans, and Wellington style boots, Chaney and his fellow civil rights workers had come here to investigate. While attending Cornell University, Schwerner had brought about the integration of his Alpha Epsilon Pi fraternity. He and his new wife, Rita, protested the building trades in New York City refusing to integrate, and the couple had moved to Mississippi to dive deeper into the movement. They met Chaney, and he and Schwerner became fast friends.

Today Chaney was having trouble catching his breath. His asthma had been acting up—the same asthma that had kept him from joining the army. He wore a white T-shirt and green trousers with torn pockets. He walked in the brown leather shoes he wore like slip-ons. His straw hat bore buttons from the civil rights movement. They were his mementos, proof his life counted for something larger.

While he was still in high school in Meridian, he had become interested in the civil rights movement, and it had cost him. At age sixteen, the principal suspended him after he refused to remove his NAACP insignia. He wore the dismissal as a badge of honor. He had recently quit his job working for his father as a plasterer's apprentice, and he had poured himself into Freedom Summer, so busy he had been unable to visit his newborn daughter yet.

Chaney and Schwerner examined the rubble with a college student named Andy Goodman, who had volunteered for Freedom Summer. Like Schwerner, he hailed from New York City. A handsome Queens College student with wavy dark hair, Goodman had grown up in a ten-bedroom apartment on the Upper West Side, which served as a haven for progressive politicians and causes. His family welcomed comic actor Zero Mostel and others caught in the crossfire of the nation's red-baiting days. Leonard Bernstein sometimes played piano, a cigarette dangling from his lips.

Goodman dabbled in theater and off-Broadway acting before majoring in anthropology, writing papers that compared the rise of African-American radicals to "the rise in temperature that follows upon sickness." In 1963, he watched his best friend, Ralph Engleman, join civil rights protests, and a year later, he heard Mississippi NAACP president Aaron Henry discuss both the plight of African-Americans and the disturbing silence of good people. Goodman told his parents he wanted to join the front lines of the civil rights movement in Mississippi. They worried he might be hurt, and his mother, Carolyn, packed bandages and iodine, but they gave him their blessing.

After surveying the wreckage at Mount Zion, the three civil rights workers hopped back in their 1963 blue Ford Fairlane Ranch Wagon with its distinctive white top. They drove to interview church members, and after saying their good-byes, they headed back to Philadelphia.

Along the way, Deputy Cecil Price pulled Chaney over for speeding and held Goodman and Schwerner in connection with the church burning investigation. He put all three of them in the local jail—only to release them at 10:30 p.m. into the hands of waiting Klansmen.

James Chaney cranked the station wagon and headed for Highway 19, the way back to Meridian. Deputy Price tailed the three men for a few blocks and disappeared. Lights from the small town gave way to darkness as the trio drove between the pine trees lining the road. They welcomed the sight of open road. Less than thirty-seven miles and they would be home.

Then Chaney spotted headlights behind him, gaining fast. He hit the gas, and the vehicles behind him raced to catch up. Soon all of them were barreling down the two-lane road.

Perhaps Chaney believed the speeding cars would soon catch him. Perhaps he believed they were sitting ducks if night riders began firing.

Whatever the reason, he took a chance. He took a hard right onto Mississippi Highway 492, possibly turning off his headlights as he had done before to slip into Neshoba County at night.

His gamble complete, he headed west on the highway, only to check his rearview mirror and see the awful truth. The cars remained in hot pursuit, and soon red lights were flashing.

If he talked about hightailing it, Mickey Schwerner would have dissuaded him. Their training had taught them to pull over for law enforcement.

The station wagon came to a halt before crossing the bridge. Deputy Cecil Price, the very man who had pulled over the blue Ford earlier that day, exited his patrol car. He walked over to the wagon and ordered the three men into his car. They followed his orders, while another Klansman commandeered the station wagon. Price and his fellow Klansmen drove to a remote road called Rock Cut.

There, one by one, Klansmen killed the three men. They loaded the bodies into the back of the station wagon and drove to a new site, burying Chaney, Schwerner, and Goodman fifteen feet down in an earthen dam.

• • •

The killing of the three civil rights workers sickened Delmar Dennis. He quit the KKK right after that—only to have an FBI agent convince him to return to the shadowy group, this time as an informant. To his surprise, he rose in the ranks of leadership upon his return, becoming a province titan and a confidant of Imperial Wizard Sam Bowers.

FBI records showed agents visited Bowers after the men's disappearance and asked if he knew anything about what had happened to the three civil rights workers. Bowers reassured agents he knew nothing, and they left.

In Bowers's meetings with Klansmen, Dennis said the leader bragged that all the perpetrators would go free. "He told us we'll have money and lawyers."

When word came on December 4, 1964, that agents had arrested twenty-one Klansmen on federal charges, attorneys urged them to stay silent. While awaiting their conversations with agents, Sheriff Lawrence Rainey famously chuckled, stuffing another round of Red Man tobacco in his cheek. Other Klansmen joined him in laughter. A photograph capturing the moment came to symbolize the nation's belief that these men regarded their criminal charges as a joke, and that nothing would happen to them.

That perception held up six days later when the US commissioner in Meridian, Esther Carter, dismissed all the charges. This let the Klansmen walk free for the next month, until a federal grand jury indicted nineteen for conspiring to deprive Chaney, Schwerner, and Goodman of their civil rights. But Carter's action set the tone for how the case would be handled by those in power within Mississippi. US district judge Harold Cox soon followed her lead by dismissing the federal conspiracy charges, except for those against Sheriff Lawrence Rainey and Deputy Cecil Price. The judge concluded these charges had to involve "color of the law" and, therefore, could apply only to law enforcement officials.

The White Knights oozed confidence. Some in the KKK joked that Cox, an ornery segregationist judge, would order FBI agents to rebury the bodies of the three civil rights workers back in the dam.

But their luck began to run out in 1966 when the US Supreme Court concluded the initial indictments were proper. The next year, eighteen went on trial, and Dennis testified against them. The jury convicted Bowers, Deputy Price, Wayne Roberts, and four others. Jurors acquitted Sheriff Rainey and seven others. The jury couldn't agree on Killen and two others.

Bowers went to prison for the most time—a mere six years. Most served half or less of that.

Shortly after the trial, Dennis said the White Knights tried to kill him. He had exposed the wrongdoing of Klansmen and yet all those he had testified against were free and back home now. He was the one run out of town.

One Mississippi newspaper headline blared that he got paid $15,000 for testifying, he recalled. "That looks so bad. People think, 'That SOB got rich.' People said I had a big sack full of money. They said I'd sell out friends for $15,000."

As Dennis wrapped up his account, I told him I was thinking about tracking down all the Klansmen charged in the Mississippi Burning case. "Most of 'em are getting pretty old these days," I said. "Either that, or they're dead. I assume I don't have anything to worry about since the Klan hasn't been active in years."

Dennis jumped in and spoke before I had even finished my thought. "I think you have a lot to worry about."

6

I shared the details I learned from Dennis with my managing editor, Bennie Ivory. When I told him about Mike Moore's interest, he asked me to write a story about it for *The Clarion-Ledger*'s upcoming project on Mississippi a quarter century since the killings of Chaney, Goodman, and Schwerner. I also mentioned the idea of tracking down the suspects, and Ivory asked me to get right on it. Within days, I was off to Philadelphia, Mississippi, to see who would speak to me.

I found former deputy Cecil Price spending his days at a trucking company run by Olen Burrage, who owned the property where Chaney, Goodman, and Chaney had been buried. Less than forty miles south, the once-blustering Sheriff Lawrence Rainey worked as a security guard in Meridian for a black boss. Across town, Wayne Roberts operated a bar known as "The Other Place," where patrons brought in their own booze in paper sacks. None of them would talk with me.

Jimmie Snowden, who had been a part of the killing party, had spent three years in prison. I located his number in the Meridian telephone directory.

I dialed and when he answered I spoke. "I'm Jerry Mitchell from *The Clarion-Ledger*. I was wondering if I could talk with you."

"The hell you say. You got any money?"

"No."

"Then why in the hell do you think I'd talk with you?"

A dial tone buzzed in my ear.

Murder. Wasn't that the curdling hint that Ken Lawrence dropped about the sealed documents?

Since that day, I had been contacting anyone who might know more about the Mississippi Sovereignty Commission. Some of them were civil rights activists who had been able to view the spy agency's records. But they had stood before a federal judge and took an oath. If they revealed any contents, the judge could put them behind bars for as long as he desired. When I pressed one more activist for what he had read in the spy records, he barked, "I suppose you want me to go to jail, Mitchell."

Tired of the runaround, I walked into my kitchen that night, grabbed the cordless telephone, and dialed Lawrence's number. "You told me before that the files show the commission was involved with murder. What do you mean by that?"

"I can't really say but trust me. The proof is in the files."

"It has something to do with the Mississippi Burning case, doesn't it?"

Silence again. A welcome silence.

"Was the commission involved in the murders?"

He remained silent and finally told me that he would explain—but only if I wouldn't quote him.

"Fine."

"All right, I'm convinced the files show that the state of Mississippi had something to do with the killing of Mickey Schwerner."

The state? I pressed the phone to my ear, listening through the rising static. "How's that?"

Lawrence replied with the words I had longed to hear. "I'll just read them to you."

I grabbed a blank envelope I saw on the kitchen counter and began taking notes.

"All right, this document is dated March 24, 1964, and it's addressed to Betty Jane Long of the House of Representatives. 'Enclosed is copy of a report from our investigative staff on subject you mentioned to me when I appeared before the House Committee. This subject had not previously appeared in our files, and we appreciate your calling him to our attention.'"

Lawrence explained that this letter from Erle Johnston, the director of the Sovereignty Commission, came just a day after the commission filed a report on March 23, 1964. "That report shows they were following Mickey and Rita Schwerner around in Meridian. It gives personal descriptions and their phone numbers."

I scribbled down every detail he shared.

"The documents make clear that Meridian police and the Lauderdale County Sheriff's Department cooperated with the commission in conducting this surveillance."

The commission's connection with the Meridian police was hardly surprising. From what I had been told, half of those in the police department belonged to the KKK.

"There's one other thing you should know."

"What's that?"

"The white Citizens' Council circulated the license plate of the station wagon that the three civil rights workers were driving in."

"You're kidding."

"Want me to explain?"

"You bet."

"A commission spy named Agent X wrote down the license tag number in February 1964."

Agent X attended the gatherings of activists and later the training sessions for Freedom Summer volunteers in Ohio, sending reports to the commission through Day Detectives. Through analyzing commission reports, Lawrence and others figured out that Agent X was R. L. Bolden, who later became vice president of the Mississippi NAACP.

Lawrence said the commission gave the license tag number to the white Citizens' Council, which circulated it widely.

He told me to follow the pattern. After agents from the commission spied on the Schwerners, they shared their reports with the Meridian Police Department, which included Klansmen. The White Knights took that information, knew which car to look for, and ordered Schwerner's killing—carried out by the brother of one of those police officers.

My mind spun, trying to soak it all in. At this point, I had only one source, on background—and I needed to find another to confirm it before I could publish a story. But who could the second source be? I had no clue.

7

The *Clarion-Ledger*'s long-awaited twenty-fifth anniversary package ran, featuring many stories on how the state had changed—or stayed the same—over the past quarter century. What pleased me most was the editorial inside the paper, urging the state to prosecute the trio's killings:

> Attorney General Mike Moore should take it to a grand jury. . . . All primary suspects are still alive. They walk the streets as free men.
>
> While there are difficulties in prosecuting an old case, there are benefits. It is more likely a jury could make a clear judgment in these times, away from the emotional days of the civil rights struggles of the 1960s.
>
> And, the case of a Klansman prosecuted in Alabama for killing children in a church bombing 12 years ago also shows it can be done. . . .
>
> Reopening the Philadelphia murder case is simply the right and moral thing to do. It's called justice.
>
> Justice demands it. Nothing more, nothing less.

• • •

The Mississippi sun broiled the crowd of more than a thousand that honored the slain men on the twenty-fifth anniversary of the killings, June 21, 1989. The three families sat on chairs on a flatbed truck outside the rebuilt Mount Zion Methodist Church near Philadelphia. James Chaney's mother, Fannie, had moved her family from here to New Jersey when the threats worsened after her son's death. Rita Bender, who now lived in Seattle, believed in the cause her late husband, Mickey Schwerner, had died for, but disliked those who pigeonholed her as his widow. Dr. Carolyn Goodman, whose son was Andy, still worked as a clinical psychologist in New York City. It marked the first time she had ever set foot in the state.

The keynote speaker of the day was Governor Ray Mabus, who tossed his jacket during the brutal heat. He marveled at the courage of the three young men. "They gave their lives for their vision. Can we do any less for ours?"

Secretary of State Dick Molpus followed. In the spring of 1964, he had spotted men lighting a cross on the courthouse lawn in Neshoba County. Months later, it seemed the whole world was descending on his hometown. Although he didn't understand all of what was happening, he understood one thing—these killers were guilty of a dastardly crime.

At five-foot-ten with dirty blond hair, Molpus hardly looked like a politician, and he hardly sounded like one as he faced the families and spoke. "We deeply regret what happened here twenty-five years ago. We wish we could undo it. We are profoundly sorry that they are gone. We wish we could bring them back. Every decent person in Philadelphia and Neshoba County and Mississippi feels that way."

His eyes met Bender's. "My heart is full today because I know that if James Chaney, Andy Goodman, and Mickey Schwerner were to return today, they would see a Philadelphia and Mississippi that while far from perfect are closer to being the kind of place the God who put us here wants them to be. And they would find—perhaps to their surprise—that our trials and difficulties have given Mississippi a special understanding of the need for redemption and reconciliation and have empowered us to serve as a beacon for the nation."

After the anniversary service, I talked with the families. What did they think of the idea of the state of Mississippi prosecuting this case?

Carolyn Goodman seemed skeptical, wondering how serious such an effort would be. She said authorities shouldn't bother if they weren't serious. Rita Bender expressed support, and so did Chaney's brother, Ben. He had been just twelve when the Klan killed his brother. He and Bender wanted to see justice and, just as important, an examination of the system that led to the killings.

Mississippi's failure to prosecute, both then and now, gnawed at me. After discovering the name of the district attorney at the time, William H. Johnson, I telephoned him. He talked of meeting at the governor's office on a Sunday afternoon—the same meeting that retired agent Roy K. Moore had described.

Johnson said the agents talked about having two confessions. "But they wouldn't tell us who the people were who confessed."

That didn't surprise me. After the Justice Department revealed that a federal grand jury would take up the case on September 21, 1964, Judge O. H. Barnett announced that a Neshoba County grand jury would meet three days earlier. Barnett, whom the FBI had spotted at a Klan rally, subpoenaed all the agents investigating the case.

FBI director J. Edgar Hoover balked at the demand, and an FBI memo later explained why: "A Klansman judge is unlikely to disqualify himself or to eliminate Klan members as an impediment to service on a grand jury or petit jury."

There was yet another reason as well. Sheriff Lawrence Rainey, who would have played a role with the grand jury, was a suspect in the case. The federal officials couldn't imagine submitting the key evidence and the identities of secret informants to one of the very killers they were seeking to prosecute.

Before hanging up, Johnson admitted the case was "a travesty of justice. No question about it."

I awoke to a dreary morning on July 27, 1989. A source had told me that today US district judge William H. Barbour Jr. would open up the long-closed records of the Mississippi Sovereignty Commission.

I had shared the tip a day before with my editors, who dubbed the spy records "our Pentagon papers." I was glad to see the day come because I knew it meant I could finally read all about state officials' dirty deeds, including what I had been told about the Mississippi Burning case. No longer would all of these secrets remain hidden in a vault until 2027.

Time inched toward 5 p.m., when the clerk's office closed, and I wondered if my source had been told wrong. What was going on?

Fellow court reporter Beverly Pettigrew Kraft staked out the clerk's office. *The Clarion-Ledger* and the *Jackson Daily News* had consolidated in the spring, and now she and I shared the duty of covering courts. I was grateful to be working with her now, instead of having to compete against her. Everyone in the newsroom knew when she had a scoop, the sound of her heels clicking up the hallway with purpose.

I decided to wait at the office of Attorney General Mike Moore, whom I knew would receive the judge's order. When the order finally arrived, Moore refused to let me have a copy, but American Civil Liberties Union lawyer Shirley Payne shared the order with Kraft.

In his order, Judge Barbour castigated the Sovereignty Commission for its evil deeds. He called the state's efforts to keep the records closed "a subterfuge for the continuing denial of the constitutional rights of the plaintiffs."

But our hopes of viewing these secret records hit a roadblock. Most of the civil rights activists in Mississippi wanted these spy reports made public, considering any false or potentially embarrassing information they contained as badges of honor. But two civil rights activists, Ed King and John Salter, believed activists would be hurt by rumors and other false information in these reports. They appealed to the Fifth US Circuit Court of Appeals, and won a delay. Reporting on what the spy agency had done in the Mississippi Burning case would have to wait. So would possible revelations of other acts by the state in some of the nation's most notorious crimes.

8

Sometimes the biggest breaks come from the least likely places. But if one stays open to surprises, one can make hay out of happenstance. I had already experienced that, when a tip from a fellow reporter had led to my first glimpse of Sovereignty Commission records. And I was about to benefit from happenstance again.

I was fulfilling a friendly obligation. A lawyer acquaintance of mine had been after me to have lunch sometime, and I had kept putting it off. When I finally did show up at his office, I was early, and he was out. I stepped deeper into his office, noticing a row of cardboard boxes tucked beneath the table. I could tell they were filled with documents. I moved closer and noticed that one document was stamped "Confidential."

I wondered what kind of case that could be and squatted down. It took me a few seconds to realize I was staring at Sovereignty Commission records. It only took me another second to realize that the lawyer I had been avoiding could be a second source for the story on the state of Mississippi spying on the Schwerners. Go figure.

A few nights later, I showed him the start of a story I had typed up from my notes:

> The state spied on Mickey Schwerner and his wife three
> months before the Ku Klux Klan killed him and two other
> civil rights activists, Mississippi Sovereignty Commission
> documents show.

He confirmed it was accurate and added that the commission files included a drawing of the location of the bodies of the three civil rights workers in the dam. That was something I didn't know.

I had one more person to talk to before finishing my story. When I stepped inside the Elite Restaurant, I felt I had slipped into a time portal. In between turquoise booths, waitresses wiped Formica tables. Diners ate their fill of veal cutlets, homemade yeast rolls, and lemon icebox pie.

The man who suggested this place had his own past. Erle Johnston had once headed the Mississippi Sovereignty Commission. A short man with thinning gray hair and a cheery laugh, he reminded me of a public relations man. Which he was.

We shook hands. "Good to meet you, Mr. Johnston."

"Call me Erle."

Johnston rambled about his days in Mississippi politics, handling campaigns for politicians such as "Big Jim" Eastland. After working on Ross Barnett's successful campaign for governor in 1959, Johnston directed public relations for the Sovereignty Commission. By 1963, he was running the spy agency.

"At first, I reported to Governor Ross Barnett. Starting in '64, I reported to Governor Paul Johnson."

This was the same Paul Johnson Jr. who ran one of the South's most racist campaigns back in 1963. On the stump, he called out to crowds, "You know what NAACP stands for? Niggers, apes, alligators, coons, and possums." The crowds roared in approval and voted him into office. What didn't make headlines was that the KKK had backed his successful gubernatorial campaign.

I asked Johnston what the Sovereignty Commission did, in the most basic sense. He explained that the agency was originally formed to fight against court-ordered desegregation, but he bragged that he had changed the mission of the commission into an agency that settled racial conflicts.

That struck me as quite the spin after all I had read about the commission.

I pressed him on the subject I had telephoned about. "What can you tell me about Betty Jane Long talking to you about Mickey Schwerner?"

"She said there was a white man there causing trouble, said he'd been spotted in the black community and asked us to investigate. So we did."

He acknowledged this happened in March 1964, months before the slayings of the three civil rights workers. When I brought up the possibility that the commission's work played a role in Klansmen killing the three men, he denied that accusation. "The role of the commission in the murders was just making reports."

What he didn't deny was that the commission shared the report with the Meridian Police Department, which the KKK had infiltrated. And if that wasn't convincing enough, the main shooter of the three civil rights workers, Alton Wayne Roberts, had a brother, Lee, who worked for that same police department.

After this interview, I telephoned Rita Bender, whose petite frame belied the fire that burned in her bones. I told her about the secret spy agency records that showed the Sovereignty Commission spied on her and her husband, Mickey Schwerner, three months before his killing in the summer of 1964. She believed this revelation confirmed what she had long thought. "I'm not surprised by this at all. In fact, I expected it."

She recalled a spring day, months before the murders, when a man knocked on her apartment door, saying he was selling vacuums. He tried to force his way inside. She shoved the door back with all her might, locked it, and told him to go away. She waited until she was convinced he had gone. After he left, she spent her time wondering not just who the man was, but who he was working for.

My story ran on September 10, 1989, under the headline, "State Spied on Schwerner Three Months Before Death." The next day, I had a message to call US Attorney George Phillips. I knew George from having chased him around for past stories, but he had never been the one to call me before. When I reached him, he sounded upbeat.

"I saw your piece yesterday on Michael Schwerner, Jerry. Interesting story."

"Thanks."

"Just one thing we were wondering about, did your story on the commission records come from that court file or some other public documents?"

"No."

"Where did you get them?"

I cursed myself for failing to dodge his question.

"I can't tell you that," I answered.

"That's all we wanted to know."

"What do you mean, George? And who is we?"

"I can't tell you."

By the time I hung up the phone, I wondered if I had just made a big mistake.

The more crushing news came from Attorney General Mike Moore. I had visited him just before my story landed, wondering how the investigation into the Mississippi Burning case was going. I hoped that my new reporting would spark him to pursue new charges in the case.

Moore's attitude, however, was grim, as if he'd already reached a decision he didn't want to have to discuss.

"I've had some of my investigators working on the case," Moore said, "and they're telling me that too many witnesses have died."

"Who's dead?"

"James Jordan, who testified for the prosecution."

"What about Delmar Dennis? He's still alive."

"Yeah, but we really feel we need more than just that."

"What about the transcript? Mississippi court rules permit you to use the testimony of any dead witness."

"You're right, but what jury would listen to dead witnesses?" He paused, then delivered his own verdict. "This case is going nowhere, Jerry."

It took me a moment to take in the finality of his words. I left his office shaking my head.

I had hoped that my latest story on the Schwerners would be able to turn the tide, to bring Moore to reconsider. But it failed to move him. In his eyes, it didn't open up any new paths, any new witnesses who could speak to the murders directly.

Weeks later, I heard that Moore was shutting down the investigation. The Mississippi Burning case would stay cold.

I felt like I had failed, but my colleagues helped me see the silver lining. We had been able to help ferret out unreported details about a twenty-five-year-old murder case that many powerful figures had wanted to keep sealed. That was something. And while the Mississippi Burning case would go dormant—for more than a decade—my nightly reading expanded into examining other cold cases.

I had become obsessed with the history of my new home state, a history that still demanded action. The White Knights, after all, had gotten away with far more than one dark night of terror and murder. Just hours after President Kennedy delivered his first major civil rights speech on June 11, 1963, an assassin gunned down NAACP leader Medgar Evers outside his Jackson home. Five months after President Johnson signed the Voting Rights Act in August 1965, the Ku Klux Klan fatally firebombed NAACP leader Vernon Dahmer because of his voting rights work. In both cases, and many more, the killers had never been held to account.

Wondering if the Sovereignty Commission records could provide more clues about these cold cases, I reached out to Ken Lawrence again. He stopped by the newsroom, where I learned that my source for the Sovereignty Commission records looked like the bespectacled bookworm I had envisioned, combing through documents with a magnifying glass.

On my desk, I had a column by Sid Salter, editor for the *Scott County Times,* which detailed several items uncovered in the commission files in his own reporting. A few paragraphs caught my eye. They mentioned that the spy agency had screened potential jurors for the defense of Byron De La Beckwith, who went on trial in 1964 for the murder of Medgar Evers.

I asked Lawrence about the jury screening and handed him the column.

"Yeah," he said, "I knew that."

"You did? Why didn't you let me know?"

"I keep telling you—there are a lot of stories in those Sovereignty Commission papers."

"Well, what can you tell me about this?"

"There's more to it than what's here."

PART II

MEDGAR EVERS

9

In my years of living in Jackson, I had driven down Medgar Evers Boulevard many times. Yet I knew almost nothing about the namesake for this four-lane thoroughfare. To learn more, I drove to the Mississippi Capitol, constructed on the grounds of what had been the state's first prison. I hiked up the marble stairs until I reached an office for reporters covering the legislature. From their high perch, they could watch lawmakers traipsing up and down the corridors, huddling in hallways with lobbyists and sneaking into committee rooms for conversations.

When I walked into the Capitol Press Room, I saw veteran journalist Bill Minor clacking his fingers on his Underwood manual typewriter, spitting out a column. He had been covering Mississippi since the 1947 funeral of one of its most racist senators, Theodore G. Bilbo. The son of a newspaper Linotype operator in Louisiana and a lifelong Democrat, Minor had long viewed himself as a champion for the little guy. While working for the New Orleans *Times-Picayune*, he came to the forefront in 1947 when the *New Yorker* wrote a profile on him, stunned to learn that Minor's story on the governor's secret police group known as the Mississippi Bureau of Investigation had failed to make national headlines.

After his time with the *Times-Picayune*, he turned *The Capital Reporter*, a collection of community announcements, into a hard-hitting investigative publication. Syndicated columnist Carl Rowan wrote, "Mississippi is a better state and Jackson a better city because Wilson F. 'Bill' . . . Minor has been socking it to fast-and-loose bankers, crooked politicians, the Ku Klux Klan and others."

I sought Minor out because he had known Medgar Evers and reported on his work from the mid-1950s to the early 1960s. At the screening of *Mississippi Burning*, Minor had brought up Evers's name.

Months before the US Supreme Court ruled in the 1954 desegregation decision, *Brown v. Board of Education*, Evers became one of the first black applicants to the all-white and all-powerful University of Mississippi School of Law. He had hoped to become a lawyer and perhaps run for Congress one day, but white Mississippi was up in arms. When Mississippi attorney general J. P. Coleman questioned where Evers would stay while attending the segregated university, he replied, "On the campus, sir. I'm very hygienic. I bathe every day, and I assure you this brown won't rub off."

The law school rejected his application, and Evers consulted with the NAACP on whether to sue. Impressed with the young professional, the NAACP hired him instead as its first full-time field secretary for Mississippi. From his start in December 1954, he put forty thousand miles a year on his car, helping revive NAACP branches, organize new ones, and register African-Americans to vote.

Outsiders painted his home state as hopelessly cursed, but Evers believed Mississippi would be a fine place to live once the enemy of hate had been defeated. "I don't choose to live anywhere else," he told *Ebony* magazine. "There is room here for my children to play and grow, and become good citizens—if the white man will let them."

No matter where he went, however, threats of violence followed. He had been followed so many times he had lost track. That was one reason he had bought his Oldsmobile 88. It had a V-8 engine so powerful it left most cars behind. The speedometer would change colors, depending on his speed. On some dark nights across the Mississippi Delta, his dashboard glowed red as he floored it to escape those hell-bent on harming him.

Evers's name began appearing on KKK "death lists" almost as soon as he took over the NAACP in Mississippi, his telephone ringing at all hours with threats. Some messages were short and emphatic: "We're going to kill you, nigger." Others were longer, but no less frightening, describing how they planned to torture him.

In May 1963, he became even more visible after the FCC cleared the way for him to respond to the white mayor's criticisms of the NAACP, which the mayor called a "northern outside group." Evers told the television audience that more than half the NAACP members were southerners. Whether Mississippi chooses to change or not, he said, "History has reached a turning point, here and over the world."

After his speech, he led civil rights marches and boycotts in downtown Jackson. More death threats followed. "They said they're going to kill me," he told CBS News. "They said they're going to blow my home up. They said I only had a few hours to live." As he edged closer to his fateful end, he told *The New York Times*, "If I die, it will be a good cause. I'm fighting for America just as much as the soldiers in Vietnam."

On June 12, 1963, just hours after President John Kennedy told the nation that the grandsons of slaves were still not free, Evers was assassinated.

It was after midnight when Evers pulled into the driveway of his Jackson home. He grabbed a bundle of T-shirts that read "Jim Crow Must Go" and opened the car door. After he had shut the door and stepped forward, a soft-nosed Winchester bullet smashed into his back. The slug struck him above his right kidney and mushroomed, breaking two ribs before tearing through a lung. Blood and flesh showered the windshield. He collapsed onto the concrete, gasping for air. The bullet continued through Evers's body and shattered a window in the house. His wife, Myrlie, had been dozing inside and now sprung awake. As Evers struggled to drag himself toward the house, Myrlie and the Everses' three children, Darrell, Reena, and Van, dashed outside. They saw the blood and screamed.

"Daddy, Daddy!" Reena yelled. "Please get up, Daddy!"

He never did. Too much damage had been done.

Minor remembered the nearly five thousand who turned out for Evers's funeral, including some of the nation's top civil rights leaders, Martin Luther King Jr., Roy Wilkins, and Ralph Abernathy. As the crowd marched toward downtown Jackson, their anger rose higher than the 103-degree temperature, and they yelled, "We want the killer. We want justice." Jackson police pushed the crowd back, beating some marchers with their batons. In retaliation, marchers hurled rocks and bottles. Minor saw one lawman clutch his pistol and say, "We may as well open fire. If we don't do it today, we'll have to do it tomorrow."

With bricks and bottles flying, Justice Department official John Doar stepped between the two groups, saying, "Medgar Evers wouldn't want it this way." At the same time, Ed King, Dave Dennis, and other civil rights leaders helped calm the marchers.

"If the cops had started shooting, it would have been a bloodbath," Minor said. "Hundreds would have been killed."

What was it that Ken Lawrence had said? That there was more on the Evers case in the commission files?

When I telephoned him to press for details, he was more forthcoming. It seemed he had overcome some of his wariness about talking about the records.

"How about the fact that the Sovereignty Commission spied on Medgar Evers, trying to catch him in an illegal act?" he said.

"Really?"

"The state was after Medgar Evers for quite a while."

"But what was the spy agency trying to accomplish?"

First, Lawrence said, they had wanted any dirt they could get on Evers, hoping to find any excuse to lock him up or discredit him. Yet even after his assassination, they didn't let up.

"They were helping out the defense," Lawrence said. "Stanney Sanders, the defense lawyer in the murder trial, contacted the Sovereignty Commission for assistance. The commission checked out all these potential jurors. It did all it could to help Medgar Evers's assassin get away with murder."

He continued. "Don't you see? The state that was supposed to be prosecuting Byron De La Beckwith for the murder of Medgar Evers was secretly assisting his defense, trying to get him acquitted."

• • •

Byron De La Beckwith.

That singsong, six-syllable name bounced around in my brain. It didn't take much reading to learn that two all-white juries had failed to agree on a verdict for Beckwith in 1964. It didn't take much more reading to learn that, by all appearances, he had gotten away with murder.

Old newspaper stories and magazine articles portrayed him as the lone, obsessed assassin, determined to kill the NAACP's number one man in Mississippi. The case against Beckwith had certainly been convincing. His high-powered rifle had been found near the murder scene, complete with his fingerprint. Witnesses placed his white Valiant, with his law enforcement–like whip antenna, near the scene. Two taxi drivers testified that he had asked directions to the NAACP leader's home a few days earlier. When FBI agents arrested him, they found a circled cut around his right eye, and Beckwith admitted it had come from firing his rifle. If all that weren't enough, his words provided a motive. "The NAACP, under the direction of its leadership," he wrote in a letter to the *Jackson Daily News*, "is doing a first-class job of getting itself in a position to be exterminated!"

In his defense, Beckwith offered an alibi. Two policemen testified he was was more than ninety miles away, in Greenwood, a half hour from the time Medgar Evers was killed in Jackson. Beckwith maintained his .30-06 Enfield rifle had been stolen days earlier.

Jurors deadlocked 7–5 in favor of finding Beckwith not guilty. At his second trial, jurors deadlocked again, this time even closer to acquittal. After that, prosecutors dropped the case.

Beckwith went free from jail and returned to the Mississippi Delta a hero. A sign across a Delta bridge proclaimed, "Welcome Home, Delay," a sight that brought him "tears of joy."

After he arrived home, his best friend, Gordon Lackey, swore Beckwith into the White Knights of the Ku Klux Klan, according to FBI records. The pair were so tight that Jackson police had investigated the possibility that Lackey, a crop duster, had flown Beckwith down to Jackson for the assassination.

In 1967, Beckwith made an unsuccessful run for lieutenant governor, telling voters he was "a straight shooter"—a line he delivered with all the subtlety of a sledgehammer. His over-the-top campaign, promising "absolute white supremacy under white Christian rule," finished with 5 percent of the vote.

Minor recalled talking to Beckwith in jail. Initially, the accused assassin had been held in the suburban Rankin County jail, where the sheriff let him come and go as he pleased and had even let him bring in his gun collection. After public outrage, Beckwith was brought to the jail in Jackson. Here a jailer tipped Minor off and let him ride up the elevator with Beckwith. The trip spooked the reporter, especially the way Beckwith responded when Minor mentioned Medgar Evers. Beckwith didn't reply in any way. He simply remained cold. "He had no remorse whatsoever," Minor said. Glancing into the man's eyes, Minor sensed the spirit of Lee Harvey Oswald, who had assassinated President Kennedy in November 1963. "For Beckwith, this was his moment in history," Minor said. "These were his fifteen seconds of fame."

When the trial took place, he said Beckwith had made a show of it. After a defense lawyer handed him the murder weapon, he took aim, causing one juror to duck. Beckwith relished the attention and greeted visitors such as former major general Edwin Walker, who had been arrested for helping lead the 1962 insurrection at Ole Miss that ended in two deaths. Minor also said that Beckwith didn't pay a dime for his defense. The white Citizens' Council picked up their charter member's entire tab, hiring three council members as lawyers: Hardy Lott, Hugh Cunningham, and Stanney Sanders, who happened to have been the same district attorney who failed to get a Greenwood, Mississippi, grand jury to indict two of Emmett Till's killers for his 1955 abduction, despite their confession to the crime.

The journalist believed Beckwith was guilty, but the all-white jury failed to convict him. Minor said prosecutors certainly weren't helped by the fact that Ross Barnett, who had served as Mississippi's governor until days before the first trial began, attended the trial and showed his support, shaking hands with Beckwith.

I shook my head at this revelation. How could the jury interpret this as anything other than a signal to acquit Beckwith?

This information fit with what Lawrence had told me, about the Sovereignty Commission assisting Beckwith's defense. I shared what I had found so far with Minor, and he became angry. "It's an outrage the state of Mississippi was prosecuting and on the other hand was trying to subvert the efforts."

Did these clues have the power to pry open the Medgar Evers case? I had no idea, but I knew I needed to follow them. They led me back to Erle Johnston, who continued to put his best spin on the Sovereignty Commission's dark deeds. He said he would be willing to talk with me as long as my story mentioned his new book on the commission.

I asked him why a state agency, led by the governor, would have aided an alleged assassin. He assured me they never would have gotten involved in the investigation, but when Beckwith's second trial took place, there was someone on the list of prospective jurors who had the same last name as agent Andy Hopkins at the commission. Johnston said that the defense lawyer contacted Hopkins and asked if he was kin, to which Hopkins replied that he might be a distant cousin.

But the Sovereignty Commission agent didn't stop there, I knew—Hopkins helped Beckwith's defense lawyers check out all the potential jurors.

When I objected, Johnston defended the agent's actions. "That was right in 1964. Everything was tense," with spy agency officials wondering if these potential jurors "were connected with people coming down south."

Mississippi's segregationist spy agency prepared a complete report on the prospective jurors, identifying them by occupation and social affiliations, he said. "One said he was a member of the [white] Citizens' Council. The rest may or may not have been."

He said Hopkins had gathered all the information through telephone calls. "It was just like looking up a committee of the Chamber of Commerce."

I questioned him about this. "If an investigator was making calls, trying to find out as much as he could about the potential jurors, wouldn't he contact their bosses, family members, or others?"

He acknowledged that was possible.

"Couldn't that have had an influence on the jury?"

He insisted the commission had zero influence on jury makeup. If these white men were denied a spot on the jury, he said, "it wasn't on account of us."

After talking with Johnston, I shared his explanation with my best source on the Sovereignty Commission, Ken Lawrence, who replied, "That's absolute bullshit. Of course what the commission did affected the jury and affected the trial. Let me read you more from the report.

"Two potential jurors are each referred to as likely to be a 'fair and impartial juror.' Here's what the commission report says about another juror: 'Believed to be Jewish. No further information available.' What do you think that tells you?"

I decided to visit with Bill Waller, who had prosecuted the case as a district attorney. He sought to weed out as many racists as he could from the jury, asking the white men seated, "Do you think it's a crime to kill a nigger?" In the newspaper coverage I had read, most reporters praised Waller, believing he had tried as hard as he could to convict Beckwith. Still, that effort looked very different in the 1960s than it would today.

In 1974, Waller took the oath of office as governor. Since then, he had moved to a modest law office near the newspaper. It was there that we spoke—and it hardly fazed Waller when I brought up the Sovereignty Commission at the start of our conversation.

He seemed well aware that the commission was involved in some way in the case, recalling that an investigator came "in and out of the courtroom every day." However, when I asked him whether the commission's work could have resulted in the hung jury, he remained skeptical.

"I don't think so, but that's a judgment call," he said. "There were sympathizers on the jury, of course."

As far as Waller was concerned, it wasn't all that interesting a question. He believed both the case and his role in it were long past. He seemed reluctant to pick back over the outcome.

But I saw it as something worth pursuing. I was just beginning to probe deeper into what the spy agency had done, and there were enough damning hints that its work had almost gotten Beckwith acquitted in the second trial.

I wondered, too, about the legal implications of what the Sovereignty Commission had done. After talking with Waller, I reached out to legal expert Aaron Condon for his take. With his dark glasses and dry wit, the University of Mississippi School of Law professor had long been feared for his demanding classes on criminal law. I loved listening to his stories, marveling at his ability to recite long passages from judicial decisions.

When I told him about the Sovereignty Commission agent contacting families of jurors, he said it could constitute improper jury contact or jury tampering. "It could be part of a background check, but it's not proper in such a way that the juror feels he is under investigation."

Possible jury tampering? Now that was a story. And it could call into question the legitimacy of Mississippi's handling of the Medgar Evers murder.

Still, before I turned in my story, I wanted to see if I could reach Beckwith himself for a comment.

If only I could find him.

In 1987, then–*Jackson Daily News* reporter Willie Raab had conducted a telephone interview with Beckwith in which the latter had urged "white-only, Christian rule" for the nation. At the time, he was living in Signal Mountain, Tennessee, just outside Chattanooga. When I dialed directory assistance, the operator found no listing for Beckwith.

I called Raab, hoping he had hung on to the phone number. No luck. The sheriff's office there was no help, either.

I telephoned the *Chattanooga Times* and explained to the operator that I was trying to find someone who might have a number for Beckwith. The next thing I knew I was talking to Johnny Popham, the legendary reporter who put fifty thousand miles a year on his green Buick covering the South for *The New York Times*. In his Tidewater Virginia accent, Popham told me he didn't have Beckwith's number. But he promised to check around.

When I checked back days later, Popham still knew nothing.

Without any further leads, I went ahead and turned in my story to my editor John Hammack. After reading it, he messaged me back on my computer, "Great story. Damn. It's a shame we can't get a hold of Byron."

10

My Sunday story appeared in *The Clarion-Ledger* on October 1, 1989, beneath the headline, "State Screened Jurors in Evers Case." The next day, I telephoned Myrlie Evers, the widow of the Mississippi NAACP leader, to make sure she heard the news. The fifty-six-year-old business professional had lost her husband and raised three children while developing an impressive career, most recently as public works commissioner for the city of Los Angeles. Back in 1970, she had even made a laudable run for Congress on a shoestring budget, where people passed the hat to raise enough money for her filing fee.

We had spoken months earlier when she had blasted her brother-in-law, Charles Evers, for giving the Medgar Evers Humanitarian Award to Angolan rebel leader Jonas Savimbi. The conflict had been the latest flareup in the longtime battle between the two over the slain civil rights leader's memory.

The memories I brought up today, however, were more difficult to revisit. She listened in silence as I told her the state of Mississippi had secretly assisted Beckwith's defense. Finally, she asked, "Could you fax me the story?"

Hours later, she called back. Outraged at the spy agency's actions, she said her late husband's assassination should be prosecuted again. "I would like to see the killer brought to justice. I know it's possible, but I don't know if it's probable." She spoke of the painful mark that the murder and mistrials had left on her soul. "It's like a deep scar that has never healed."

Talking with her helped me understand Medgar Evers as a husband, as a father, as more than a civil rights martyr. All these years later, his family was still hurting, still searching for justice.

I had been hoping that what I had found out about the Sovereignty Commission's actions might convince authorities to reopen the case. Now I realized that what Myrlie Evers had to say was far more important, more powerful, and more persuasive. I reported her remarks in the newspaper, and a day later, I wasn't surprised when I picked up *The Clarion-Ledger* to see an editorial, written by a separate department from our newsroom:

> Mississippians should view with loathing the revelation that the second trial of the murder case of slain civil rights leader Medgar Evers was tried on an uneven field. . . .
>
> It strains credulity that members of a pro-segregationist organization, pre-screened by a state pro-segregationist agency, would impartially consider the rights of a black civil rights leader both groups openly despised.
>
> Hinds County District Attorney Ed Peters should re-open the case. It's not without precedent. Former Alabama Attorney General Bill Baxley in 1977 won a murder conviction 14 years after a racially motivated bombing killed four children in a black Birmingham church.
>
> Baxley later helped plan the successful prosecution of a white supremacist who 22 years earlier plotted the bombing of another black Birmingham church.
>
> The death of Evers . . . is a symbol of Mississippi's most sinister past that lingers like an ugly stain.
>
> By going to court, the state could proclaim to the

nation that indeed Mississippi has made a new beginning
and is a place of hope and justice for all law-abiding citizens without regard to race or philosophy.

Peters should heed this opportunity to do the right
thing and not continue to let this crime go unpunished.

In the days that followed, I continued writing more about the Sovereignty
Commission, while interviewing some of the jurors from the Beckwith trials. The defense struck Joseph Harris from the jury after the segregationist
spy agency reported that it believed he was Jewish. "Everybody who had
a college education, his own business and was not backwoods Baptist," he
told me, "was immediately excused from jury duty."

The more I wrote, the angrier some readers became—not at the commission but at me. One called to tell me I was a traitor to the white race.
Once when I picked up the phone, a man screamed, "When are you going
to stop writing about this dead nigger?"

One Sunday, as I was walking my daughter, Katherine, to the car, an
elderly man blocked our way to the church parking lot. "Why are you
writing about the past?"

"Actually, I'm writing about new things we're learning about the past,"
I responded.

His eyes narrowed. "Why don't you write about something going on
right now?"

"It *is* going on right now. It's news."

The man crossed his arms, unmoved. I stepped around him, heading
with my daughter to the car.

Despite such complaints, I kept working. After a full day's work of
covering courts for the newspaper, I would slip upstairs to our library and
pore through microfilm of old newspaper articles.

Myrlie Evers's request for justice attracted support from African-American
leaders. On October 9, 1989, Hinds County supervisor Bennie Thompson voted for a resolution, urging the reopening of the case. No one joined
him, but she took it as a positive. "I'm pleased that there is enough interest

and that someone had enough courage, even today, to bring this issue to a vote, even though it was a 'no' vote. Perhaps it's a beginning."

A beginning indeed. Charles Evers, who had taken over his brother's job at the NAACP after his assassination, now ran the WMPR radio station in Jackson. His office resembled a museum with photographs of him and his brother playing football at what was now Alcorn State University. There were also ones of him with boxing champion Muhammad Ali, blues legend B. B. King, and a fascinating mix of politicians, including Richard Nixon and Ronald Reagan. There were a series of black-and-white photos of him campaigning with then-presidential candidate Bobby Kennedy amid the palm trees of Los Angeles. Hours later, Kennedy was assassinated. "He was like a brother to me," he said.

I asked him about his flesh-and-blood brother, Medgar, whom he called "Lope." That nickname, he explained, came from a dancing church deacon his brother disdained. The brothers grew up in a family of nine, working in the sleepy sawmill town of Decatur, which stretched less than a mile in any direction in the hills of east Mississippi. "Lope hated the cold," he told me, "so I'd get in bed first and warm it up for him."

When World War II came, Charles spent his time in the Pacific while his brother, Medgar, traveled to Normandy, dodging bullets and stepping over dead bodies at Omaha Beach. Medgar battled the Nazis, only to return home and fight racism all over again, this time in the form of Jim Crow. Charles joined him in that battle, as the pair committed to fight back against the laws barring African-Americans from voting booths, restaurants, and restrooms.

On his twenty-first birthday in 1946, Medgar Evers joined his brother and other black veterans in heading to vote—only to be met by white men, who pulled out their guns. The Axis soldiers had failed to kill them. Now it seemed a Mississippi mob wanted to finish the job. "Those days were almost unbearable, but somehow, we withstood it," Charles Evers told me. "There was so much racism, bigotry, and ignorance."

The brothers attended Alcorn, and students marveled at their differences. Charles was bombastic, brazen, and charming, winning people over with his easy laugh. Medgar was straight-laced and serious, preferring studious women to the sassy ones Charles loved to woo. Medgar believed in working hard and being professional. Charles believed in hustling. He studied just enough to get by while Medgar buried himself in books and newspapers, learning more about the world beyond Mississippi.

In 1955, the push for voting rights cost Charles his job at a radio station, and he headed for Chicago, where he operated several nightclubs, some of them serving as fronts for gambling and prostitution. When news came that his brother, Medgar, had been assassinated, he loaded his suitcase with clothes, a rapid-firing carbine, and two .38-caliber pistols. By the time the plane landed on the runway in Jackson, he had made up his mind. He would take over his brother's job with the NAACP, and he would kill any white person who ever tried to kill him.

Days later, he flew to Washington, DC, for his brother's funeral at Arlington National Cemetery. As he watched Medgar's coffin descend into the grave, all he could think about was his brother inside, cold and alone. This time, Charles had no way to warm him up.

Days after the Board of Supervisors' vote in Hinds County, the Jackson City Council passed a resolution by a 4–2 margin calling for the re-prosecution of Evers's killing: "The activities of the Sovereignty Commission regarding and related to the Medgar Evers murder prosecution raise the presumption that the trial therein was not conducted in the fair, just, and impartial manner required by law."

The council had no power, no way to force the district attorney to do anything, but Myrlie Evers counted the vote as a victory. "Jerry, would you mind reading me the resolution?"

"Not at all."

After I finished, she asked, "Would you please read it again?"

Less than three weeks after my first story on the Medgar Evers case ran, an FBI agent I knew telephoned. "Jerry, I want you to tell me who your sources were with the Sovereignty Commission stories."

My sources? Why does the FBI want to know my sources?

"Keep the judge happy. Go ahead and tell me."

This remark tipped me off. The judge in the Sovereignty Commission case had obviously put the FBI up to this.

After a few moments of silence, the agent chuckled.

I half-laughed, still uneasy. "You know I can't tell you anything."

He said agents had quizzed all of those with access to the files. None had admitted to helping me. The call ended after that, but the news of the FBI conducting a formal investigation spooked me, making me wonder what was going to happen next.

Everyone who had viewed these Sovereignty Commission files had been forced to sign an oath, knowing they could be found in contempt by the federal judge in the case if they shared any of what they read. The judge had the power to haul me in front of a federal grand jury and question me about those leaks. And if I refused to reveal my sources, the judge could find me in contempt and even throw me in jail.

11

A day before Halloween, I crossed the street and headed to the office of Hinds County district attorney Ed Peters. If Myrlie Evers was going to succeed in pushing for a new trial, it would have to come through him. So far, he had been dodging my calls.

A former Golden Gloves boxer, Peters was a raging bull in the courtroom. His unbridled passion led his enemies to claim he would do anything to win, even break the rules. As district attorney, dozens of accusations had been made against him. But if Ronald Reagan was the Teflon president, Peters was the Teflon prosecutor. In 1975, a grand jury indicted him on an extortion charge, but a jury acquitted him. A federal task force followed, examining allegations of protection payoffs. More allegations followed—he took drugs, he took bribes, or he gave hand signals to witnesses. Peters denied all the claims, and no one proved otherwise.

On top of that, Peters had run into more than his share of conflicts with the African-American community. He came under fire when he declared that with all factors being equal, he would always pick a white juror over a black juror in a death penalty case because a white juror was more likely to favor the death penalty.

I wanted to talk to him today, not to ask about his past, but about the future of the Medgar Evers case. I wasn't optimistic coming in. Two years before, Peters had told a reporter, "There's no way under any stretch of the law that case could be tried again. Anyone having taken the first class in law school ought to know that." Still, I wanted to see what he had to say now that new interest was gusting up.

When I caught the white-haired prosecutor in his office, Peters surprised me. He volunteered that he was thinking about having a grand jury look into the case. The prosecutor explained that a grand jury could be tasked with determining if jurors had been influenced by the Sovereignty Commission's actions.

"It's not illegal to check the background of jurors," he said. "The question is if it amounted to an unfair trial."

That, however, was just the first step. Even if the trial were unfair, he said that a litany of legal hurdles would remain. First, he said, the US Constitution guaranteed defendants the right to a speedy trial. Next, he explained, Mississippi had a rule requiring defendants to be tried within 270 days of their arraignments. Either could halt the prosecution in its tracks.

The more Peters talked, the more it sounded like he had already decided against pursuing the matter.

Days later, I stopped by the circuit clerk's office to see what remained from the Medgar Evers case. A clerk there dug into the dark crevices of the courthouse. All she could come up with was a dusty old file. She handed it to me, and I read the label, "State v. Byron De La Beckwith."

I flipped through the file, which contained only a few pages. There wasn't even a copy of his 1963 murder indictment. The clerk mentioned that Assistant District Attorney Bobby DeLaughter had been here before me, looking at the same file.

That surprised me because I thought the district attorney was already leaning against the case, pursuing a grand jury just for show.

I knew DeLaughter well. He was a top prosecutor for Ed Peters, and he was one of the first sources I met in 1987 when I began covering the court beat for *The Clarion-Ledger*. A dark-haired Baptist deacon with a low-key demeanor, DeLaughter seemed, on the surface, an unlikely candidate to handle this case. His great-uncle had been a powerful Mississippi lawmaker who helped sponsor the legislation creating the Sovereignty Commission in the first place.

But DeLaughter had earned my trust in recent years. If he wanted to pursue a case, he wouldn't give me the runaround to find out. His office was just upstairs, so I headed up to talk.

DeLaughter confirmed that he was heading up the district attorney's investigation, and he described it as a broad one, looking not only at what the Sovereignty Commission did, but at the murder case itself. "We want to determine what, if any, witnesses are available and any evidence is still available for prosecution."

That sounded far different than what Peters had said, making me believe the idea came from DeLaughter rather than his boss. But the younger prosecutor's words soon matched Peters's pessimism. DeLaughter said hopes of reopening the case against Byron De La Beckwith looked dim at this point. There was no trial transcript from either of the 1964 trials. The murder weapon and other evidence was missing. And then there were the legal challenges, such as a speedy trial, which he believed made the case almost impossible to prosecute.

All this talk of legal challenges sent me back to my favorite law professor, Aaron Condon. I wanted to hear his thoughts about the difficulties the case faced. In particular, I wanted to ask him about the note DeLaughter had closed on—the speedy trial question.

Condon told me the constitutional right of a speedy trial wasn't as big a hurdle as prosecutors were telling me, because the murder charge against Beckwith had been dismissed after the second trial. He said that meant the speedy trial clock had stopped ticking, then and there.

When I shared this with DeLaughter, he seemed stunned. Condon had been one of his professors in law school.

"How can he say that?" DeLaughter asked. He shook his head and said he was going to reach out to Condon. He talked, too, of reaching out to the Mississippi attorney general's office for help researching the law. There was no way for the case to go forward, he said, unless these obstacles could be overcome.

I put my pen down, and we talked a little about our families. I told him that Karen and I had another baby on the way, and that Katherine, now four, was anxious to be the big sister. He told me that his ten-year-old son, Burt, was enjoying baseball. When the subject of Medgar Evers arose again, he confessed there were many details about the killing that he had yet to learn. "I don't know much about the case, but I do know this—no man deserves to be shot in the back in front of his family."

On November 1, 1989, retired *New York Times* reporter Johnny Popham came through with the unlisted telephone number for Medgar Evers's accused assassin, Byron De La Beckwith. I presumed it was too late at this point, that Beckwith wouldn't be willing to talk to me now that the DA had reopened the case. But I had to try.

I dialed the number, and a voice with a sugary-sweet drawl answered. It was him. I introduced myself.

Byron De La Beckwith hesitated. "Now, who are you again?"

"Jerry Mitchell with *The Clarion-Ledger* in Jackson, Mississippi."

"*The Clarion-Ledger*? Now that's a fine newspaper."

After some back-and-forth, I decided to bring up the Mississippi Sovereignty Commission. He praised it as a "good and wholesome" organization. "I'll be glad when they put it back in force. I was very disturbed with those who brought it to a close."

He said that if the Sovereignty Commission made a comeback, it would help "reestablish Dixie as a Southern Confederate republic." Back in 1956, he had unsuccessfully applied to work for the commission. He assured the governor then that he was an "expert with a pistol, good with a rifle and fair with a shot gun [*sic*]," vowing to "tear the mask from the face of the NAACP and forever rid this fair land of the DISEASE OF INTEGRATION!"

Beckwith's tune hadn't changed a note, all these years later. As he started to decry foreign immigrants, I tried to move him along, bringing up his 1964 trials. "Now, you went on trial twice . . ."

"Yes, for killing that nigger," he said. "Every once in a while, I see his picture in the paper. He is a high yellow, a very light-skinned nigger. His brother is as black as soot. There's no true bloodline. They're just mongrels. God hates mongrels. To adulterate is to mix blood. It's forbidden in scripture and forbidden in society."

The longer he talked, the more racism he spewed. Part of me wanted to object, to argue back, but the other part of me, the journalist, knew that the best thing I could do would be to keep him talking. I steered him back to the subject at hand, that District Attorney Ed Peters's office was now examining the case again.

Beckwith said he had no concerns at all because Peters was an "honorable man." Then he muttered, "White folks are supposed to look after white folks."

He revealed that he was wrapping up a book about his life titled *Glory in Conflict*. "I've been tried for my life twice. Each trial lasted ten days." And each had failed.

"So, who killed Medgar Evers?" I asked.

"I don't know who killed him, and I don't care."

His voice was blunt and dismissive, and it sent my thoughts toward Myrlie Evers. Over the past month, I had spoken with her several times, and each time I could hear the pain in her voice. For her, the past would never be the past.

I asked Beckwith if he felt any sympathy toward the family.

"I feel about as much compassion for the Medgar Evers family as a nigger getting run over by a streetcar in Chicago." He cackled. "Do they still have streetcars in Chicago?"

His laughter seemed to hang in the air as the conversation ended. What kind of man cracks a joke like that, finding joy in the grief of a family? A man named Byron De La Beckwith.

I decided to circle back to Ken Lawrence after talking with Beckwith. I told him about all that Beckwith had said. None of it surprised Lawrence, but he surprised me when he told me that the FBI had come to question him about the Sovereignty Commission leaks.

"I told the agent I never gave you any of the files."

That was true, but I was worried about how dogged the FBI agents had proven.

Lawrence said the judge in the case believed that he had leaked the secret files to me and that he had reassured the agent that wasn't true. Lawrence explained that the information he had shared with me were indeed spy files, but they were files leaked to him before the Mississippi legislature shut down the agency in 1977. This gave him some leeway on those files. But he wouldn't be able to share the documents related to the Sovereignty Commission spying on Medgar Evers.

I would need to see these documents to be able to keep momentum building toward a case, so I decided to reach out to another potential source on the Sovereignty Commission files. The source, a businessman, acknowledged having access to some of the secret spy records.

Technically, it was against the law in Mississippi to possess these spy records, which might have halted our conversation in its tracks a few years earlier. But the good news was that the judge in the case had ruled the law in question unconstitutional, making it unenforceable. The other good news was that my new source, unlike the others, hadn't signed an oath to keep information from the files secret. This could unlock the door that Lawrence was stuck behind.

When I asked my source about Mississippi spying on Medgar Evers, he responded positively. He said he had seen those records, and in fact he had copies.

"Copies?" I asked.

My heart skipped a beat.

Then he spoke the magic words. "Would you like me to fax them to you?"

The fax machine whirred, spitting out the curling paper. I began to read the Sovereignty Commission documents, which showed that Mississippi's governor at the time, J. P. Coleman, had ordered law enforcement officials in 1958 to spy on Evers in hopes of "catching him in an illegal act." These secret records described Evers as a "race agitator" and listed his phone number, license number, height, weight, and address. The documents included a description of his car and his personal history.

Coleman's order surprised those I talked to. By Mississippi standards, the retired judge from the Fifth US Circuit Court of Appeals had been a racial moderate. In 1955, he managed to win his race for governor without joining the white Citizens' Council. Years later, he drew criticism for welcoming the FBI to investigate the 1959 lynching of Mack Charles Parker.

When I reached Coleman, he said, "I honestly don't know of anybody, including Mr. Evers, who ever got put under surveillance while I was chairman of the commission."

Then he admitted, "I've long since forgotten whatever I did know. Once you get into something thirty years after it's happened, it's like Uncle Remus's tar baby. You never get loose from it."

What many had forgotten was that Coleman had himself urged Mississippi lawmakers to create the Sovereignty Commission. In archives, I found his 1956 inauguration speech, where he declared, "If the rules of racial separation are intact when we leave office, our place in history will be secure."

When I asked him why he pushed for this commission, Coleman said he knew lawmakers would create such a law anyway. That was why, he said, he made sure he appointed "cool-headed, level-headed people who would take a constructive approach to things that were happening."

He downplayed the spy agency's work. "To be honest, the Sovereignty Commission was a pretty harmless outfit."

Harmless to whom?

When I reached Erle Johnston, he acknowledged that Evers had been a target. "The commission by its normal process kept surveillance on many, many people who were activists or militants in the civil rights movement. The only thing surveillance meant was you wanted to know what they were doing and saying and planning."

Johnston's explanations rang hollow, veering into doublespeak. He reassured me that if Medgar Evers "wasn't planning anything, there wasn't any surveillance."

I telephoned Myrlie Evers, who remembered that police followed her husband for years before his death. "I certainly knew we were being watched." It had created an atmosphere of fear long before Medgar's assassination.

After her husband's killer went free in 1964, she worried that her family's home would never feel anything less than haunted. The bloodstains were still visible on the driveway, and the pain and memories became too much. She and her children moved to California.

"I felt the guilt of leaving Medgar, even though his remains were not there. I felt the guilt of leaving the struggle as I perceived it. Mississippi is home. It always has been. It always will be."

These days, she spent much of her time with her second husband, Walter Williams, in their Bend, Oregon, home, where tall pines give way to towering peaks. She called him her "Gentle Giant," a six-foot-four longshoreman and labor organizer who became a powerful voice for African-American equality in Los Angeles during World War II. After Medgar Evers's assassination, he saw Myrlie Evers and her children on TV, wishing he could take care of her. Thirteen years later, he got his wish. He stayed by her side and was happy to let her keep the last name Evers. "I loved Medgar," he told me, "before I loved Myrlie."

Weeks before Christmas in 1989, Myrlie Evers returned to Mississippi. She came to talk with prosecutors about pursuing a case against her husband's assassin. Just a month earlier, she had gathered with Rosa Parks, Emmett Till's mother, Mamie Till-Mobley, and others to dedicate the Southern Poverty Law Center's new Civil Rights Memorial in Montgomery, Alabama. The granite monument featured the names of forty martyrs, Medgar Evers among them.

District Attorney Ed Peters and Assistant District Attorney Bobby De-Laughter welcomed Myrlie Evers to their office on December 4. Peters was already planning on letting a grand jury decide this month if the Sovereignty Commission had influenced the jury verdict in Beckwith's second murder trial. But when they met, for the most part, DeLaughter remained mute while Peters detailed his reasons the case could not be pursued. He showed Myrlie a file folder with a handful of documents from old court files. There was, he insisted, no evidence left to pursue a case.

Myrlie told the district attorney that she did not want a prosecution for show. She wanted another trial for only one reason—to convict Beckwith.

After her meeting, she asked me if I trusted Peters.

"No," I replied. "But I trust Bobby."

She told me that her meeting had disheartened her. She concluded that prosecutors would never pursue the murder case. Her brother-in-law, Charles, had come away with a similar message after his conversation with the district attorney. "He told me to leave it alone," Myrlie said.

Ten days later, the grand jury met and was unable to prove that the jury in Beckwith's trial had been influenced. The case was going nowhere.

12

A few days after Myrlie Evers's meeting at the district attorney's office, I telephoned the same source who had given me the reports on the state of Mississippi's surveillance of Medgar Evers. The last time I spoke with him, he had said, "Come on over and see me some time, Jerry."

On December 11, 1989, I took him up on his offer. I walked past his polite secretary and entered his office. We chatted for a long time before he pointed to six blue notebooks, sitting on his bookshelf. Nothing suggested these could be Mississippi's notorious spy files—they were just nondescript notebooks. And yet, as the businessman explained, here they were.

He pointed again at them. "They're yours."

The scene felt plucked out of the Edgar Allan Poe short story "The Purloined Letter," where the thief hides a devastating dispatch in plain sight. As I loaded the blue notebooks into the back of my Honda CRX, my heart raced. I thought about what these records might mean to the Medgar Evers case and to Mississippi, the dark secrets of the past spilling out for all to see.

As soon as I reached a pay phone, I dropped in a quarter and called the city desk. An editor answered, and I blurted out, "I got 'em. I got 'em."

"You got what?"

"The Sovereignty Commission records."

I spent Christmas Day and the rest of the holidays reading through stacks of secret spy records, much to the chagrin of my family. I was skimming through the rest of the 2,400 pages of files because I had a meeting in a few days with my editors, already anxious to know the contents of all the records.

Much of what I read stunned me—how far Mississippi officials went to stamp out any attempt to cross the color line. When one frantic mother wrote Governor Paul Johnson Jr. about her teenage daughter's biracial romance, Sovereignty Commission director Erle Johnston fired off a January 1965 memo to an investigator, suggesting that if the boyfriend was twenty-two or older, he could be drafted. That effort failed when it turned out the boyfriend was only twenty.

My heart ached when I read about two young white boys caught up in a racial paradox. Mississippi's "one-drop rule" wouldn't let the brothers attend the all-white public school because they were descendants of Confederate army deserter Newt Knight, whose common-law wife was African-American. But Mississippi wasn't going to let these pale-skinned boys attend an all-black public school, either—because that would suggest integration. So, each school morning, the two brothers watched the buses go by, unable to join their would-be classmates until they had passed their tenth birthdays.

When Korean War veteran Clyde Kennard tried to enroll in 1958 at the all-white college in Hattiesburg, Mississippi, a group of white men plotted to kill the African-American chicken farmer by wiring dynamite to his car's starter. When that plan fell through, Kennard was arrested for illegal possession of liquor after constables reportedly planted the bottles in his Mercury station wagon. When Kennard refused to give up his quest for higher education, he was arrested again, this time accused of buying stolen chicken feed. The all-white, all-male jury deliberated all of ten minutes before convicting Kennard, who received the maximum seven years in prison while the admitted thief received no punishment.

In 1963, then-governor Ross Barnett released Kennard from prison because he was dying of colon cancer. Medgar Evers wept at the sight of his friend, Kennard, who weighed less than ninety pounds when he died, months later, on the anniversary of the Declaration of Independence that promised "all men are created equal."

Although I had yet to find anything that would aid the Medgar Evers case, I did find a bombshell. It was about the newspaper I worked for, *The Clarion-Ledger,* and its sister paper, the *Jackson Daily News.* The files showed how the papers worked hand in hand with segregationist leaders and the Sovereignty Commission.

If that wasn't damning enough, *The Clarion-Ledger* received a stream of spy reports from the Sovereignty Commission. The commission convinced the *Jackson Daily News* to publish one of its reports verbatim. The scheme worked, forcing a civil rights worker out of Mississippi.

To ensure help from some of the African-American press, the commission put a few black editors on the payroll, including Percy Greene, who operated the *Jackson Advocate.* At the commission's request, he printed a Sovereignty Commission story verbatim, linking Martin Luther King Jr. to communists.

The Clarion-Ledger then picked up that story as planned. "In this manner the story will be more effective because a Negro will be the author exposing the Communist associations of other Negroes," Erle Johnston wrote March 24, 1964.

This stunned me. Days later, I confronted Johnston about planting the story in the black newspaper. He defended the agency's actions. "We felt like sometimes if we could publicize information about some particular person who was making noises, his influence could be reduced."

He denied zeroing in on the civil rights leader. "We never did target King at all. He was untouchable. It wasn't him. It was the lesser fry we were interested in."

Yet even his denial sounded like a confession.

All of this activity from the commission was aimed at taking down the civil rights movement, no matter who the target was. There was no question about that. And Mississippi's leading papers were happy to help.

I knew almost nothing about *The Clarion-Ledger*'s past, and the more I was finding out, the more horrified I was.

I telephoned Hodding Carter III, whose family ran the Pulitzer Prize–winning *Delta-Democrat Times* in Greenville. His father had stood up to the white Citizens' Council, calling them "the uptown Klan." He recalled the era in which *The Clarion-Ledger* and *Jackson Daily News* were racist organs of the segregationist establishment. "What the newspapers did was a tragedy. It was a subversion of the press in the name of ideology. It was as sickening as communism. Anything went."

Myrlie Evers shared Carter's animosity toward the newspapers, which she said rarely missed an opportunity to bash her husband and the NAACP. On the day of Evers's death, the *Jackson Daily News* wrote that the bullet that killed him landed next to a watermelon on the kitchen counter—a cutting racist reference amid tragedy.

Eleven days after her husband's assassination, *The Clarion-Ledger* published its most infamous headline: "Californian Is Charged with Murder of Evers," which ran after FBI agents arrested Byron De La Beckwith. One editor had rubbed his hands together in glee after discovering that Beckwith, who had spent almost his entire life in Mississippi, happened to have been born in California. Anything to suggest this had been done by an outsider.

Bill Minor told me the Hedermans, a teetotaling Baptist family that owned the two newspapers, had a powerful say in state government and also backed the white Citizens' Councils. The papers, he said, were among the worst in the nation. The editor of the *Jackson Daily News*, Jimmy Ward, referred to black civil rights workers as "chimpanzees" in his columns, and on the same day that many newspapers featured the March on Washington and Martin Luther King Jr.'s historic "I Have a Dream" speech on August 28, 1963, *The Clarion-Ledger* printed the headline, "Washington Is Clean Again with Negro Trash Removed."

Minor said the newspapers began to change in the 1970s when Rea Hederman took over *The Clarion-Ledger*. He hired talented reporters, black and white, and set out to help change a state that had long battled against change. He succeeded in turning the paper around, and awards followed. In 1982, his family sold *The Clarion-Ledger* and the *Jackson Daily*

News to Gannett, and in turn he bought *The New York Review of Books*. A year after the sale, *The Clarion-Ledger* won the Pulitzer Prize for its successful push for education reform. Since then, the newsroom for the now-combined newspapers had become more diverse, with Bennie Ivory now serving as editor for *The Clarion-Ledger*, the first African-American to do so in the paper's history.

When I touched base with Ken Lawrence, he told me these were Sovereignty Commission files that he had assembled as a court exhibit to show the terrible things the spy agency had done. I told him how surprised I had been to learn about the racist past of the two newspapers. "What they did was despicable," he said. "If you're asking my opinion, I think *The Clarion-Ledger* needs to apologize for all the things it did."

I took this idea to heart when I spoke with Ivory and my bosses about the commission files, sharing that I thought we should write a story on ourselves as part of our package on the Sovereignty Commission. The editors agreed, but Executive Editor John Johnson balked at my suggestion that we write an editorial apologizing for all the newspaper had done. Even worse, Johnson gave me and two other reporters, Michael Rejebian and Leesha Cooper, only three weeks to finish the project of combing through the commission files. Other reporters had spent months at work on their long-term projects. Now this one involving "our Pentagon papers" was getting just a few weeks?

"Mississippi's Secret Past" hit the newsstands on January 29, 1990. The project exposed many secrets from the records, including the state's harassment of anyone suspected of involvement in civil rights activities, collecting spy files on at least 10,000 people. For years, the commission succeeded in getting them smeared in the newspapers, fired from their jobs, or worse. Ivory held the story up in front of the staff as an example of an exemplary project. But the feeling kept gnawing at me—that we could have accomplished even more.

Back on the court beat, I visited the district attorney's office and knocked on Bobby DeLaughter's door. He invited me in, and I noticed he was reading police reports. "They're from the Medgar Evers case," he told me.

I hadn't seen them before, and I wondered if there was something in those reports that could help move the case forward. I hoped, too, that DeLaughter was thinking the same thing.

"I'd love to look at those old reports some time, Bobby."

"Not right now," he said. "Give me a few months."

By that time, he predicted the case would be closed.

Those words surprised me. I was beginning to think that he had hopes of reopening the case. But he sounded resigned to leave it as it was, another unpunished killing from the civil rights movement in Mississippi.

13

After watching another Mississippi public service commissioner sentenced to prison for corruption on February 16, 1990, Edd Jussely, who handled public relations for Mississippi Power & Light Company, cornered me. He had been reading my stories on the Medgar Evers case and asked me what the latest was. He was hoping for any shred of good news.

I shared my concern that the case was going nowhere. He told me not to give up, and he said he had some information. Edd had used to work for a television station in the Mississippi Delta, and he said he had often spent time chatting with local law enforcement officers. He remembered hearing from them that "a couple of cops had lied for Byron De La Beckwith, saying they saw him in Greenwood at the time."

"They lied? Are you sure?"

"Absolutely. Just ask Bill Minor."

After work, I dropped by the veteran journalist's home in north Jackson and asked him about the alibi witnesses. He, too, believed they were lying. In fact, he had received a letter prior to Beckwith's first trial in February 1964, warning that a "possible perjured witness" would "swear Beckwith was somewhere else at the time of the murder." The writer wanted Minor to expose this concocted alibi, saying white Mississippi would be on trial with Beckwith. "Often in the past, out of group loyalty or sympathy for the motive, members of our group have identified with inter-racial acts of violence by defending or rationalizing such acts, obstructing due process of law, and jury verdicts contrary to the evidence presented. . . . [If] the evidence in the forthcoming trial should indicate that . . . Beckwith is guilty as charged, and the jury's verdict is not in keeping with this evidence, judgment for . . . Beckwith and for us will not end with the trial."

Minor had followed up at the time, but he hadn't been able to prove anything. I told him I would look into it. If the alibi witnesses had lied, maybe they had slipped up in the decades since. The only problem was that there was no trial transcript to review the testimony. The clerk's office didn't have a copy, and neither did the Mississippi Supreme Court. Transcripts are usually created for appeals, but Beckwith had never been convicted. Lawyers would likely have created a transcript in advance of the second trial, but who would have held on to one after all these years?

A few days later, I telephoned Myrlie Evers to see what she recalled about the officers' testimony. She told me because she was a witness in the case, she couldn't stay in the courtroom and hear what they said. She did, however, have a surprise in store. She told me that my search for a transcript had finally come to an end.

"You have a transcript?"

"Yes, I received it from the district attorney's office after the trial was over. I have kept it ever since."

I could hardly believe it. "Would you mind making a copy and sending it to me?"

"I would be happy to, Jerry."

The 1964 transcript laid out the testimony of the two police officers, James Holley and Hollis Creswell. They testified that they saw Beckwith at a service station at 1:05 a.m. on June 12, 1963, while they were on patrol in Greenwood, Mississippi. That testimony gave Beckwith a solid alibi, putting him more than ninety miles away from where Medgar Evers had been killed in Jackson about a half-hour earlier.

What struck me was how precise the officers' time was. They never

wrote the time down and never connected the time to anything memorable. In fact, they told jurors that Beckwith was doing nothing unusual
that night. He was just standing there, having the attendant fill up his car
with gas.

As officers in a small town, they saw hundreds of people they knew
each day. Why would they remember seeing Beckwith at this particular
time?

Holley, who still lived in Greenwood, now served on the city council.
He had a crew cut, a potbelly, and a cheerful smile. When I caught up with
him, he told me he had seen Beckwith at 1:05 a.m. on June 12, 1963, the
same time he had testified to twenty-five years ago. When I asked him the
whereabouts of his old partner, he had no clue.

In the newsroom, we kept stacks of telephone directories for towns
across Mississippi. I searched until I discovered one for Greenwood. Flipping through it, I saw no listing for Hollis Creswell, but I noticed a half-
dozen listings with the same last name. I picked one and dialed.

When a man answered, I tried to sound as southern as I could. "Is
Hollis there?"

"No, you've got the wrong number. You want my cousin. He lives over
near Maben. I've got his number. Let me get it for you."

Clutching an unfiltered Camel, Hollis Creswell swore to me that Beckwith
was innocent and that he saw him the evening Evers was killed. "I can see
Beckwith as clearly that night as I can today. I have no reason to tell a lie
for him."

Sitting at a small Formica table in his kitchen, the seventy-
five-year-old retired policeman detailed his health woes, including a
stroke, heart trouble, and diabetes, before resuming his diatribe. "If I tell
the truth, I'll tell it a hundred years from now. If a man does tell a lie, he
can't tell it twice. I'll tell the truth the third time, the fourth time, the fifth
time—whatever it takes. I'll tell it next week or five minutes before I die."

I sat amazed at his soliloquy on Beckwith's innocence, because I had
yet to pose my first question. The ash on the cigarette was up to an inch
when I asked him, "When did you see Beckwith?"

He couldn't recall the date or even the year when he saw Beckwith, but he swore to me he could never forget the time. "It was about five till one a.m."

Could never forget the time? This was a different time than he testified to.

Creswell told me he remembered heading with his partner to eat supper at a store that was closing at 1 a.m. "We would stop there at midnight or after at the grocery store and buy bologna and crackers. We did that quite often."

He said someone was pumping gas for Beckwith, who had his foot propped on the concrete next to the pump. "I waved at him, and he waved at me."

At first, Creswell told me he knew Beckwith "quite well." But when I pressed him further, he insisted the alleged killer "was no personal friend of mine."

He complained about authorities reinvestigating Evers's murder. "If I thought the man was guilty, I'd say so, but I don't believe it. I won't believe it. If he told me himself, I wouldn't believe it." He kept interrupting himself to swear that he was telling the truth. The more he swore, the more suspicious I grew.

"I got summoned to the trial," he said. "I told the truth at the trial."

Before the interview ended, he made his views clear. "If my brother committed murder, I wouldn't testify and lie for him. If I see you or the blackest nigger in the country shortly after a murder happens, I'll testify to what I saw."

Nothing like spewing the N-word to prove your lack of prejudice.

I went back and read the trial transcript again. All the details that Creswell had given me—seeing Beckwith with his foot propped up, Beckwith waving at him and him waving back—were missing from his 1964 testimony. He'd also given me a different time, "five till one a.m." Holley had told me he stayed in the patrol car while his partner went in to buy cigarettes—the opposite of their original testimony. Sure, the passage of time could have muddied memories, but I began to suspect it was something more.

I telephoned Holley, and he sounded as chipper as ever. When I quizzed him about his sighting of Beckwith, he said, "I saw Delay sometime around one a.m. Maybe a few minutes before." That was a change from what he told me the first time we talked. He had moved toward what Creswell said the other day, which made me believe the two were chatting.

The more I read in the transcript, the more I suspected the officers had been colluding all along—and poorly. In their testimony, both insisted that they had seen Beckwith at 1:05 a.m., and both had connected their precise time with the closing of a grocery store that sold sandwiches. Both talked of hurrying to get something to eat, except there was a problem— they said the store closed at 1 a.m.

As I reread Creswell's testimony, it looked like the original plan may have been for the officers to testify that they had seen Beckwith at five till one, which would fit with rushing to a store that closed at 1 a.m. But after Creswell insisted to jurors he saw Beckwith at 1:05 a.m., he and his partner were stuck with that time.

"I looked at my watch, and I told him [Holley] it was 5 minutes . . . after 1 o'clock. He said, 'Well, we had better go on over before he closes up.'" Although he told jurors originally that the store closed at 1 a.m., he now—to save the story—insisted that the owner didn't "have any fixed time to close."

And that wasn't even the most absurd part of their testimony. During the trial, Beckwith's lawyers tried their best to link the sighting of Beckwith to the night of Evers's assassination, but there was an important detail the lawyers left out: Beckwith wasn't arrested that day. Or the next. In fact, more than ten days passed between Evers's murder and Beckwith's arrest. It would have been well over a week before the officers could have ever connected their glimpsing of Beckwith to the murder of Medgar Evers.

In my mind, that gap in time made it almost impossible to believe that their sighting of Beckwith could have stuck in memory, especially since they insisted he had done nothing unusual. Why would both police officers have remembered such a precise date and time for such a forgettable event, especially if they were already in a hurry?

District Attorney Bill Waller cross-examined Holley about that absurdity, asking about his memory of other dates around Medgar Evers's assassination on June 12.

"Who did you see at 1:05 a.m. on the night of the 10th of June?"

"I don't know," the officer replied.

"Did you see Mr. Beckwith at ten o'clock Sunday night, June the eighth or June the ninth?"

"I don't recall."

"Did you see him at seven o'clock on June the eighth?"

"I don't recall seeing him at that time."

"When do you recall having seen Mr. Beckwith at any specific time and place?"

"I don't."

"Who did you see at one ten on the morning of June the twelfth?"

"I don't know, sir."

"Who did you see at one fifteen?"

"I don't recall seeing anyone."

"Who did you see at two o'clock?"

"I don't recall."

"Do you know of anybody you saw that whole night on that whole shift?"

"Not specifically, no, sir."

With that, Waller ended his questioning. I could hardly believe how clumsy Holley and Creswell had been on the witness stand and how no one, in all this time, had held them to account on it.

14

After interviewing the retired officers, it only made sense now to speak with the man for whom they'd provided an alibi—Byron De La Beckwith. Nothing attracted me to the idea of another conversation with the man I considered a racist killer, but I knew if I didn't, the case would remain stuck, and he would remain free, just as he had been for the past quarter century. I also knew I'd get the most out of him if I went to talk with him in person.

I had an upcoming personal trip to Nashville, and I considered swinging by to interview Beckwith on the way. The only question on my mind was how he would react. Had he figured out yet that I was the one who wrote the stories that got the case reopened?

When I called him up to ask if I could interview him on April 8, 1990, Beckwith became inquisitive. "Now, if you want to come and have us treat you as a guest in our home, I have some questions you need to answer."

"Sure."

"Where did you grow up?"

"Texarkana, Texas."

"And what are you parents' names?"

"Jerry and Jane Mitchell."

As soon as the words left my mouth, I regretted saying them. If he had just asked, I could have revealed my ethnic background—some mix of English, Scotch-Irish, German, French, Native American, and God knows what else tossed in. I was, after all, a southerner.

"And where did you go to college?"

"Harding University."

He knew about the Christian college, located north of Arkansas's capital of Little Rock. "Are you a Christian?" he asked.

"I am." Although we had yet to discuss the matter, I suspected his version of Christianity differed greatly from mine.

Each answer shared more personal information he could use against me, yet I kept responding. There was no turning back.

"Where do you live?"

"I live in south Jackson."

He didn't press for a street address, and I was grateful.

When he grew quiet, I spoke. "Do you mind if I stop by Sunday afternoon?"

"Now, what time do you expect to arrive?"

"I should be there no later than three."

"That would be fine. Now what do you look like, so we can know who to expect?"

"I'm redheaded, and I have a beard."

"A beard?"

He seemed concerned about this information but probed no further. "Thelma and I will be waiting for you."

Before leaving town, I told prosecutor Bobby DeLaughter that I was going to interview Beckwith. "Anything you'd like for me to ask him?"

"Sure, why don't you ask him if he ever attended a Klan rally down by the swinging bridge in Byram?"

I told him I would, and I also mentioned that I now had a copy of the trial transcript. He made clear that he wanted it, and I promised I would get him a copy, one way or another.

That night, I told my wife, Karen, now eight months pregnant, that I was going to interview Beckwith. She recoiled. "Are you trying to get yourself killed?"

"No, not at all."

"Didn't you write the stories that got the case reopened?"

"Yes."

"Then I'm sure he wants you dead."

"But he doesn't know I'm the one who wrote the stories."

She glared at me. "How do you know?"

I realized I had no answer for that question. The best I could say was that it didn't *seem*, in our earlier conversations, that Beckwith had any idea.

She teared up. "I don't want to be a widow, raising our children."

I didn't know what to say. She grabbed my arm and pleaded with me, picking out the most powerful words she knew to make me stay. "If you go, I'll never forgive you."

I closed my eyes, stung by her words. I remembered Myrlie Evers telling me that when their children were young, she had challenged her husband's dangerous work. Yet he had kept going.

I opened my eyes and said, "Karen, I have to go."

As I snaked up the side of Signal Mountain, driving through the afternoon's shadows, I was unable to shake my wife's warnings. I felt torn by her concern and my journalistic instincts. I tried to concentrate on my line of questioning for Beckwith.

"Did you kill Medgar Evers?" would be the most obvious, and dangerous, thing I could ask. But what I really wanted to know was what made him tick, what influences had turned him into the worst racist I had ever encountered.

The fact that he lived in Signal Mountain, just across from Lookout Mountain, was hardly surprising. Up until recent years, Klansmen had openly raised money at intersections in this area, collecting donations from drivers.

I gazed at the address I had scribbled down, 1510 Albion Way. I figured

I had the right place when I spotted a David Duke bumper sticker on the back of a car. I knew I had the right place when I saw a Confederate battle flag flapping in the breeze outside a white wooden-frame house.

Pulling into the gravel driveway, I spotted Beckwith sitting in a chair. The wiry five-foot-eight man stood and hailed me. He wore a white shirt and dark tie with white circles. I noticed the creases and cracks of his sixty-nine years, much of that life spent selling cigarettes, fertilizer, guns, candy, and a few million packs of Juicy Fruit.

I shook his hand, surprised by his steady grip. As I let go, I realized it was the same hand accused of pulling the trigger that killed Medgar Evers.

He smiled and gestured a half foot from his chin. "I thought your beard would be out to here. It's nicely trimmed."

He waved me inside his home. "C'mon in. Thelma and I've been waiting for you."

Beckwith welcomed me like a long-lost cousin. Perhaps it was my red hair, which reminded him of the founder of the white Citizens' Council. Perhaps it was my alabaster skin, making obvious my Scotch-Irish heritage. Perhaps it was my conservative Christian upbringing, which he presumed meant I shared his views about God. Whatever the reasons, he believed he had found a kindred spirit, and for that reason, he shared his secrets.

Inside his home, his southern charm flourished. He guided me past a gold-plated rifle into a back room, where he sat in a floral chair, holding court and sipping from a drink that bubbled furiously like a mad scientist's potion. Thelma, his second wife, poured me a glass of this concoction—a mixture of orange soda and food-grade hydrogen peroxide. This, he promised me, would remove the poisons the government had been pumping into my body through fluoridated water. "Fluoridated water has been killing babies. It's being suppressed by the government and national TV."

He talked of his southern heritage, his grandfather riding in the Confederate cavalry. He told me his full name was Byron De La Beckwith VI, and he grew up on the Glen Oak Plantation in the Mississippi Delta, fishing from the banks of the Yazoo River. The only white child on the plantation, he talked of being raised by "nigger servants." He told me as long as they stayed in their place and whites stayed in theirs, relationships worked.

At age twelve, he became an orphan, raised by two bachelor uncles. Unlike hunters who bagged big game, he preferred to shoot squirrels and "varmints," such as vultures, garfish, and poisonous snakes—killing, as he put it, "for my own pleasure."

He talked of being a failure in school. "School used to bore the living hell out of me," he said. "I didn't learn a damn thing in high school or college, except how to get along and be a good ol' boy among good ol' boys."

He talked of fighting in the Battle of Tarawa in World War II. On November 20, 1943, Beckwith provided cover fire for fellow Marines invading Betio Island, a part of the Gilbert Islands and the second stop for US forces in their island-hopping campaign against Japanese forces. When his gun jammed, he grabbed another, and when that one failed, too, he mimicked its firing—only to have thirty-eight pieces of lead rip into his left thigh. "Machine gunners don't live a minute and a half in the heat of combat, if that long."

He returned to Mississippi with a Purple Heart and a new bride. Locals regarded him as an oddball since he was polite to a fault, often wore white shoes, and rarely kept quiet. A southern belle, he recalled, had once told him, "Mr. Beckwith, when you shut your mouth, we're going to have a lovely conversation."

Eager to belong, he joined any club that would have him. He reeled off their names—the Sons of the American Revolution, Sons of Confederate Veterans, Veterans of Foreign Wars, the American Legion, and so many others I lost track. His lineage, he told me, enabled him to join the Sons of the American Revolution, an organization he was excited to learn included President Eisenhower, until fellow members pulled him aside and told him Eisenhower was "a Swedish Jew."

He said that it was revelations like this that jump-started his political awakening. "I found out all the horrible, insidiously evil things that went on in local, county, state, federal, and worldwide government."

The words that changed him most came from Judge Thomas P. Brady, whose speech decrying the US Supreme Court's 1954 decision to desegregate public schools inspired him to join the white Citizens' Council. Beckwith said the most powerful members of society—bank presidents, judges, lawyers, congressmen, and other politicians—made up the council. "That was my first love," he sighed, as if reminiscing about a high school sweetheart. "The Citizens' Council was the first ray of light Dixie had seen since we fought through Reconstruction and captured the right to vote, the right of white people to run the South."

He said the council was "invented by Robert B. Patterson," a World War II paratrooper and a captain for the Mississippi State University football team that went undefeated in 1940. "He's a redheaded devil just like you are."

"Is he alive?"

"You bet your life he's very much alive. He certainly did save the South a lot of embarrassment."

These days, he said, there has been a "great awakening of council activity in St. Louis, but it's under a little different name"—the Council of Conservative Citizens.

He denied being a Klansman but made clear his admiration. When he was five, walking the streets of a Northern California city where he lived, he glimpsed Klansmen with "big, beautiful white caps that made them look seven feet tall. They had on their beautiful flowing robes, and they were in the cafés and drugstores during the business parts of the day so that people of the whole state of California would know they were Klansmen."

He told me to be thankful for the KKK. If the group didn't exist, "you'd be a damn mulatto, quadroon, or octoroon instead of a white man, a Nordic man of blood and culture. You'd just be a damn mongrel."

I shuddered at his racist remarks, trying my best to steer him to the answers I needed. "Did you know Sam Bowers and Delmar Dennis?"

"I got to know them all. You see, the top Klan was made up of Masons, Knight Templars, and Shriners. The hierarchy of state government was made up of Masons, Knight Templars, and Shriners."

When I asked him about being charged with murdering Medgar Evers, he instead suggested the real killer was Lee Harvey Oswald. I figured he would deflect, but I almost laughed out loud at the absurdity of his answer.

Instead, he talked of his own later conviction in 1975. He had been caught with a time bomb made up of six sticks of dynamite. In his car,

New Orleans police found a map marked all the way to the home of Jewish leader A. I. Botnick, who headed the regional office for the Anti-Defamation League. This time, a jury convicted Beckwith. He insisted to me that he had been set up, saying that he had traveled to New Orleans to appraise china his grandmother received as a gift from Jefferson Davis's widow. He blamed his conviction on the "little Jewish prosecutor" and the "nigger women" on the jury.

At a certain point, I just let Beckwith speak, rather than trying to shape the conversation. He was a torrent of warped and hateful views. He said that any opponent of the white Christian way of life should be punished "quietly, secretly, and mysteriously. The Klan must once again become a submarine and stop acting like a tank." As he described his version of Christianity, it was utterly alien—a place where only faithful white people could be saved, where those of African descent are no more than soulless animals, and where those of Jewish descent are the literal offspring of Satan. He told me that all those stories I had heard in Sunday school were lies. He clasped a black leather Bible in his hand, opening the book to make a point with his jagged finger. "Niggers are beasts. It says so in here in the book of Adam."

He explained he was part of the Christian Identity Movement, flipping over to the book of Genesis and reading aloud about the Garden of Eden. "It says here, 'There was no man to till the soil.' The word 'man' in Hebrew is 'adam,' which literally means 'blood in the face.' Now, blood in the face means when you blush. Now you ain't never seen a nigger or a Jew blush. We all know that the white race is the only one that can blush."

The more he talked, the more I felt I had stumbled upon a backwoods preacher before the snake-handling part of the service began. He said our white ancestors were the true children of God, that Jesus was a "Hebrew," and that "anyone who calls Jesus a Jew is blaspheming." He mentioned the Caucasus Mountains. "That's why we're called Caucasians," he whispered, as if sharing a centuries-old secret.

The veins in his neck jutted out. He went on an anti-Semitic rant, claiming Jews possessed satanic powers, and that one day, the "true Israelites" would destroy these Jews.

He paused from his tirade long enough to finish his bubbling brew. His wife entered the room, and he held up his glass. "This sure was good what you gave me. It was just delicious. Fountain of youth."

She came near, and he gushed over the woman he married seven years earlier. "I fell in love with her. She was the first Miss Chattanooga."

He talked of his home state of Mississippi and bragged about it having more churches per capita than any other state. "That's a fact—till the niggers started having all those holy roller meetings and NAACP meetings in those churches. Then they began to burn down." He paused. "You know, niggers are careless with matches."

He cackled, his voice echoing through the house. He was his own perfect audience. I felt overwhelmed, stunned that such a person could exist, let alone that he could be celebrated—and worse—protected by those in power.

Outside the window, the sun had already slipped behind the redbud trees and darkness had begun to cover the mountain. I mentioned it was time to go, and his wife slid a turkey sandwich inside my briefcase.

He grabbed a flashlight, opened the door, and stepped outside. "Let me walk you to your car."

"That isn't necessary."

He walked ahead of me anyway, his flashlight slicing through the gloom. When I opened the driver's door on my Honda and moved to step in, he blocked my way. He glared at me, shadows covering his face.

"God will bless you if you write positive things about white Caucasian Christians. If you write negative things about white Caucasian Christians, God will punish you."

He paused, then locked eyes. "If God does not punish you directly, several individuals will do it for him."

He stepped aside, and I closed the door.

I was glad to have something, even just a pane of glass, between him and me.

I couldn't start the engine fast enough. As I drove down the street, I never looked back. I pressed the gas and sped down the mountain, hoping to make it out of town before the darkness closed in around me.

15

Visions of Byron De La Beckwith, flashlight clutched in hand, invaded my dreams. It had been foolish to seek him out alone—Karen was right. But, lucky or not, I had gotten away safely, and now I had new mysteries to untangle. After returning to Jackson, I visited the downtown library and found the speech Beckwith had mentioned. The white Citizens' Council had distributed the speech, known as "Black Monday," to schoolchildren across Mississippi.

Black Monday referred to May 17, 1954—the day the US Supreme Court ruled that segregated public schools were unconstitutional. The speech had been delivered by a self-described genius named Judge Thomas P. Brady, who later served on the Mississippi Supreme Court. He told a bizarre racist version of history in which he claimed whites were responsible for developing a calendar and pursuing astronomy in ancient Egypt and for carrying out architecture and art in ancient India. He insisted that these societies had started white and that racial amalgamation had destroyed them.

This was nothing more than fake history, a desire by white supremacists to believe they were behind the world's greatest achievements when, in reality, these ancient civilizations were anything but white. Searching for something on white supremacy, I discovered James Coates's book *Armed and Dangerous: The Rise of the Survivalist Right.* According to history, Assyria had conquered Israel (the northern ten tribes) and eventually assimilated them. But Christian Identity claimed these tribes escaped captivity, making their way instead to Europe.

Beckwith had also claimed Adam and Eve were white people and that the serpent, Satan, had sex with Eve, who gave birth to Cain, "the first Jew." This ridiculous belief must be why Beckwith kept insisting Jews had satanic powers.

I flipped to the index, discovering people Beckwith had mentioned, including Richard Butler, a Christian Identity preacher whose Idaho-based Aryan Nations had inspired horrible violence. I telephoned Butler, who talked of "white race traitors" and a Jewish conspiracy, insisting, "There's nothing wrong with being racist. The Japanese are very racist. The blacks are very racist."

Christian Identity created a straight line for followers, letting them embrace hate and violence with a clear conscience because they believed God was on their side. They turned mainstream Christian thoughts, such as the end-of-the-age Apocalypse, into a modern-day race war. In the years to come, Identity followers would carry out the 1996 Olympics bombing in Atlanta, gay bar bombings, abortion clinic bombings, and a Midwest rampage that killed two and injured ten—all of them black, Jewish, or Asian.

Similar messages made their way into the hearts and minds of many white Americans through publications such as Beckwith's favorite newspaper, *The Spotlight.* The radical right tabloid, passing itself off as a patriotic publication, supposedly boasted a circulation higher than the conservative magazine *National Review. Spotlight* promoted "America First," criticized welfare, pushed immigration limits, and opposed free trade. To conceal its racism, the publication referred to "Jews" as "international bankers" and praised former KKK leader David Duke, without, of course, mentioning his past.

Beckwith had pointed with pride to the Council of Conservative Citizens for carrying on the work that the white Citizens' Council had done for years, opposing "race mixing" and publicizing stories that claimed black Americans were inferior. A quarter-century later, the organization's website would inspire Dylann Roof to walk into the Emanuel AME Church in Charleston, South Carolina, and kill nine African-American members.

I hadn't told my editors about my plan to swing by and interview Byron De La Beckwith while I was in Tennessee. When I returned to the office, I figured my editors would be excited about my interview with the alleged assassin of Medgar Evers. I figured wrong.

After I had turned in a profile of Beckwith, along with a separate story on his involvement in Christian Identity, Executive Editor John Johnson chewed me out, telling me I never should have gone out there. I knew in hindsight that I should have discussed this in advance, but I explained it was a last-minute decision I made.

"Are you going to print my stories?" I asked.

"No, we're not going to run them."

Rain pelted me as I headed to the parking lot that night. An interview with Medgar Evers's reputed assassin, and the newspaper won't print it? I felt as miserable as the weather, wondering what to do next.

Weeks later, Jack Nelson, the Pulitzer Prize–winning chief of the Washington bureau for the *Los Angeles Times*, came to Jackson and invited me to join him for lunch. He told me about his upcoming book, *Terror in the Night*, which would show how the White Knights in the mid-1960s expanded their targets beyond African-Americans to include a terror campaign against the Jews. He asked me about the Medgar Evers case, and I mentioned my recent visit with Beckwith.

"You know Beckwith bragged about killing Medgar Evers at a Klan rally, don't you?"

"No, I didn't know that."

Suddenly, the question that Bobby DeLaughter had suggested for Beckwith clicked in my mind: *"Why don't you ask him if he ever attended a Klan rally down by the swinging bridge in Byram?"* DeLaughter, I realized, must have some evidence that incriminates Beckwith.

After lunch, I telephoned. "Bobby, is it true you have a statement from someone at a Klan rally who says Beckwith bragged about killing Medgar Evers?"

"Yes, if we can ever find Delmar Dennis."

"Delmar Dennis?" *That's who's been holding this up?* "I've got his phone number."

DeLaughter asked to speak with Dennis before I talked with him again.

"Fine with me, Bobby. As long as I can do a story."

DeLaughter told me that Dennis had quoted Beckwith in a little-known book called *Klandestine*. In a tirade at the Klan rally, Beckwith had allegedly said: "Killing that nigger gave me no more inner discomfort than our wives endure when they give birth to our children. We ask them to do that for us. We should do just as much. So, let's get in there and kill those enemies, including the President, from the top down."

When I reached Dennis, he said the quotation in the book was accurate. "Beckwith definitely bragged about killing him."

He said he had been told that the assassination of Medgar Evers had been a Klan job. He said he had also been told that Klansmen approached some of the jurors, and that's why Beckwith went free.

Dennis asked me to not publish his name for fear that Beckwith might kill him. I told him I would have to discuss the matter with my editors. In a rare departure from newspaper policy, they agreed.

The early version of my story included Dennis's name and a reference to *Klandestine*, but I deleted those references before I turned it in because editors said we would keep his identity a secret. When they learned about *Klandestine*, they became upset, feeling that if my story had been published, the newspaper would have been embarrassed since the quotation had already appeared in the book.

My editors told me to rewrite the story, so that it would now mention both Dennis and the book. "This will be your last story on the Beckwith case," Johnson told me. "You've gotten too close to the story."

Before my story ran, I telephoned Dennis and apologized, explaining that we would need to run his name now. He brushed it off as no big deal. "It's all right."

I also telephoned Beckwith about Dennis's statement to give him a chance to respond. The white supremacist took the news in stride, calling the claim "Hereford droppings." He said, "Somebody is trying to make some money out of this at taxpayers' expense." Then he mentioned that he had been invited to speak at a recent KKK rally in Jackson, but he had decided against coming. "Some damn fool might try to put me in jail."

I didn't realize it, but by the time I called him, Beckwith had already agreed to let DeLaughter interview him in Signal Mountain. The white supremacist canceled after our conversation. It hadn't been my intention to get in the way. But I did find comfort in the sense that Beckwith finally seemed spooked, and in the fact that the investigation was finding its second wind.

Dennis's statement represented a major breakthrough, a new witness in a quarter-century-old case desperate for new witnesses. Beckwith had always insisted he was ninety miles away and had nothing to do with Evers's killing. Now here was someone saying Beckwith bragged about murdering the civil rights leader.

I caught up with Myrlie Evers. "For the first time, Jerry, I feel hope."

But while hopes for a possible prosecution took flight, I sank into a depression. Executive Editor John Johnson made good on his threats to take me off the story. I spent each workday covering courts, but I could no longer pursue my passion of the past seven months, the Medgar Evers case.

Life went on, in all its highs and lows. I celebrated my son's birth. I wept at my grandfather's funeral. But my days felt long and uninspired, my future suddenly in doubt. I didn't know if I was going to stay at *The Clarion-Ledger*, or even in journalism for that matter. I dropped by Johnson's office to make one more case, but he told me in no uncertain terms that, even if Byron De La Beckwith were indicted, I couldn't cover the trial. I knew then that I would have to leave the paper where I had worked for the past four years.

First, however, I would keep my word to DeLaughter. Underneath my desk, I grabbed copies of the three volumes of the transcript of Beckwith's

1964 trial, loaded them into a grocery sack, and delivered them to his south Jackson home. He was waiting on his front steps.

Weeks later, I ran into him in the courthouse as I went through the motions on my beat. He had just returned from interviewing Delmar Dennis, and he said the session had been a fruitful one. He was already thinking through next steps, and the next big question would seem to be the missing murder weapon. When the case was first reopened back in 1989, DeLaughter had told me that it would be difficult to prosecute the case without the murder weapon.

Now at the courthouse, DeLaughter and I ruminated about where the gun might be. My thoughts went to evidence lockers, long cleaned out. He hypothesized that the rifle might have wound up in the home of some collector. I watched his face as he answered. The more he talked, the more his eyes twinkled.

"You're really going to reopen this case, aren't you, Bobby?"

He smiled. "I can see the light at the end of the tunnel."

16

On the morning of June 15, 1990, fellow reporter Michael Rejebian led me into Managing Editor Bennie Ivory's office. Ivory told us that an anonymous caller had contacted him after seeing an ABC *Primetime Live* broadcast the night before, which had centered on the reopening of the Medgar Evers case. I had given this interview to ABC before being taken off the case. The broadcast also included interviews with District Attorney Ed Peters, who said he didn't know where the murder weapon was, and with Byron De La Beckwith, who chortled as he declared, "I didn't kill that nigger, but he's sho' dead. He ain't comin' back."

Ivory said the anonymous caller claimed to know where the Evers murder weapon was. The caller, however, would only speak to me, the reporter he had seen on *Primetime*.

"You're back on the story," Ivory said.

I could have hugged him. I had never heard five more welcome words.

When I reached the caller, he agreed to reveal the gun's location—but only in person.

"Where are you?"

"Signal Mountain, Tennessee."

That's where Beckwith lives.

The man said he was a law enforcement officer but refused to share his name. As the conversation continued, he mentioned I was from the Lone Star State.

"How did you know I was from Texas?"

"I checked you out."

After hanging up, it dawned on me that he could have learned about my roots from one person in Signal Mountain—Byron De La Beckwith. If that was the case, the officer's insistence that I show up in person seemed like a possible—or blatant—setup.

In Ivory's office, the editors and I debated strategy. Should I go to Signal Mountain? If so, what precautions should we take?

We all agreed that we needed to check out the tip. I couldn't go alone, however. Rejebian would travel with me, and we would meet the officer tomorrow, a Saturday.

When I told my wife about our return trip to Signal Mountain, she begged me not to go. "You're really crazy. You want to be killed."

Upset, she telephoned my parents. My father told me, "It's a trap. Don't do it."

I told them both I had to go. That the whole case could hinge on this information. I repeated that another reporter was coming with me, and that we would be careful.

With my family concerned about my safety, I decided to telephone Bobby DeLaughter for his advice. I told him we had a tip about the gun's location and that the tipster wanted to meet us in Signal Mountain. "Does it sound like a setup to you, Bobby?"

"I don't know."

The more I pressed him, the less he said, refusing to give advice one way or the other.

Rejebian and I decided to go. We opted against traveling in my car, and instead we made the trip in his white Chevy Blazer.

We arrived in Signal Mountain at about 2:30 p.m., pulling into the parking lot of a shopping center. I found a pay phone and dialed a pager number I had been given.

As we waited for the call back, the fear I'd been holding off all morning settled in. But soon, just as planned, an officer dressed in uniform arrived to meet us.

He told us to get back into the Chevy and follow him. This hadn't been part of the plan. We obliged, but the longer we trailed him, the more my concerns grew.

We followed him to the end of a remote street where weeds stretched six feet high. He pulled his squad car so far around that he blocked our way back out.

"I don't like the looks of this, Mike."

"I don't, either."

The officer stepped out of his squad car, and when I saw his gun strapped to his waist, I wondered if we had just made a horrible mistake. But it was too late for us to do anything else.

Mike and I got out of the Blazer, and the officer kept moving closer. The next thing we knew, he was patting both of us down, telling us he was searching for weapons and tape recorders.

After he was finished, he finally spoke. "Are y'all going to nail him?"

I exhaled in relief after hearing the question. The words didn't seem like those of a Beckwith sympathizer. Still, I chose my words carefully. "That's up to the DA's office."

"Do you know Ed Pete?" he asked.

Rejebian and I traded puzzled looks, and he broke the silence. "Ed Peters? The district attorney?"

"Yeah. That's the one. That's why this case isn't going to be prosecuted."

The officer said that Peters already *had* the murder weapon. "The gun is on his mantel, right next to a framed article from the *Jackson Daily News*."

Rejebian and I bowed our heads in disbelief. We'd had no idea what to expect coming into the conversation, but it certainly wasn't *this*.

"Peters said on national television he doesn't know where the gun is," Rejebian said.

"I know, but Peters has it."

"So where did you get this information?" I asked.

"From Beckwith," he said. "I was watching *Primetime Live* with him. When they said on the program that the gun was missing, Beckwith started laughing. He said it wasn't missing, it was on Ed Peters's mantel."

The conversation moved from the murder weapon to the man accused of pulling the trigger. The officer fidgeted with his sunglasses, telling us to beware of Beckwith. The man was dangerous. Beckwith collected bombs and guns in his basement, the officer said, along with years of rations, for the coming "race war."

When I mentioned that Beckwith had delivered what felt like a threat as I was getting ready to leave Signal Mountain, the officer confirmed my fear. He said the white supremacist wanted to get me personally. He repeated Beckwith's words for me now: "That redheaded son-of-a-bitch from Texas had better watch out."

On the drive home, Rejebian and I sifted through each detail of the conversation. If this man watched TV with Beckwith and was, it seemed, even friends with him, why had he reached out to us? That was unclear, and unnerving. We didn't believe the officer's claims about Peters having the murder weapon, but we agreed that when we returned to Mississippi, we still needed to check out the tip.

"Peters wouldn't have the gun on his mantel," Rejebian said.

"Stranger things have happened," I said.

I had stopped guessing what might happen next.

Back in Jackson, Rejebian returned Monday to his beat. On his usual rounds of covering the city of Jackson, he spoke with Police Chief Charlie Newell. When the chief asked what he did that weekend, Rejebian mentioned looking for the rifle in the Medgar Evers case.

Newell happened to be familiar with the weapon and its history. He shared that a "Judge Moore" had acquired the murder weapon years after the trial, at a time when the gun was no longer considered evidence. The judge turned out to be the late Russel Moore, the father of Assistant City

Attorney Matthew Moore. When Rejebian confronted the lawyer, the younger Moore confirmed off the record that his father had taken the rifle as a souvenir.

"Do you still have the gun?" Rejebian asked.

"No, my brother-in-law came and got it."

"Who's your brother-in-law?"

"Bobby DeLaughter."

Rejebian rushed back to the office and explained what he had found. It seemed impossible. What were the odds that the prosecutor in a case would collect the murder weapon from his own in-laws? And *why*?

I telephoned DeLaughter at the district attorney's office, only to find he had left for the day. I called his home, reaching his wife, Dixie, whom I knew from *The Clarion-Ledger*, where she worked in circulation. "Bobby's at baseball practice. You can catch him there."

Rejebian and I sped to Leavell Woods Park in south Jackson, where the prosecutor was wrapping up coaching a Little League team. We sat on the warped wooden bleachers, sweltering in the 95-degree heat. Several times DeLaughter cocked his eye at us.

When practice was over, he strolled over, chuckling. I had told him in advance about our clandestine meeting in Signal Mountain, and he had seen it as a wild goose chase. That made a lot more sense now.

"Did y'all find the gun?" he joked.

"Yeah, *you've* got the gun," Rejebian responded.

Blood appeared to drain from DeLaughter's face. He sputtered. "I-I-I don't want the target of the investigation to know what we do or don't have."

"Beckwith already knows you have the gun," Rejebian said.

DeLaughter shook his head in disbelief. He walked away, and I followed him to his car. "Why didn't you tell me, Bobby?"

"I would have told you sooner, Jerry, if it hadn't been for your editors," he said. I knew he was still stinging from what happened with Delmar Dennis, but I was struggling to understand what was going on.

Back in the office, Rejebian telephoned Matthew Moore and told him that DeLaughter had said he would have told us sooner about the gun if it hadn't been for our editors. Moore told Rejebian everything he knew on the record.

With Moore now talking, I called DeLaughter. He admitted that prosecutors had the gun, saying they had not said so earlier because they didn't want Beckwith to know they were collecting evidence in the case. They wanted Beckwith to relax and keep shooting off his mouth.

I wanted to believe DeLaughter, despite the strange circumstances. Myrlie Evers wanted to believe, too, but she was stunned. "I certainly hope that more 'missing' information will surface."

She wanted to know why DeLaughter hadn't told her, and I could only share what he told me. "Bobby says he kept it a secret because he didn't want Beckwith to know."

The irony was that Beckwith had already surmised the gun was in the hands of prosecutors. And now I had to call him for comment. When he answered, he told me he was taping our telephone conversation and demanded I do the same.

I told him prosecutors had the gun, and he began mocking them.

"They do? Well, that's astounding. If they didn't have the gun, something is dreadfully wrong in that locker where they keep evidence."

He said authorities might have a gun *like* his, but pointed out "there were two million guns like that in circulation at the end of World War One. If they don't have a gun like that, they are very poor scroungers."

I got what I needed to close out our article on the murder weapon. Then, before the conversation ended, Beckwith insisted he had never threatened me before. Which meant the officer who tipped us off must have talked again to Beckwith. *How strange.*

It was almost midnight when Rejebian and I left *The Clarion-Ledger* that night. We could barely wrap our heads around the day's events.

"God wanted us to have this story," I said.

And so, it seems, did Byron De La Beckwith.

17

After we broke the story about the supposedly long-lost murder weapon, African-American leaders in Mississippi, including future congressman Bennie Thompson, called for a federal investigation into the prosecutors' handling of it. Civil rights advocates knew Judge Russel Moore well and had reason to be suspicious. He had played a role in some of Mississippi's worst moments. In 1961, he had convicted Freedom Riders and sent them to Mississippi's worst prison. And when Beckwith went on trial, Moore attended the proceedings.

In the days that followed our report, DeLaughter told me more about how he had come to acquire the gun. Some time back, he said he had heard Moore say the rifle in his house had been used in a civil rights case. While poring through crime scene photos for the Evers case, the prosecutor was able to make the connection. "Damn, I remember him telling me about a rifle. I wonder if that could be it."

DeLaughter said he wrote down the murder weapon's serial number from the police reports. "That night after I got home, I called Mrs. Moore and asked her if she knew anything. She knew about the rifle but didn't remember the specifics. So I drove out there that night, she showed me where it was—on the top shelf of a bedroom closet."

DeLaughter saw the scratched initials of authorities on the gun and compared the serial number to the one he had written down. "The hairs on the back of my neck stood up. I thought, 'This is it.'"

Rather than check the murder weapon into evidence, DeLaughter took the rifle home, wrapped it in a blanket, and stuffed it into their bedroom closet, his wife, Dixie, later told me. When I asked DeLaughter about concerns that he was trying to deep-six the case, he reassured me that he knew it didn't look great, but "if there had been a cover-up, I would have done something other than save it for prosecution."

He explained that prosecutors had ended up in a catch-22. They had been truthful in saying, early in the investigation, that they did not have the gun. But "once we were in possession of the gun, if we had changed our response from a negative answer to a 'no comment,' this would have done nothing but signal a change."

Medgar Evers's brother, Charles, defended the district attorney's office and thought the fuss over the gun was a sideshow. "I'm sick and tired of these politicians politicizing off of my brother's name," he told me. "With the evidence *The Clarion-Ledger* has brought and with the evidence the district attorney has uncovered, [Beckwith] is going to be indicted."

On July 13, 1990, the Justice Department concluded there was no violation of federal law. "Maybe now," DeLaughter said, "people will be glad we have the gun rather than poor-mouth the fellow who saved it."

DeLaughter cornered me the next time I came by the district attorney's office. He was already looking forward. He told me that while he had copied the trial transcript I shared with him, prosecutors needed a certified copy of the original transcript in order to be able to use the testimony as evidence.

This signaled progress, and I welcomed the good news. Over the past year, I had seen a shift in the way he spoke about the Medgar Evers case. At first, he spoke about what a shame it was that a man had been shot in the back in front his family. Now he was talking about how this prosecution could right a historical wrong.

When he pressed me on where to find the original transcript, I suggested he talk with Myrlie Evers. Mine was just a photocopy, but if anyone's transcript was official and admissible, it would be hers.

Days later, she telephoned me, saying she had received a call from De-Laughter, quoting him as saying, "We're at a dead end. We can't work any further. We don't have a transcript."

"Keep working," she replied.

"You have a transcript?"

"Yes."

On October 12, 1990, she arrived in Jackson to deliver the 963-page transcript in person to prosecutors. At her insistence, I met her at the airport with a photographer. She told me she knew she was handing over a critical piece of evidence, and she wanted to make sure this act was documented. The last thing she wanted was for the transcript to turn up "missing."

A month later, she and former prosecutors testified in a hearing that authenticated the transcript. That act cleared the way for the grand jury to consider murder charges.

When I reached Beckwith for comment, he said, "I've got forty more years. I don't know how much longer you've got."

He cackled. "You're a reckless driver. You be careful now as you're driving down the road. I don't want you to have an accident or wreck or someone molest you. Would you think people would do that to you?"

"Do you think they would?"

"Have they ever?"

"No."

"They haven't?"

He laughed again. "Well, somebody told me to live and learn."

From that morning forward, I began checking under my car hood. I was no longer taking any chances.

18

A grand jury began hearing evidence on whether to indict Byron De La Beckwith. On December 13, 1990, eighteen members packed a room inside the Hinds County Courthouse, led by a grand jury foreman named Dr. Carl Gustav Evers. He wasn't related, but he had been at the University of Mississippi Medical Center the night Medgar Evers was brought into the emergency room with a fatal gunshot wound.

After the grand jury saw much of the evidence, including the rifle used to kill the NAACP leader, his widow, Myrlie Evers, sat before them, sharing how she and her children had watched President Kennedy speak that night on television and were waiting up to talk with Medgar about it. Instead, an assassin's bullet struck him, leaving the carport covered in his blood. She watched friends load him into the back of their family station wagon and speed him toward the hospital. In the throes of death, he twisted and yelled, "Turn me loose. Turn me loose."

Grand jurors took in her words, and some wiped away tears. The passage of a quarter century had failed to dim her pain.

In the wake of the tragedy of Evers's murder came changes. African-Americans in Jackson became school crossing guards and police officers for the first time. Courtesy titles such as "Mr." and "Mrs."—long denied to black Mississippians—began to be used. Restaurants opened their doors to all.

Myrlie Evers said, "The person who pulled the trigger with the intent of eradicating Medgar Evers certainly did get rid of the person, but his person and what he stood for continued, not only to live, but to thrive."

Even so, every bit of change had been hard won, and certain wounds—like Beckwith's mistrials—continued to sting. Myrlie Evers made clear that it was time for Mississippi to correct the record.

After listening to her, grand jurors heard statements from witnesses who said Beckwith had bragged to them about killing Medgar Evers. In this group, the prosecutor also called an unlikely witness, Edgar Ray Killen, the onetime KKK leader who strolled into the grand jury room wearing a dark suit and a cowboy hat.

After Assistant District Attorney Bobby DeLaughter asked a few questions, Killen interrupted. "Can I ask why I'm here? I'm really mystified by being here."

"This grand jury is investigating the shooting death of Medgar Evers on June 12, 1963," the prosecutor replied.

"I'm really mystified because I didn't even know Mr. . . . whatever his name is—Beckwith."

"That's interesting, Mr. Killen, because I didn't mention the name of Beckwith in connection with the murder; you did."

"Well, I ain't never heard of him except in the news."

"Have you ever been a member of the White Knights of the Ku Klux Klan of Mississippi?"

"Many people testified that I was."

"Do you deny saying in 1964, following the arrest of you, Sam Bowers, and the other Klansmen for the three murders in Neshoba County, that there was no reason to worry—that the Evers murder was a Klan project and the killer is free today because of Klan contacts with some of the jurors, and that same thing was going to happen in your cases?"

"Well, first, I didn't know Sam Bowers was in the Klan."

"You're telling us that you did not know that the imperial wizard himself was in the Klan?"

Some grand jurors chuckled.

"As far as, you know, Sam coming up to me and saying, 'I'm the imperial wizard,' no, he didn't do that."

"Of course he wouldn't. As a matter of fact, when you join the Klan, you take a solemn blood oath of secrecy, don't you?"

DeLaughter pressed Killen again on Beckwith.

"The only time I ever seen Beckwith," Killen said, "was when he come by the courtroom when we were on trial and shook hands with us."

"I thought you said earlier that you never heard of him."

Before wrapping up, DeLaughter called Beckwith's two potential alibi witnesses before the grand jury. The strategy carried a bit of a risk because if the grand jury believed these retired police officers, there would be no indictment.

Hollis Creswell walked in, put his hand on the Bible, and swore to tell the truth. He insisted he saw Beckwith at "five minutes till 1 o'clock," but couldn't place the time that he heard about Medgar Evers's death, "somewhere around 4, 4:30. I don't remember."

DeLaughter pressed for more details about seeing Beckwith.

"I'm not positive on whether he was in front of the car or behind the car, but I am positive that he was standing with his foot propped right on that median right there."

"Which way was Beckwith facing?"

"He was facing this way. Facing the car."

"Did you wave to him?"

"No, I know he didn't. I'm sure he didn't."

DeLaughter asked him about telling me that Beckwith had waved at him and that he had waved back.

"I ain't sure of that now, but I made that statement. I know if he waved to me, I waved back at him."

"Did he wave at you?"

"I don't know. That's been too long ago."

"Do you deny making a statement earlier that you waved at him?"

"No, I don't."

District Attorney Ed Peters joined in the questioning, and so did grand jurors. How was Creswell so sure he saw Beckwith that night since Beckwith wasn't arrested until more than ten days later?

"Just like I told you," Creswell replied. "We heard that news [of Evers's killing]."

"On the news they didn't tell you that he [Beckwith] was the killer. They just told you the fact that he [Evers] was dead."

"Well, no, they didn't."

"You didn't hear that fact . . . until ten days later. . . . How can you remember something like that ten days later?"

"I remember it was the same night—the same morning."

"Did you make a report of that?"

"Naw, I didn't because I had no reason to."

After he finished, he walked outside, and his former partner, James Holley, entered. He fared no better.

Darkness had fallen by the time the grand jury stepped into a nearby courtroom and turned over their indictments to a judge. The judge announced no indictment would be made public until after any arrests. That meant Myrlie Evers and the rest of us might have to wait several days to find out if Beckwith had been indicted. She told me she felt "full of butterflies, waiting, not knowing."

More than an hour later, she telephoned me at home, unable to contain her joy. "You know the thing that you and I have been waiting for?"

"Yes?"

"It happened."

I could hardly believe the news. Byron De La Beckwith had just been indicted.

19

Clarion-Ledger Managing Editor Bennie Ivory knew that Byron De La Beckwith had talked at length with me. Now he wondered if the white supremacist would chat with another *Clarion-Ledger* journalist. Reporter J. Lee Howard took on the challenge and telephoned Beckwith.

Before agreeing to meet, Beckwith subjected him to a litany of questions about his racial heritage.

"I'm white," Howard answered.

"Are you sure?"

Howard tried to introduce himself more thoroughly, at one point mentioning his stint in the Marine Corps. "Semper Fi," Beckwith said. "Why didn't you tell me? I've always got time for a Marine."

On December 16, 1990, a Sunday, Beckwith welcomed Howard inside his Signal Mountain home, telling him, "I am guilty of no crime whatsoever, and it will be proven that that's the case whenever I am tried by a fair and impartial jury of my peers."

His definition of peers? "Like I am—right, white, and on the Christian side of every issue."

He suggested the Medgar Evers case had been resurrected because "the niggers have run out of something to do."

The next day, Howard returned to Beckwith's house for lunch. While Howard downed broiled chicken and syrupy sweet tea, Beckwith received a call from a different reporter, who told Beckwith that he had been indicted. When Beckwith returned to eat his now-cold meal, he was furious, digging into his turnip greens like a man on fire.

He shrugged off his possible arrest, saying prosecutors "do what they've been told by a handful of Jews and white trash, several Negroes, and non-white immigrants. The crowd in power in Mississippi are the sons and daughters of the mothers and fathers that put Negroes in the white schools in 1954. They're the same people that for the glee and the profit, deliberately and enthusiastically fomented strife on the white Christian republic of Mississippi, Dixie, and the whole United States. They are the same people who are the sons and daughters of the Jewish temple gods who killed Christ at Calvary."

Through gasps of air, he sputtered. His wife, Thelma, clasped his waving hand and told him to relax. "I tell you, honey," she said, "whatever they do to you, it will come back on them."

Beckwith started up again. "More and more people are getting mad about race mixing and anti-Christian sentiment, and if more of these pockets of pus splatter all over me, they're likely to do something about it. I have not yet begun to fight. I've got to stop and lick my wounds. But I'll get my strength back and come back at 'em again and again. If I sin against Thee, ever-lovin' God, well, he's going to kick my ass. These other races, creeds, and colors, we're supposed to control them. That's why God put us down here."

Beckwith asked Howard to leave, saying he had important business to attend to. Thelma dabbed her nose with a tissue. "Oh, this is going to kill him. He's been a good man all his life. I'm so mad."

Soon after Howard left, deputies arrived. While being taken into custody, Beckwith couldn't resist a joke. "You want to search my pockets to see if I've got a bomb?" Yet by the time deputies reached the sheriff's office, leading the white supremacist past a waiting press contingent, he had lost his sense of humor. He snarled at a photographer, "You want me to shove that camera down your throat?"

That night in the newsroom, sensing that we were watching history unfold, we made our way to the presses, grabbing copies of the first newspapers off the press. They bore the headline BECKWITH ARRESTED IN THE EVERS CASE.

Returning to the newsroom, I sat on top of a desk. Moments later, Ivory slid in beside me and asked, "Can you believe this?"

"Still doesn't seem real."

He shook his head. "Never thought I'd see the day that Ed Peters would have Byron De La Beckwith arrested."

20

The .38 pistol gleamed in the moonlight as Delmar Dennis drove his pickup truck into the darkness of the Smoky Mountains. The onetime FBI informant traveled in silence for miles before telling me he might not testify in Byron De La Beckwith's upcoming murder trial. He said his possible testimony had been on his mind, and he was worried. Two hours away in jail, the accused assassin was fighting extradition, as he put it, "tooth, nail, and claw."

Dennis, tall, stocky, and balding, told me he was more concerned about Beckwith's friends than the old man himself. The former KKK leader said that the radical views of Christian Identity made them "more dangerous than the Klan. They think they're doing God's will."

He talked about a rabid sect within Identity called the Phineas Priesthood. "Have you ever heard of the Phineas Priesthood?"

"No, I haven't."

"You know the story of Phineas in the Bible, don't you?"

"Not that I remember."

"Well, this is one they don't teach in Sunday school."

He shared the story of Israelite men bowing down to Baal and having sex with Moabite women. Upset by this sight, Phineas, the grandson of Aaron the High Priest, ran a spear through a copulating couple.

Dennis said by carrying out this act, Phineas halted a plague and received a priesthood. "This is where they get their name. They believe they have God's authority to kill."

He said their targets included "race mixers" and others, including white traitors. He pointed me to a book, written by white supremacist Richard Kelly Hoskins, called *Vigilantes of Christendom: The History of the Phineas Priesthood.* He also mentioned a February 1991 publication by the same author called the *Hoskins Report,* a strange mix of stock reports and white supremacy. Inside, Beckwith had written a letter to the editor, ending with the phrase "Phineas for President."

"Don't you see?" Dennis said. "Beckwith is a Phineas priest."

He pointed to the .38 on his dashboard and told me it was loaded. "There was a time I didn't carry a gun much." But if a Phineas priest attacked him, he said he would have no warning. "Nothing is quite so dangerous as a religious fanatic who thinks he's doing the Lord's will."

Back at the office in Jackson, I consulted every white supremacy expert I could find. None had heard of the Phineas Priesthood.

When I reached the Center for Democratic Renewal in Atlanta, they pointed me to Leonard Zeskind of Kansas City, who ran the Institute for Research and Education on Human Rights and had researched white supremacy for decades. He shared that he had run across references to Phineas in recent white supremacist writings. He said these Phineas priests "regard themselves as God's assassins. They believe they have authority from God to kill interracial couples, gays, bankers and anyone else they view as God's enemies." The priesthood, he said, signaled a new direction of the violent right, which now sought largely to escape detection through smaller groups and "lone wolves," a shift from the larger organizations of previous decades.

Vigilantes of Christendom began with the words: "In Denver, Colorado, an anti-Christian radio announcer stepped from his Volkswagen and was greeted with a hail of gunfire. In North Carolina, men entered a homosexual parlor, shot the occupants and burned the parlor down on top of them. In the Midwest, interracial couples jogging together fell one after another before the carefully spaced shots of a distant sniper. In Seattle, a bomb exploded in a porno movie theater. In Washington State, a Brinks car is held up and money taken to finance further acts against the establishment. . . . In D.C., a White prostitute and her Black pimp are found shot to death. It makes little difference whether you agree or disagree with the Phineas Priesthood. It is important that you know that it exists, is active and in the near future may become a central fact in your life."

The words chilled me. These were terrorists, even if society didn't call them that.

I telephoned the *Vigilantes* author at his office in Lynchburg, Virginia, to try to learn more about his beliefs. When I questioned him about his white supremacist writings, he fired back, "Go to the store and find out how many books are written on the black race, the history of the Orientals, the history of the Jews and how many there are of the history of the whites."

I tried another tack, suggesting at the least that the Phineas Priesthood was controversial. He responded, "You're making something controversial over Bible teachings. That's crazy."

When I asked him about Beckwith, he slammed down the telephone.

I called Beckwith's wife, Thelma, to see if I could get more information. She seemed like a genuine southern belle until she opened her mouth. She sometimes railed for hours, cursing the Jews and screaming at me. Other times, she was perfectly calm, but still a screw loose, as when she told me she knew her husband was innocent because she was a psychic. Once, when I checked my voice mail, I heard her trying to complete a person-to-person call to me.

"He's not here," the operator told her. "Would you like to leave him a message?"

"Why, yes. You just tell him to go to hell."

She sounded cordial today. She confirmed her husband was indeed a "priest," but she denied he belonged to the Phineas Priesthood, even though Hoskins had given a copy of *Vigilantes* to Beckwith, inscribing it, "To the Master."

All these revelations made it possible for me to write a story on the Phineas Priesthood and Beckwith. He had made clear what he thought just before his arrest on Signal Mountain: "I'm willing to lay my life down to rid evil from this country. I'm willing to kill the evil in this country that would push me out."

On October 3, 1990, I learned of at least one person he considered evil. After losing his extradition battle, he was now forced to appear in a Mississippi courtroom. Upon entering, in handcuffs, he spotted me and exclaimed, "Speak of the devil!"

21

Desperate to soak up as many details as I could about Medgar Evers's killing, I spent my days and nights reading the 1964 trial transcript. In one portion, a telephone company employee testified that Medgar Evers had an unlisted number. That didn't surprise me.

But it reminded me of the testimony of two cab drivers I had just read. I flipped back and re-read the words of Herbert Richard Speight and Lee Swilley, both of whom worked for White-Top Cab. They testified that Beckwith had showed up at the Trailways bus station in Jackson about 4 p.m. the Saturday before Evers's assassination, which took place after midnight on Wednesday.

"He approached me and asked me if I knew Negro Medgar Evers, N-double-A-C-P leader," Speight said. "I told him I did not."

When the cab drivers were unable to give Beckwith directions to the civil rights leader's home, Beckwith went back inside the bus station to a pay phone and returned with a map taken from the telephone book. First Beckwith asked about a possible address on Lexington Street. Speight told him that "couldn't be where the colored fellow lived because it's an all-white section."

Beckwith returned with an address on Buena Vista Avenue and then one on Poplar Boulevard, which Speight told him were also white neighborhoods. Before the cab drivers left, Beckwith explained why he needed the directions. "I've got to find where he lives in a couple of days."

This in itself was damning, but I wondered why he had to find the civil rights leader so quickly. It sounded like he had a deadline.

I telephoned Klansman turned FBI informant Delmar Dennis. He repeated what he had told me before—that he was told the Evers's assassination had been a KKK job. It wasn't a stretch to believe. When Beckwith walked free in 1964, the White Knights burned crosses in most of the eighty-two counties across Mississippi. The event signaled victory for the KKK.

Talking to Dennis, I wondered aloud about the timing of the killing. I knew President Kennedy had delivered his first national civil rights address just hours before Evers was killed.

"Could that have been the deadline Beckwith was referring to?" I asked.

"Yes, it could," Dennis replied. "You have to realize the Klan never thought of itself as local. It viewed itself as a national organization. This assassination wasn't just a message to Mississippians."

His remarks dovetailed with what Dan Prince, who had rented from Beckwith before being kicked out, had told me. Beckwith admitted killing Medgar Evers, Prince said. "He stated to me that his business was killing people and it was national, and he wasn't going to let some local mess it up."

I dove back into the transcript and noticed something I had missed about the testimony of Speight, one of the cab drivers. At one point, he corrected himself, saying Beckwith had actually told the cab drivers he was looking for "Medgar Evans."

Beckwith had the name of his target wrong?

I tried wrapping my mind around that. If Beckwith had the name wrong, then the belief he was an obsessed assassin was wrong. Instead, it sounded like he was carrying out orders.

When I thought back on Beckwith's remarks regarding Medgar Evers, they began to make more sense. Many murderers voice fury toward their victims, even years later, but Beckwith breathed indifference. "What did I want to be bothered with a little ol' NAACP nigger when I was calling on the wealthiest planters in Mississippi, Tennessee and Alabama, selling fertilizer? What time did I have to take up my day with what the little ol' nigger was doing down in Jackson or wherever he was doing what he was doing?"

I wondered about the streets Beckwith had called out. He had to be getting the names from the telephone book. I drove to the Mississippi Department of Archives and History building and looked at a 1963 Jackson telephone book. Inside, I found four Everses. None was Medgar Evers, because his number was unlisted. The last name Evans, however, took up two columns. None had the first name of Medgar.

I searched through the names for the streets Beckwith mentioned to the cab drivers, trying to reconstruct what he did. After studying the phone book for some time, it appeared to me that after going through the list of Evanses, he started back in reverse order and stopped at the first Evans that had initials and also began with an "FL" (or 35) prefix.

I remembered that a prefix signaled numbers from a specific area. But why would Beckwith have stopped at that prefix? I flipped the phone book pages until I found the telephone listing for the NAACP office. It, too, bore the "FL" prefix.

The first two streets matched this pattern, but Poplar Boulevard was missing from all the Evanses listed in the phone book.

So where did Beckwith come up with Poplar Boulevard? I paused for a minute and tried to think like Beckwith might have thought that day. Wait a minute. What if Beckwith knew someone on that street? And what if that person lived near Medgar Evers?

I returned to the archives help desk, and this time asked for a 1963 crisscross directory for the city of Jackson. In the days before the Internet, it was the handiest device for finding people. The crisscross directory was often packed with information, including the names of everyone at every single address in a city.

When an archivist brought it, I flipped through the pages till I found Poplar Boulevard. I scrolled my finger across the names of the people who lived on the street until one jumped out—Samuel E. Lackey.

Lackey? Beckwith was close with another Lackey—Gordon Lackey— who supposedly swore Beckwith into the White Knights of the KKK. Beckwith later told an FBI informant that Lackey was "his guiding force" in murdering Medgar Evers.

Not long after Beckwith was indicted, I took a trip to Greenwood to visit Lackey. He was tall, white-haired, and fit-looking, still teaching martial arts classes in Greenwood. Before his class began, I approached him and asked what he knew about Medgar Evers.

Lackey did little to conceal his hatred of the slain civil rights leader. "Medgar Evers was not a praiseworthy character, not a role model. He's like Louis Farrakhan." He claimed Evers had called for revolution at a Mississippi Delta farm, saying, "My brothers, it is time for the fertile black cotton rows to run red with white planters' blood."

Evers never made these remarks. I knew that. What fascinated me was that Lackey's words sounded like what a Klansman would say to justify murder.

When I asked him who killed Evers, Lackey bristled. "Anybody of any political hue or cry could have." He spat out the words in fury, even after all these years.

I brought up a 1966 FBI document in which an informant said Lackey had bragged about assisting Beckwith in killing Evers. He laughed. "That's total fabrication. I've never once been questioned by the FBI on my role. They never asked me. They never asked if I had any desire."

I asked if he was related to Samuel Lackey, who lived on Poplar Avenue in Jackson in 1963.

"That's my uncle," he said.

After our conversation concluded, I realized he had never denied playing a part in the assassination. *My role*, he'd said, without hesitation.

• • •

None of this surprised Myrlie Evers, who told me that her husband, Medgar, appeared on a number of KKK "death lists" after taking the job as field secretary for the Mississippi NAACP. "Medgar was constantly being followed or spied on. One time he even wrote down a tag number."

"Oh?"

"Yes, I still have it somewhere."

After searching through an old trunk, she found the file and read it to me: Hinds County tag H18955. "The car was a '61 or '62 Pontiac, he wrote. It was blue with a white top. Medgar described the man as tall, wearing a black-and-white checkered shirt."

The car tag matched those of cabs back then, and the general description matched the White-Top Cab. While the physical description didn't match the five-foot-eight Beckwith, it could describe Lackey. The fact that others were spying on Evers added to the growing proof that Beckwith conspired with others.

I asked Bobby DeLaughter about a conspiracy to kill Evers. He thought that was a real possibility. I asked him if he thought Lackey was involved.

"I think he was in it up to his eyeballs," he replied. But he said that he knew of no way to prove it in a trial. There wasn't enough evidence, and DeLaughter believed Beckwith pulled the trigger. Going after Lackey at this point might do nothing more than muddy the water in this prosecution.

Fliers spread like dandelions across Batesville, Mississippi, and the rest of Panola County, where jurors would be picked in a few weeks for Beckwith's September 1992 trial. The fliers, which landed in hundreds of driveways, called Beckwith a political prisoner. Each flier was attached to a Liberty Lobby's *Citizens Rule Book*, which told these possible jurors they could find a defendant not guilty, regardless of the evidence. I thought Beckwith was behind this, but authorities lacked proof.

In court, prosecutors and defense lawyers were still wrangling over last-minute motions. The defense had already asked the Mississippi Supreme Court to halt the trial on constitutional grounds, but I knew that justices rarely intervened in such cases.

While eating lunch at Taco Bell, I read the latest motion from De-Laughter, who accused Beckwith of trying to thwart justice again, this time with the fliers. As I started to walk out the door, Beckwith's forty-seven-year-old son, Byron VII, also known as "DeLay Jr.," stopped me. "Jerry, have you got a minute? We'd like to talk with you."

I joined him and his twenty-three-year-old son, Byron VIII, at the table. The younger Beckwith asked, "Do you think my granddaddy did it?"

I hesitated, but finally acknowledged that I believed Beckwith was guilty.

DeLay Jr. nodded. "I appreciate your honesty."

He began railing against the prosecution, sounding much like his father. The former marine talked about others being involved in the murder of Medgar Evers, but they weren't the ones being prosecuted. He never shared their names, suggesting his father had merely acted on orders and was now being made the patsy. "It's like a mobster movie. All of a sudden, one fellow takes the fall."

I had come to believe that there was a wider conspiracy than the lone gunman story. But I was also certain that his father was more than just a fall guy. He was a true believer and a willing assassin, even if others had encouraged him to pull the trigger.

22

The Mississippi Supreme Court halted the trial for Byron De La Beckwith before it ever began. In their September 21, 1992, decision, justices voted 5–2 to grant a defense request to hear the constitutional issues of speedy trial and due process.

Beckwith had insisted he couldn't afford a lawyer, so the trial judge appointed him two of the best criminal defense lawyers in Mississippi, free of charge. Merrida Coxwell Jr. burned hot in his passion for justice for the downtrodden. Jim Kitchens, who carried the air of a genteel southerner, happened to be one of the few white lawyers that belonged to the Magnolia Bar Association, the organization for black attorneys in Mississippi.

In a hearing before the justices, Coxwell asked them to dismiss the indictment. He told them the delay in the Beckwith case had been longer than any in the state's history.

DeLaughter argued there was new evidence and denied claims that delays had given the state a tactical advantage to prosecute Beckwith. "Just because the tide turned against him does not mean there was any ill motive on the part of the state."

Myrlie Evers, who had flown in from Oregon, sat in the audience. I did my best to listen to the justices' questions to determine if I could detect their leanings. Their makeup had changed slightly since the 5–2 vote, but unless some votes changed, Beckwith would never go on trial.

After the hearing, she asked what I thought would happen next. I shared that a source inside the court had told me that justices were leaning toward dismissing Beckwith's indictment and letting him walk free.

"They are?" she asked.

She put her hand on my arm. "We've done all we can, Jerry."

In the weeks that followed, false rumors spread across Jackson. At one point, gossip circulated that the justices had thrown out Beckwith's indictment, stoking fears of a possible riot.

Nine days before Christmas, the Mississippi Supreme Court ended the falsehoods with a 4–3 vote. Instead of throwing out the murder charge, justices allowed the trial of Beckwith to go forward, citing the new evidence.

But the three dissenting justices were far from happy with the decision. In his dissent, Chief Justice Roy Noble Lee called the decision "an egregious miscarriage of justice," describing it as "the worst pronouncement of the law during my tenure on the Mississippi Supreme Court bench." What he didn't mention was he had once been a leader in the same white Citizens' Council that had paid all of Beckwith's legal fees during his first two murder trials.

Despite the victory for the prosecution, justices concluded that Beckwith must go free on bond. He was heading home to Tennessee.

I telephoned Myrlie Evers and explained what the court had done.

"Do you think Beckwith will run, Jerry?"

"I don't know, Myrlie. I don't know."

When Beckwith arrived back in Signal Mountain, he said he was glad to be where "people are all white and all Christian." But when a television camera crew appeared, he pulled a pocketknife on them. He settled back into his racist networks, and soon after returning was sworn in as president of the Confederate States of America, a bizarre white supremacist group that claimed southern states had never reunified after the Civil War.

I read the acceptance speech of Beckwith, who talked of the upcoming race war. I had no doubt that he and his followers were delusional. I also had no doubt that some delusional people kill.

After the judge for Beckwith's upcoming trial hinted he might move the trial back to Jackson, the same fliers aimed at influencing potential jurors began to appear across the capital city. I paid a visit to white supremacist Richard Barrett in Learned, Mississippi, to see what he knew about the fliers. He shared an envelope from Beckwith postmarked February 26, 1993. Inside was the same flier and booklet that had appeared in many driveways across Mississippi. Beckwith wrote on a sticky note attached to the flier: "It cost me $750 to $1,000 to have them tossed out. Thousands of these must appear in certain areas like shingles on your roof."

Beckwith *was* behind the fliers. Now I had the proof.

I wrote a story detailing how Beckwith paid to have these packets distributed, and prosecutors used the revelation to get the trial moved back to Jackson. The jurors would still be picked from Panola County. And I had hopes that bringing the scheme to light would now mean that Beckwith and the Klan would stop trying to manipulate the jury.

Months later, I realized how wrong I had been. On December 18, 1993, fliers once again blanketed driveways in Panola County like snow, urging potential jurors to vote not guilty: "If you think Byron has suffered enough at the hands of these hate-filled cowards who have never fired a shot, then use every opportunity to deal the liars and enemies of our country a lethal blow by supporting the release of this fine Christian gentleman."

Still, I could hardly believe how far the case had come. Peters and DeLaughter had not backed down in the end. The Mississippi Supreme Court had not dismissed the case. Beckwith had not been able to squirm free, nor had he opted to flee. The trial was finally happening.

23

Byron De La Beckwith stared at the dozen jurors sitting in the chairs as testimony began January 27, 1994—thirty years to the day that his first trial began in the same courtroom. Back then, white men had occupied all the seats. Today offered a much different sight. In addition to women serving on this panel, black jurors outnumbered white jurors two to one.

Circuit Judge L. Breland Hilburn presided over the trial. With his dark hair and full beard, he bore a slight resemblance to Union general Ulysses S. Grant.

For Beckwith, the trial served as a reunion with fellow white supremacists. Richard Barrett attended and so did longtime Klansman Burris Dunn, along with Bill Pickel, a leader for the Americans for the Preservation of the White Race, a KKK front group. Sam Bowers kept his distance, communicating through notes he slipped through Beckwith's son.

Standing at a wooden podium, DeLaughter did his best to make this a simple murder case. "You will see from the evidence that this is not about trying to set an old wrong right. You're going to see from the evidence it's not about politics. It's not even going to be a civil rights case that incidentally involves a murder. What you will see from the evidence of this case is about a man whose life was snuffed out June 12, 1963. What the evidence will show is this man Medgar Evers was shot and killed. That bullet was aimed out of prejudice, propelled by hatred, and fired by a coward from ambush at night."

DeLaughter pointed at Beckwith, leaning his left arm over the chair. "He embarked upon a one-man mission to purge society of anyone and everything that stood for integration," the prosecutor said. "You will see letters written by this defendant where he proclaims that the enemies of the white race must be purged from society and the leaders of the NAACP exterminated."

Defense lawyer Merrida Coxwell Jr. fought back, arguing that prosecutors wanted to convict Beckwith for his opinions. "By the time this case is over, you will have seen that it was physically impossible for Mr. Byron De La Beckwith to have killed Medgar Evers because he was as far from this location as you are from your homes right now," he said. "The fact that his fingerprint was found on a gun doesn't mean that Mr. Byron De La Beckwith fired the shot."

Myrlie Evers became the prosecution's first witness. Although this would be her third time to testify, it would be the first time a prosecutor called her "Mrs. Evers." She had wanted then–district attorney Bill Waller to do so in 1964, but he worried how the all-white jury would react because Mississippi's segregationist society denied courtesy titles to black Mississippians. She had warned Waller that if he called her anything but "Mrs. Evers," she would correct him in front of the jury. In the end, he never called her anything.

Today, as she sat on the witness stand, memories flooded her mind. She talked of her late husband pushing to desegregate schools, swimming pools, restaurants, and libraries. "He wanted us to be able to go to department stores and be able to be called our names instead of 'boy' or 'girl.'"

She described that fateful night, hearing that horrible blast and the children falling to the floor as their father had taught them. "I bolted up and ran to the door, and there was Medgar at the steps with his keys in his hand," she said. "I screamed, I guess uncontrollably, and the children ran out shortly after I did."

She gazed at Beckwith, the man she believed assassinated her husband.

He was an old man, wearing a three-piece gray suit. He wasn't smirking the way he had been in the first two trials. On his lapel, she noticed a Confederate battle flag pin—a cause some Americans still seemed hell-bent on fighting more than a century later. She glared at him, hoping to catch his eye, and when he looked away, she kept staring. She wanted him to see that she was here to make sure justice was done. She wanted him to see that she was no longer a grieving widow but a powerful woman who had done her part to bring a more just society into reality. She wanted him to see that when he fired that gun, he helped spark a movement that never ended.

As prosecutors detailed their evidence, the dead came to life. Prosecutors and volunteers played the parts of witnesses from Byron De La Beckwith's first 1964 trial. Through them, jurors heard about the murder weapon found in a honeysuckle thicket, the rifle smelling of gunpowder, and someone fleeing after the shot was fired. Prosecutor Tommy Mayfield played the part of the ornery cab driver so well that spectators laughed aloud at one point, just as they had three decades earlier.

Ghosts continued to swirl as jurors handled the .30-06 rifle used to kill Medgar Evers. Some refused to touch it.

After testimony from a tackle shop owner saying he traded Beckwith a rifle scope, gun collector Ines Thornton McIntyre III told jurors that when he saw a photograph of what looked like his old .30-06 weapon, with its modified stock, in the *Jackson Daily News*, he telephoned Jackson police. The serial number of the gun he traded Beckwith in 1960 matched the one on the murder weapon.

John Chamblee, a bald and lanky former Jackson police detective, said that to figure out where the assassin stood, police shined a flashlight on the clear, warm night and discovered a sniper's nest. "There was dew on the grass all around," but none where "some person had been standing behind the three small trees and bushes."

Beckwith scribbled notes in a loose-leaf notebook while defense lawyer Jim Kitchens sought to fend off the prosecution's witnesses by arguing that Jackson police failed to rule out other suspects. Chamblee responded that he was not responsible for tracking down those leads.

"Is there more that you don't remember than you do remember?" Kitchens asked.

"I'm afraid you're right."

In the courtroom, Myrlie Evers watched the trial with her children Darrell and Reena. Darrell had been nine when his dad was killed. He remembered racing his father up and down the street on his bicycle, pedaling as fast as he could while his father ran on foot. His dad always won. Sitting in the courtroom, Darrell glared at Beckwith. "He not only shot my father, he shot me. He shot my sister. He shot my brother. He definitely shot my mother."

Reena put her arm around her mother. She had been eight when her father was killed. He had long doted on her. She loved his warm hugs and the Cracker Jacks he bought her. Most special of all were her memories of dancing with Daddy as she played Chubby Checker's "The Twist" on her turntable.

Van, who was three at the time of the death, had been unable to make the trial. As the youngest, he had fewer memories of his father, recalling most clearly the bubble gum cigars that his father would buy him. But a few years before the trial, Van had taken up a unique opportunity to memorialize his father. When Van found out prosecutors needed a second autopsy because the original autopsy report was missing, he volunteered to go. At the time pathologist Dr. Michael Baden opened the casket, it was as if Medgar Evers's body had been buried for three weeks, instead of three decades. Van was able to come in and spend time with the father he hardly remembered. He gazed at this man, who at thirty-seven was almost Van's own age. For the first time in decades, he touched his father's face.

A fluorescent light glowed as Dr. Baden showed jurors the X-rays of Medgar Evers's body, pointing to the presence of lead fragments and a starburst effect. The veteran director of forensic sciences for the New York State Police said, "The bullet clearly came from a high velocity missile that struck bone. My opinion is that it is definitely consistent with coming from such a [.30-06] bullet."

A defense lawyer questioned the pathologist's conclusion, asking whether a powerful handgun like a .357 Magnum could cause the same damage. Baden said no. He explained that bullets fired from rifles travel twice as fast as those from handguns. The evidence clearly implicated the rifle. And as other witnesses would soon attest, the rifle clearly implicated Beckwith.

Gripping his wooden cane, Ralph Hargrove hobbled past the jury box before settling into the witness stand, where he had testified as a police detective for decades. Bailiffs dimmed the lights, and the white-haired man relaxed. The screen showed a fingerprint from the .30-06 rifle and Beckwith's right index fingerprint. Hargrove tapped the matches with a pointer. "I could have picked two more."

"Why didn't you?" DeLaughter asked.

Hargrove cupped his right ear to catch the question. "Because I didn't need them. With fourteen points of identification, that's more than enough to identify the latent fingerprint as the fingerprint of Mr. Byron De La Beckwith."

Detectives had found the rifle stuffed in a thick hedge of honeysuckle near the sniper's nest set up to kill Medgar Evers. When they brought the gun to Hargrove, he'd found the gun had been wiped clean, but when he dusted beneath the telescopic sight, the fingerprint appeared—exactly where a man might hold his rifle while cleaning it.

Hargrove showed jurors now-fading color slides of a younger Beckwith with a fading half-moon scar over his right eye. Police believed the mark had come from the rifle's recoil when he fired the fatal shot. In 1964, Beckwith testified he got this scar while target practicing with the same rifle several days before "all this Evers business came up." He'd relished his moment in the spotlight, unable to resist a sick joke. "If I have ever killed anything besides time, we haven't been able to cook it at home."

After Hargrove finished, the judge gaveled for a recess. The meek detective stepped down from the witness stand and confided to me that he worried about sympathizers on this panel. "It don't take but one to hang a jury."

· · ·

Even as Mississippi sought a better future, the ugly past came to the fore. My colleague at *The Clarion-Ledger* Grace Simmons found out that a white alternate juror in this trial had been accused in litigation of threatening a black employee and saying her husband belonged to the KKK. It was a claim her husband did little to refute. In response to the allegation, he said: "A white man's got the same right to be a member of the Ku Klux Klan as a colored man being a member of the NAACP."

District Attorney Ed Peters asked the judge to remove the alternate juror. The judge deferred his decision, but now I wondered about the rest of the jurors. Myrlie called me that night to voice the same concern. We both knew that the Klan had tampered with juries before.

During questioning, jurors had sworn to the judge they knew no one associated with the KKK. That alternate juror, who would serve on the jury if anyone got sick or had to leave, had apparently lied about that. Could others be doing the same, concealing their racial views in hopes of helping Beckwith go free?

Ralph Hargrove was right. All it took was one juror.

24

The trial of Byron De La Beckwith became the hottest ticket in town. The balcony, where the judge relegated the press, filled with reporters from around the globe. My mentor for this journey, journalist Bill Minor, came and so did writer Willie Morris, the de facto guide for the out-of-town press. He insisted they eat frog legs at Crechale's and check out the courtroom's bathrooms, where the words "White" and "Colored" peered ghostlike through the dark painted doors.

On the witness stand, retired FBI firearms expert Richard Poppleton testified about tests on the fatal bullet. It was so powerful it had killed Medgar Evers and kept going, smashing a window and flying through the wall. It had then bounced off the Evers's refrigerator and landed in their kitchen, right on the kitchen counter.

Several nights before Medgar Evers's assassination, two teenagers noticed a white Plymouth Valiant with a long antenna parked not far from Evers's home. Now, three decades later, they sat on the witness stand and stared at a blown-up photograph of Beckwith's Valiant. They each identified a Shriner's emblem on the back of Beckwith's rearview mirror as the one they saw that night.

Barbara Holder, no longer the twenty-two-year-old carhop, clutched her metal cane as she weaved to the witness stand. Her once shoulder-length dark hair had given way to patches of gray and a close-cropped look. Wearing large orange sunglasses, Holder described how she worked at Joe's Drive-In in Jackson for six years. "I even did a little cooking."

The drive-in was only a few hundred feet from Evers's home, with a patch of woods in between. On the evening of June 11, 1963, just hours before he was assassinated, she recalled seeing a white Valiant. Rather than pulling into a parking spot, "it backed up to the corner of the lot," the whole time keeping the license tag out of view, she said. "It looked like a patrol car because it had a long aerial, and it was awfully muddy."

Back then, drivers turned on their headlights to signal carhops for service. The Valiant's lights stayed off the whole time it was there. At one point, the car pulled up next to the building, and the driver ducked inside the restroom. She recalled him being five-foot-seven or five-foot-eight with dark clothes and dark hair.

Defense lawyer Merrida Coxwell questioned why she had failed to give police such a detailed description before.

"Probably because I can't remember two weeks ago, but I can remember thirty years ago."

The courtroom laughed.

When Beckwith's nephew, Reed Massengill, who had just published a biography about his infamous uncle, took the witness stand, Beckwith inserted a device to aid his listening. Minutes later he tossed it out. He had heard enough.

Prosecutors introduced a number of letters into evidence that Beckwith had given Massengill for his research. While jailed for Medgar Evers's murder, Beckwith heard about President Kennedy's assassination and wrote his son, "Whoever shot Kennedy 'sho [sic] did some fancy shooting. . . . I bet Ole Medgar Evers told Kennedy when he got down there, 'I thought you'd be along pretty soon.' Haw, Haw, Haw."

Prosecutors also presented the June 15, 1957, letter to the editor in which Beckwith wrote, "The NAACP, under the direction of its leaders, is doing a first-class job of getting itself in a position to be exterminated. I thank God for the association of Citizens' Councils of America. Soon the cancerous growth, the NAACP, shall be cut out of the heart of our nation, and we will all live happily ever after."

Despite his concerns about testifying, Klansman turned FBI informant Delmar Dennis took the witness stand. So did Beckwith's former tenant Dan Prince.

With a handbag draped across her matronly arm, Mary Ann Adams testified that after someone introduced her to Beckwith, praising him as "the man who killed Medgar Evers," she refused to shake his hand and called him a murderer. "He got extremely agitated and angry—said he had not killed a man, but 'a damn chicken-stealing dog and you know what you have to do with a dog that has tasted blood.'"

Then there was Peggy Morgan, dressed in pink and wearing dark glasses. She testified about traveling to Parchman prison with her husband and Beckwith, to visit a Klansman convicted of murder. On the way, she said Beckwith talked about killing Evers and then warned against sharing his admission because he wasn't "scared to kill again."

Another former FBI informant, Elluard Jenoal "Dick" Davis, fidgeted with his blue tie as he sat in his dark suit on the witness stand. During a 1969 supper in Winterhaven, Florida, he said Beckwith used the term "selective killings" as a solution to the right wing's problems. "He said he would never ask anyone to do anything that he hadn't already done himself."

The most powerful testimony came from last-minute witness Mark Reiley, an air traffic controller from Chicago who had happened to hear about the retrial while stranded at home in heavy snow. While watching CNN, he heard Beckwith was being tried for Medgar Evers's murder and contacted the district attorney's office.

Reiley told jurors about his memory of Beckwith as an inmate at the Louisiana State Penitentiary in Angola. Reiley was working as a prison guard then and testified that he had found a father figure in Beckwith at the time, listening up to eight hours a day about Christian Identity. When a black nurse appeared one day, Beckwith cursed her as a "nigger," and the woman got angry, Reiley said. "He was screaming at her, 'If I can get rid of an uppity nigger like Medgar Evers, I would have no problem with a no-count nigger like you.' "

By the time Reiley stepped down from the witness stand, six witnesses had sworn they heard Beckwith admit he killed the civil rights leader. And with that, the prosecution rested.

25

Five days after the testimony began, Byron De La Beckwith savored a steak at a four-star restaurant in Jackson. When news spread that night of his presence, managers did all they could to hasten his exit.

Instead, the white supremacist lingered, savoring whiskey, shaking hands, and reassuring those gathered that he would walk free again. One well-wisher slipped him a wad of cash for his "defense fund," despite the fact he wasn't paying a penny for his attorneys.

While Beckwith dined in style, jurors ate salad and fried chicken. The only way they could buy soft drinks was if a bailiff accompanied them. Bailiffs had barred all TV, newspapers, and conversations to prevent any possible exposure to publicity about the case.

The next morning, the defense sought to establish Beckwith's alibi. The lawyers began by introducing the 1964 testimony of Roy Jones, an auxiliary police officer from Greenwood, Mississippi, who had since died. There were more than a few similarities between his version of seeing Beckwith and the alibi statements by then-officers Hollis Creswell and James Holley. All involved eating sandwiches from the same place. All involved the same Billups service station.

Jones testified he saw Beckwith driving in his Valiant in an alley by Billups at 11:45 p.m. "He was sitting right there with his lights on, just like he was waiting for a car to go on by, so he could pull out."

Like the two officers, Jones failed to link the time to anything memorable. I wondered what jurors would believe. I wondered, too, what they would think if they read the same FBI reports I had, one of them describing Jones attending a KKK meeting.

After recounting Jones's story, the defense lawyers told the judge that Creswell was too sick to testify. I suspected it had more to do with him wanting to dodge another brutal cross-examination from prosecutors as he had experienced in front of the grand jury.

Holley became the sole live witness to provide an alibi. The sixty-five-year-old retired police officer testified he saw Beckwith in Greenwood at 1:05 a.m., returning again to the original time he told me.

District Attorney Ed Peters rose to question Holley. The former boxing champ wasted no time in getting in his first jabs. He asked the retired officer if he was on a first-name basis with Beckwith.

"No, sir."

"Why do you call him DeLay?"

"I call him Mr. Beckwith most of the time."

Peters read from the 1964 testimony, where Holley repeatedly referred to Beckwith as DeLay. "Your buddy, right?"

"My friend. Just like I hope you and I are friends."

"Pardon?"

"I said just like I would hope that you and I are friends."

"What have I ever done to be your friend?"

"You ain't done anything not to be my friend."

Chuckling could be heard at the back of the courtroom.

Peters asked Holley to name any other time that he recalled seeing Beckwith. Holley couldn't name one.

The district attorney hammered Holley about a meeting he'd had with Jackson police detectives. Holley spent time with them in the days following the murder—right when Jackson police were investigating Beckwith—yet Holley had neglected to mention his alibi for Beckwith during that meeting. Peters questioned why a sworn police officer would fail to tell fellow officers such important alibi information, which would put the accused killer ninety miles away from the murder scene.

"I would've been butting into his investigation," Holley said.

"You would've been butting into his investigation?"

"Right."

Then Holley pivoted, responding that the detectives had never asked. Peters kept pressing. "How long was your buddy DeLay in jail?"

"I don't exactly know."

"Eight months? Ten months?"

"Somewhere along there."

"And you let your buddy DeLay stay in jail all that time and never once told a single person investigating it, 'You've got the wrong guy in jail'?"

"I did not."

Rubbing his crew cut with his left hand, Holley said he talked to his partner, Creswell, who remembered the 1:05 time because he was worried the grocery store would close and they wanted to get a sandwich.

"Why was that so important?" Peters asked.

"The store closed at 1:30."

Now the store closed at 1:30 instead of 1:00. This contradicted both what he had told me and his 1964 testimony.

Peters confronted him. "Didn't y'all get together just about 1:05?"

"Sure, we talked."

"You got your times straight?"

"We went over it."

"That's why your testimony looks just alike because you got together and said, 'This is the way our testimony is going to be.'"

"It was the truth."

When Holley admitted the two officers had discussed what they knew, Peters asked, "How many times did you go over it?"

"Probably one time. We were both together and saw the same thing."

Peters had one last question for the officer. "You still consider us friends?"

A smile turned up on the corners of Holley's mouth. "Sure."

"If I ever get in jail," Peters asked, "will you promise not to leave me there for eight months if you knew where I was at the time of the crime?"

The audience howled, and the defense moved for a mistrial. The judge denied the request but told jurors to disregard the district attorney's last question.

I looked at the jurors, unable to read their faces. Did they feel this retired officer was telling the truth?

The next morning, Beckwith arrived in a Christmas red sport jacket, and I felt certain he would take the witness stand and talk. Instead, defense lawyer Jim Kitchens announced, "Mr. Beckwith, because of his advanced age and very poor memory, has elected not to testify."

Peters groaned, collapsing on the prosecution table. He had enough material to cross-examine Beckwith for four days. Now it would go untouched.

Beckwith's silence surprised everyone, including Myrlie Evers, who told reporters, "Those familiar with this man know this is the first time in years he has not ranted and raved and talked. The fact that the man did not take the witness stand says a lot about the defense."

26

On the last day of the trial, Assistant District Attorney Bobby DeLaughter stepped in front of the jury. In keeping with the court's procedure, prosecutors went both first and last in closing arguments, getting the same amount of time as the defense lawyers, who spoke in the middle.

"This assassination, by a sniper from ambush, is something that's timeless," DeLaughter told jurors. "This is something that spans the races. It is something that every decent human being absolutely should be sickened by, whether you be black or white or Hispanic. It doesn't matter. Murder by ambush is the most vile, savage, reprehensible type of murder that one can imagine."

The prosecutor detailed Beckwith's preparations. Cab drivers heard him ask for directions. Neighbors saw his Valiant in the days before the killing. Police found his sniper's nest, his rifle, and his fingerprint. "When he thought he had beat the system thirty years ago, he couldn't keep his mouth shut with people he thought were gonna be impressed with him."

Beckwith propped his chin as DeLaughter showed jurors a picture of Medgar Evers in his casket. DeLaughter told jurors that all this African-American leader had wanted was for his people to be able to experience equality, to get a decent education for their children, to be accepted as human beings, instead of being called boy or girl. After such a murder, "there is just a gaping wound laid open on society as a whole, and even when justice is done, that kind of a wound will leave a scar that won't ever heal."

DeLaughter asked the jury to find Beckwith guilty "because it's right, it's just, and, Lord knows, it's just time." He asked, "Is it ever too late to do the right thing? For the sake of justice and the hope of us as a civilized society, I sincerely hope and pray that it's not."

Defense lawyers hoped the passage of time might convince the jury that it had been too long. "You're being asked to look further into the past than any other jury I know of in the twenty-seven years of my law practice," Jim Kitchens told them. "Evidence has been lost, misplaced."

He said the Magnolia State was a different place then. "They're called the turbulent sixties. We regret the turbulence. The views held then we would disagree with today. Martin Luther King was a great man."

Beckwith rubbed his eyes in disgust. He had said before that King deserved to die.

Kitchens recounted the alibi testimony. He said the former policeman had told jurors the truth and "if he wanted to lie to you, he wouldn't lie about that. He lives in a mixed neighborhood. A black lady is watching his house while he's gone."

The defense lawyer said Holley considered Beckwith and everyone else to be his friend. "He even wanted to be Mr. Peters's buddy, even though Mr. Peters was trying to beat him down to a pulp."

Kitchens questioned whether the 1917 Enfield .30-06 was the murder weapon, since the FBI could not say the bullet that killed Evers came directly from that rifle—only a rifle like it. "There is a one in two million chance that gun fired that shot." He then suggested that a high-powered pistol had carried out the dirty work.

"You are not here to decide whether you like Byron De La Beckwith, whether you agree with him, whether you want to take him home with you, whether you want your children to meet him, whether you want to join his organization," Kitchens said. "Three people said he was in Greenwood when they killed this good man."

When Kitchens called Evers a "good man," Beckwith sighed and crossed his arms.

"Forget Byron De La Beckwith," Kitchens continued. "Forget that you don't like him. Judge the case on the evidence. If the system doesn't work for everybody, it doesn't work for anybody."

Defense lawyer Merrida Coxwell spoke next, calling the case a jigsaw puzzle that prosecutors had been unable to piece together. "Is there any proof that the gun fired the shot?"

He recalled the former police officer's testimony. "Alibi is just another way of saying the person simply wasn't there. It means the man wasn't there. There is no question Byron De La Beckwith did not kill Medgar Evers."

Closing arguments ended with District Attorney Ed Peters describing Beckwith as "a back-shooting, bushwhacking coward" and urging jurors to convict. "Don't let him walk out of this courtroom and brag about it again. Strip him of that badge of honor and have a murder conviction hung around his neck."

The prosecutor mocked the alibi testimony, by imitating the officer's inability to give any other time besides the time of the alibi when he had supposedly seen Beckwith. "I don't remember him one other place, but I remember him there."

He told the jurors, "Give the Evers family, give the state of Mississippi some justice. After thirty years, all we want is justice."

Jurors began their deliberations at 1:30 p.m., and they returned to the courtroom five hours later. I studied their faces and sensed something was wrong. The cheeks of one middle-aged white woman glowed red. The jurors were split and angry.

The district attorney looked like he had been sucker-punched. I felt the same way.

27

Rain battered the blackbirds atop the statue of Moses on the roof of the Hinds County Courthouse when I arrived the next morning, February 5, 1994. Depression sunk so deep in my bones, I slipped on whatever clothes I could grab, a sweatshirt, jeans, sneakers, and a trench coat. Most journalists in the betting pool had predicted Byron De La Beckwith would be convicted of murder in a few hours. When deliberations dragged on, many left. Yesterday's high spirits had given way to gloom.

Last night, Myrlie Evers had telephoned, and we talked about that dark night her husband, Medgar, had been gunned down. After his murder, the carport filled with neighbors, friends, and curious onlookers. When two white teenagers wandered up, she cursed them and accused them of doing the deed. When Jackson police arrived, she accused them, too. "If I had had a machine gun," she told me, "I would have mowed them all down—every white person I could."

When I said it was good that the anger had passed after a time, she confessed she still struggled with it. I said I understood, but the truth was I understood nothing. I had never seen a loved one gunned down in my driveway. I had never felt hate steal a member of my family.

Before she hung up, she told me, "No matter what happens, Jerry, we have won."

As I entered the courthouse, I wiped my wet sneakers on the mat and gazed back through the glass at the storm. If Beckwith walked free, nothing would be won.

Minutes later, I ran into Assistant District Attorney Bobby DeLaughter and told him, "That was the best closing argument I've ever heard."

"Thank you."

He was standing next to his new wife, Peggy. When the elevator opened, they stepped inside. As the doors began to close, I saw him cross his fingers in hope. Yes, there was still hope.

About a half hour later, a deputy rushed over and whispered to another deputy. I happened to overhear a single word, the only one I needed to hear—"verdict."

The jury had a verdict.

Beckwith's grandson held his head in his hands while his redheaded wife rubbed his back. Myrlie Evers clutched the hand of her daughter, Reena, and her son Darrell put his arm around her.

The jurors soon filed in, and I studied them as they entered. There was no anger visible now, only solemn faces.

The foreman clutched the decision on a yellow piece of paper. He handed it over, and the judge studied the verdict before giving it to Circuit Clerk Barbara Dunn.

Before I could glean anything from their faces, she began to speak. "We, the jury, find the defendant guilty as charged."

In that moment, Myrlie Evers would later tell me, she felt all the hate rushing out the pores of her body. She and her daughter held hands and wept. Darrell let out a whoop, and a few in the audience said, "Yeah, yeah."

Beckwith sat still in his Confederate gray suit while his family burst into tears. His wife sobbed.

The judge pounded his gavel. "Order in the court."

As the courtroom grew silent, I heard waves of joy cascading down the hall until they reached a foyer full of people, black and white. The crowd erupted in cheers, and I felt a chill. Somehow the impossible had just become possible.

Beckwith stood before the judge, who sentenced him to life in prison as mandated by law. The judge then dismissed everyone from the courtroom, and journalists rushed to interview anyone they could find.

The people I wanted to talk with were behind doors—the jurors. Hours later, I reached their foreman, Elvage Fondren, a seventy-year-old minister and retired barber who heard Martin Luther King Jr. speak in Memphis days before his April 4, 1968, assassination.

Fondren told me that during deliberations the night before, the jury had been split 8–4 in favor of Beckwith's guilt. But by morning, "Everything seemed to be so still. It was a different mood—solemn, quiet."

The next morning, jurors prayed, and Fondren followed with his questions about James Holley's testimony. Why would an officer make an "innocent man" stay in jail for eight months? In the end, the jury concluded the officer was lying.

After the jurors voted again, Fondren counted the secret ballots, which all read "guilty," and they clasped hands. "There was an invisible presence I can't explain that really came over all of us. This is when all of us broke down and began to shed tears."

Myrlie Evers had prayed for this day, and now that it had come, she could hardly believe it. After she and her family entered the room filled with reporters, she thrust her fist into the air. "All I want to do is say, 'Yay, Medgar, yay.'"

"About time," Darrell Evers said.

She wiped away tears. "My God, I don't have to say accused assassin anymore, I can say convicted assassin, who laughed and said, 'He's dead, isn't he? That's one nigger who isn't going to come back.' But what he failed to realize was that Medgar was still alive in spirit and through each and every one of us who wanted to see justice done."

Reena Evers-Everette turned her eyes toward heaven. "Hi, Daddy. We did it." She turned back to the reporters and remarked that while "a large gap of pain cannot be erased, it can be soothed. And I got a whole lot of medicine soothed on me today."

Medgar Evers's brother, Charles, never set foot in the courtroom during the murder trial, but he rejoiced when the verdict came. He later told me that "if Beckwith had met Medgar, he would never have killed him. The system killed Medgar. Beckwith just pulled the trigger."

When I finally stepped outside the courtroom, I noticed that the rain had stopped. I felt lighter, relieved of the burden I had not realized I had been carrying for the past five years. It was over. It was really over. Byron De La Beckwith had been convicted of murdering Medgar Evers.

28

Months after the conviction, Jackson lawyer Harry Rosenthal visited Beckwith in his concrete jail cell. The inmate welcomed the balding Jewish lawyer, calling him "a fine Christian man," because Rosenthal had been the one who posted the twelve thousand dollars for Beckwith's bond.

Prior to this visit, I had shared a copy of an FBI report with someone who gave it to Rosenthal. In that report, an informant said Gordon Lackey talked of helping Beckwith kill Medgar Evers. In the report, Lackey even claimed credit for pulling the trigger.

Rosenthal handed Beckwith the report and watched his reaction.

The white supremacist's eyes darted across the page. "That's not true."

The lawyer urged Beckwith to reexamine the document. "It has facts you need to look at."

This time after reading it, he handed the page back to Rosenthal. "That's not the way it was."

He motioned Rosenthal closer and whispered. "We drew, and I ended up with the short straw."

Days after the guilty verdict, my phone rang. It was Hinds County sheriff Malcolm McMillin, the only person I knew with framed pictures of

Martin Luther King Jr., Confederate president Jefferson Davis, and the Three Stooges in the same office. He barked in his baritone voice, "Watch your ass."

"What's going on, Sheriff?"

"When we took Beckwith away, he kept saying two words, over and over."

"Two words?"

"Yes, two words."

"What two words?"

"Jerry Mitchell."

I fell silent.

"Like I said, watch your ass. If you have any problems, call us."

He offered advice. "If there's a place you usually frequent or go for drinks, I'd be looking around for anybody out of the ordinary."

He advised me to go home a different way, just in case.

His words reminded me of that dark night in the Smoky Mountains, where Delmar Dennis had told me if a Phineas priest struck, there would be no warning. "Nothing is quite so dangerous as a religious fanatic who thinks he's doing the Lord's will."

Despite the sheriff's warning, I drove home the same way. I was headed down a road now. There was no turning back.

PART III

VERNON DAHMER SR.

29

The new charge in Medgar Evers's murder brought hope to more than one hundred families. They had seen their mothers, fathers, sisters, and brothers die at the hands of hate—gunned down, drowned, burned, and blown up. The trail of civil rights cold cases stretched beyond Mississippi and beyond the South to much of the rest of the nation. Many of these families had been calling for justice long before a grand jury indicted Byron De La Beckwith in December 1990, but his charge gave them the leverage they felt they needed to prod authorities into reopening these cases.

Months after Beckwith's indictment, a man named Dennis Dahmer (whose last name is pronounced "DAY-mer") telephoned me. As a child, he dreamed of becoming a doctor, but after his father's murder, he felt lost, struggling in the classroom. When he saw his mother weep over his grades, he rallied. He became a salesman with a Fortune 500 corporation and later started his own business, selling bioresearch laboratory equipment. But for him, the defining day of his life remained January 10, 1966—the day the KKK attacked his family. If not for the courage of his father, Vernon Sr., who died defending them, he said, Klansmen "probably would have killed us all."

I drove an hour and a half south from Jackson to Forrest County, named after a Confederate general who led the KKK. After arriving at the

Kelly Settlement, north of Hattiesburg, Mississippi, I pulled into a gravel driveway, where huge oak trees shaded the front lawn of a modest redbrick home. Dennis Dahmer greeted me with a beaming smile, ready to talk. I followed him inside, where I met his mother, Ellie, a retired schoolteacher. She told me about her husband—a farmer, an entrepreneur, and a civil rights leader. She pointed to a picture of him on the wall, a barrel-chested man in a suit and dark tie.

When I looked closer, I could see the resemblance to the son standing beside me. "Jerry, we know that you helped out the Medgar Evers family," Dennis said. "We were wondering if you would help our family out and write about my father."

"I'd be happy to," I replied. "What can you tell me about him?"

Dennis led me to the window and showed me the two-hundred-acre farm, where he and his seven siblings had been the work crew. He said they drove a Ford tractor, picked cotton, raised vegetables, fed cattle, and ran timber through their sawmill. When times became tough, they hunted in the woods, bringing back dove, quail, and squirrels for dinner.

Although he never served in the military, Vernon Dahmer ran his household like the army. He expected his children to answer with "sir." After explaining a chore once, he expected it done without reminding. If they failed, he would say, "Use your head for something more than a hat rack."

When World War II came, tens of thousands of army recruits poured into nearby Camp Shelby. With disposable income in their pockets, the recruits needed a general store in the surrounding African-American community. Dahmer built one next to his house, stocking shelves with fresh produce and other items. He also opened a sawmill, providing lumber for the construction of new buildings and houses.

After the war ended, he joined the NAACP. He became the leader of the group's local branch and became friends with Medgar Evers and others. While the NAACP remained focused on litigation, Dahmer believed the change would come through voting rights. He welcomed in young SNCC workers Curtis Hayes and Hollis Watkins, who lived with the family and worked on the farm. National NAACP officials complained about Dahmer befriending a rival civil rights group, but Dahmer told Evers he had no intention of sending his visitors away, since they were tackling the tough task of voter registration.

Ellie Dahmer, whose husband called her by her middle name, "Jewell," tried for years to register to vote. Each time she appeared, Circuit Clerk Theron Lynd slid her a section of the Mississippi Constitution that she was required to interpret before being able to vote. Each time, Ellie, a teacher, responded with the correct answer. Each time, he refused to let her vote, insisting she was wrong.

This test, along with poll taxes, had been put in place by Mississippi's 1890 constitution, which white politicians created to restore white supremacy. The plan gave them a method for reducing African-American voting to a fraction of what it had been. Local clerks like Lynd became the gatekeepers, approving white voters while rejecting black voters.

In 1962, the Justice Department brought a lawsuit against Lynd, and Vernon Dahmer and others testified against him, proving the clerk was guilty of racial discrimination. A year later, the Fifth US Circuit Court of Appeals found him guilty of contempt of court. Lynd, however, ignored the decision and kept barring black voters. The Dahmers kept fighting for the vote, even as the Klan grew more active.

After the news arrived of Medgar Evers's assassination on June 12, 1963, Dahmer and his wife began sleeping in shifts. He would take the first part of the evening, clutching his shotgun as he scanned the horizon for creeping shadows. She relieved him at 1 a.m., so he could rest before dawn beckoned. The Dahmers received death threats and retaliation due to their work—along with economic coercion, as their insurance company canceled their home insurance.

Eventually, on August 6, 1965, the Voting Rights Act became law— due in part to the diligence of the Dahmers—and federal registrars flooded Lynd's office and the rest of Mississippi. Vernon and Ellie Dahmer both registered, and soon they quit sleeping in shifts. "The threatening calls had stopped, the acts of violence," Dennis explained. "We pretty much figured it was all over with. Blacks had accomplished the right to vote."

Black Mississippians, however, still had to pay poll taxes before they registered to vote in state elections. In the wake of the Voting Rights Act, and in the run-up to the first election in which he and Ellie would be able to vote, Dahmer reached out to county officials to make poll tax collection in the area easier. Officials gave him permission to allow those living in the Kelly Settlement to pay their poll taxes at his small grocery store. On January 9, 1966, a local radio station announced the arrangement.

Just a day later, two carloads of Klansmen made their way to the Dahmer home in the frigid early morning hours. One group launched firebombs into the family's grocery store. Another group sailed firebombs into the Dahmer family home. One bomb hit the family's 1964 Ford Fairlane, setting it ablaze and causing the horn to stick.

The noise woke Dennis, twelve at the time. He opened his bedroom door, only to encounter a wall of fire. He climbed out a window, wearing only his underwear.

Ellie Dahmer stirred to the blare of the car horn, smelling smoke. She yelled out, "Vernon, I believe they got us this time."

He jumped out of bed and grabbed a shotgun, loaded with double-aught buckshot. "Get the children out while I hold them off!"

She darted inside the bedroom of ten-year-old daughter Bettie. The fire had almost reached the ceiling, and her pajamas were ablaze. She grabbed her daughter and ran. When she reached the back window, she opened it, only for the window to fall back shut and jam. She couldn't open it. Bettie screamed they were going to die.

Vernon Dahmer dashed to the front of the house, where the flames were fiercest. Klansmen shot up the house, and Vernon blasted his shotgun back at them. But even as he dodged the spray of bullets, the fire kept raging, with Vernon in the middle.

Ellie Dahmer hurled her shoulder against the jammed window. Both she and the window hit the ground outside. By the time she made it back to her feet, her husband was at the window, handing Bettie to her. Vernon struggled down after, joining Dennis, who had already escaped.

Gazing around, Dennis realized Harold, his twenty-six-year-old brother, home from the army, was still inside. His father tried to climb back inside, but he had been burned too badly. Dennis jumped through the window and pulled his brother out.

"We couldn't get our shoes, coats, money, or anything, the fire was coming so fast," Ellie Dahmer recalled. "We couldn't get to the doors because the doors were on fire."

Flames from the grocery store shot higher, and the family now realized that Vernon Dahmer's eighty-three-year-old "Aunt Rainey," Lurania Heidelberg, had been sleeping in back of the store. They feared that she had been burned alive and called out to her in the night. Aunt Rainey yelled back from the woods, saying that she was all right. She joined them in the nearby barn, where they all stared helplessly at the blaze.

They stayed in the barn for as long as they could, fearing that the Klansmen might return and shoot them all. Vernon Dahmer, whose face and arms were burned, sat down on a bale of hay and told his wife that "everything was going to be all right."

But it wasn't all right. Bettie had been badly burned on both arms. She was so sick she was vomiting. When he couldn't bear waiting any longer, Harold Dahmer left in the family's pickup truck, which the fire had somehow missed. A relative returned with her car to take them to Forrest General Hospital.

Ellie Dahmer worried about her daughter, Bettie, and now she was growing more concerned about her husband, Vernon. He was having to breathe now from an oxygen tank because of the damage to his lungs.

"I thought he was getting better," Ellie told me.

She choked with emotion, her lips quivering. "I guess you see what you want."

She recalled a newspaper reporter asking her husband then, "Was this important enough to die for?"

Her husband replied, "A man needs to do his own thinking. And if you don't vote, you don't count in this society."

After he and Bettie fell asleep, Ellie Dahmer rested her head next to his on the hospital bed. "The next thing I knew," she recalled, "he raised his head up and yelled out, 'Jewell,' and fell."

As she finished recounting her story to me, tears welled in her eyes. "He was dead."

30

More than one thousand people marched through the rain and mud to attend the funeral service of Vernon Dahmer at the Shady Grove Baptist Church. Hundreds shivered outside, still able to hear the words of NAACP executive director Roy Wilkins through a public address system. In a soft voice, Wilkins spoke of how Vernon Dahmer had left behind him "two legacies: the legacy of his courage—he was unafraid— . . . and the legacy of his family, the members of which will carry on where he left off."

Condolences arrived from around the world. President Lyndon Johnson sent a telegram, telling Ellie Dahmer that her husband's work exemplified "the best tradition of democracy—helping his fellow citizens register and vote. His family can be justly proud as his work was a fine example of good citizenship. It is my hope that your faith and support of your family and loved ones will assist you in this time of great need. Mrs. Johnson joins me in expressing our deep sympathy."

A few weeks later, voter registration cards arrived in the mail for Vernon and Ellie Dahmer. He had fought his whole life for the right of all Americans to vote, but he had never been able to cast a ballot.

• • •

Mirroring the work they had done in the Mississippi Burning case, the FBI sent in swarms of agents to investigate the Vernon Dahmer case, many of them working for seventy-six straight days. Hours after the attack, FBI agents arrived at what had been the Dahmer home, the embers still glowing red in the dark. With the first rays of light, agents began to comb through the yard and ashes. They studied the family's Ford pickup, which had survived the fire. The pickup had taken shotgun blasts to the windows, and agents also noticed bullet holes from an apparent .38-caliber gun. Some of those bullets had pierced the truck's gas tank, but somehow failed to ignite it.

When agents searched the truck bed, they found a plastic jug that reeked of gasoline. On what had been the family's front lawn, they found spent shotgun shells and a charred Rohm Magnum revolver. They also found a racist Halloween mask that one of the killers had worn.

While the Mississippi Burning investigation had been headed up by inspector Joe Sullivan, the Dahmer case was led by Roy K. Moore, the head of the FBI in Mississippi. Moore and his agents hit their share of dead ends in the early days: They tried to lift fingerprints from the charred revolver, but none remained after the inferno. They took plaster casts of tire tracks, but came back with no clear matches.

It did not take long, however, for Moore and his agents to figure out that the killing had been the work of the White Knights. More than two miles down the road, agents located a Ford Galaxy that had been blasted by a shotgun and had two flat tires. A man from Ellisville, Mississippi, who owned the Ford, claimed it had been stolen while he was working at the Masonite plant in Laurel, Mississippi, where many Klansmen worked.

In just a few days, agents were able to compile a list of possible attackers. But as they closed in, they became targets of the KKK. A black coffin was delivered to one agent's wife. A rattlesnake was put in the car of another. Armed Klansmen shot out agents' windows.

Furious at the KKK's unceasing violence, now almost two years after the Mississippi Burning killings, Moore battled back. In the Mississippi Burning case, Sullivan and other agents had worked meticulously for months to break open the case and then many more months before bringing arrests. But in this case, Moore decided to fight fire with fire, according to retired FBI agent Jim Ingram. "Roy had a different philosophy than Joe Sullivan."

Eleven days after the KKK firebombed the Dahmer home, Moore sent in a request to the FBI's New York City office to use informant NY-3461 for his operation in Mississippi. That informant happened to be Gregory Scarpa Sr., the longtime mobster turned FBI informant. He carried the nickname the "Grim Reaper," at least in part because he had reportedly killed eight people.

Weeks after Dahmer's killing, Scarpa and an FBI agent entered Byrd's Radio & TV Service. Inside they found the bug-eyed owner, Lawrence Byrd, a suspect in Dahmer's killing. Scarpa and the agent chatted amiably with Byrd, before buying a TV. They asked for Byrd's help loading it into the car, and Byrd obliged. Outside, Scarpa shoved Byrd into the car. He and the FBI agent hauled Byrd to a remote area, where the onetime mobster pistol-whipped him. After that, Byrd gave the FBI a twenty-two-page confession.

FBI agents took the names in Byrd's confession and began looking for the weak links. They found one in Cecil Sessum, identified as an exalted cyclops in the White Knights. Agents obtained a confession from Sessum, who admitted his involvement in the attack. He told authorities that the group of armed Klansmen had pumped gasoline into a dozen jugs before heading toward the Dahmer home. Agents then zeroed in on Billy Roy Pitts, after learning from Byrd that the revolver at the crime scene belonged to Pitts. When agents pressured him, he fled to the home of his brother, a preacher, who urged him to turn himself in. Pitts pleaded guilty to murder and began talking. He told agents that before the attack, he and fellow Klansmen had gathered at a black cemetery, where Sessum urinated on a grave, saying, "The only good nigger is a dead one." Pitts testified that Imperial Wizard Sam Bowers headed up the operation. He had ordered the attack on Dahmer and his family.

On March 28, 1966, FBI agents arrested thirteen Klansmen and later Bowers. Sessum went on trial for murder. He insisted his confession came after agents beat him, made him kneel on Dahmer's grave, and put a pistol to his head. The FBI denied the claim, and the court upheld his conviction.

Juries ultimately convicted four men—Sessum, Byrd, William Thomas Smith, and Charles Clifford Wilson—on murder or arson charges. Imperial Wizard Sam Bowers and the other Klansmen all walked free. Even those who entered prison wound up being freed by Mississippi governors, who found they could win easy political victories by lightening their sentences. By the time Dennis Dahmer called me in 1990, not a single person was behind bars for the murder of Vernon Dahmer Sr.

31

Hearing the story from the Vernon Dahmer family inspired me to pursue the case, just as I had the Medgar Evers murder. There was little doubt that justice had never been done. And if one name stuck in my mind as a target, it was Imperial Wizard Sam Bowers.

Under Bowers's command, the White Knights of the Ku Klux Klan killed at least ten people in the 1960s, including Vernon Dahmer—more if one included Medgar Evers. The White Knights's violence exceeded that of any other KKK group in the nation. And even amid the killings, Bowers seemed untouchable.

Less than a month after his Klansmen had killed Dahmer, Bowers had appeared before the House Un-American Activities Committee, which was investigating the KKK's activities in the South. He refused to answer all questions, except the question of where he was born, citing the Fifth Amendment right against self-incrimination.

At one point, Donald T. Appell, chief investigator for the committee, asked Bowers point blank: "As Imperial Wizard of the White Knights of the Ku Klux Klan of Mississippi, did you ever authorize the extermination or elimination of a human being?"

Bowers conferred with his lawyer.

"You seem shocked by that question," said Louisiana congressman Edwin E. Willis, who chaired the subcommittee. "Why don't you say 'no' under oath?"

Bowers again conferred with his counsel.

"Sir, for the reasons previously stated, I respectfully decline to answer that question."

When the barrage of questions ended, Bowers left the hearing room, unscathed and unfazed. Fellow Klansmen welcomed their leader as he emerged through the doors, triumphant.

Despite Bowers's defiance and air of invulnerability, I was surprised at how much evidence the FBI was able to piece together as he was brought to trial. Several witnesses recalled hearing him order the firebombing of civil rights leader Vernon Dahmer. And while he ended up walking free, it seemed like there were enough leads for me to work with.

I decided to start with Klansman turned FBI informant Delmar Dennis. He hadn't been involved in the initial trial, but the last time I had spoken with him—while investigating Byron De La Beckwith—he had mentioned the Dahmer firebombing. I telephoned him again.

Dennis explained that after the attack on the Dahmer family, he spoke by telephone with Bowers. To make sure the FBI didn't know what they were talking about, they communicated by code. After the call ended, they met in their usual place—secluded woods halfway between Meridian and Laurel.

Dennis scribbled on a piece of paper, "Somebody scored a big one last night," and handed it to Bowers. After the imperial wizard read the note, he struck a match and held the note over a flame. As charred bits spun in the breeze, the edges of his mouth grew into a grin. Bowers told him the Dahmer job was "more solid" than the Mississippi Burning case because "these men won't talk."

I marveled at his story. "Has this ever come out before?"

"No," he replied.

"Why not? This seriously implicates Bowers."

"I was still working undercover for the FBI when the killing took place."

"So they wouldn't let you testify in the Dahmer case?"

"No, the FBI didn't want to blow my cover."

"Why not?"

"I was going to testify in the Neshoba trial."

"So Bowers ended up walking free?"

"Yes, he did."

As I looked further into Sam Bowers, he struck me on the surface as an unlikely person to head the Ku Klux Klan. His more prominent grandfather was a Mississippi congressman who had spent his days railing against the white supremacist organization. His other grandfather bore the name of Abraham Lincoln. About a decade before launching the White Knights, Bowers had been on the brink of planting himself an early grave. After a liquor arrest and a bad business investment, he drove his pickup truck into the darkness, his only companion a loaded pistol. But before he could pull the trigger, something overwhelmed him. He came to believe that force was God calling him—a classic moment of conversion. Except that in Bowers's case, he came to believe that God was calling on him to embark on a holy war for white supremacy.

These days, I learned, Bowers was still running his company, Sambo Amusement Company, and teaching a Sunday school class each week at Hillcrest Baptist Church in Laurel. If he had any worries about being charged with Dahmer's murder, he wasn't showing it.

Although the KKK no longer blazed across the state, Bowers had maintained his white supremacist connections, meeting in 1991 with the "most notorious racist in America," Tom Metzger, who regarded the imperial wizard as a hero. Metzger had been ordered to pay a $12.5 million verdict for inciting skinheads into beating an Ethiopian student to death.

I knew if I called Bowers, he would simply hang up. I felt my best chance to talk with him would be to show up in person.

The next morning, I arrived in the small town of Laurel, which boasted more churches than restaurants. I realized that Bowers's business was in the middle of a black neighborhood, which seemed incongruous for the Klan leader. But then, perhaps that was a source of antagonistic glee for Bowers, much like the business's name.

When I reached the address, there was no sign, only a nondescript wooden shack, where white chips of paint coated the lawn like spray-on snow. As I pulled my car into the driveway, I felt a chill, as if ghosts still haunted the place.

When I stepped to the door, an eye peered through a peephole. A brusque voice asked, "What do you want?"

"I understand you lease machines here."

"Yes."

The door opened, and I saw a tall, dark-haired man who looked nothing like the short, dapper KKK leader I had seen in black-and-white photographs. The man escorted me into a room with walls covered by cheap plywood. The place looked more like a workshop than an office. I spotted a pinball machine torn open, a patient waiting for parts.

"Is there any particular kind of machine you would like to lease?" he asked.

"I'm interested in video games," I bluffed, hoping to get to see Bowers in person.

"We have any kind of video game you want—Pac-Man, you name it."

"I'd really like to talk with Mr. Bowers about it."

"I understand, but he's not going to be back today."

I left without what I'd come for, and the next day, I telephoned Bowers's office. At the very least, I was hoping to get him to comment for a story I was planning on the Dahmer family and how they were calling on authorities to reopen the case.

Bowers answered the telephone, and when I identified myself as a reporter, he became startled. Fearing he might hang up at any moment, I decided I couldn't wait to hurl the hardball question. I had to ask it now.

"Did you meet with Delmar Dennis after the attack on Vernon Dahmer and remark that the job was 'more solid' than the killings of the three civil rights workers?" I asked.

His voice rose. "I don't have any information on what you're trying to do."

The telephone clicked, and I heard a dial tone.

32

Vernon Dahmer Jr. drove me to the Shady Grove Baptist Church, which his ancestors helped start before slavery ended. As I stared at him, I felt I was gazing at a ghost. He had his father's distinctive features—a barrel-chested frame, closely cropped hair, and a narrowly trimmed mustache across his upper lip.

Dahmer Jr. had been in California, where he was stationed with the air force, at the time of the attack on his family. Six of Vernon Dahmer's seven sons served in the armed forces, four at the time of his killing. "Combined, we had seventy-eight years in the defense of this country during the Korea and Vietnam eras," Vernon Jr. said. He showed me a photograph of him and the three brothers, George, Martinez, and Alvin. They were dressed in their uniforms, staring at the rubble of the house where they'd been raised. They had defended their nation—only to return home and find that none of their countrymen were defending them.

After learning of his father's killing, Vernon Dahmer Jr. had flown back to Mississippi to handle the horrible details—the funeral, the family's finances, the search for another place for the family to live—all while onlookers and the curious press swarmed around the cinders. "I didn't have time to cry."

Dahmer Jr. told me he would serve as a spokesman for the family as they pushed to get his father's killing re-prosecuted. He asked me about my relationship with Myrlie Evers.

"We have a good relationship," I said. "I trust her, and she trusts me. I hope you and I can have the same kind of relationship."

He smiled. "I would like that. Do you have time for me to show you something?"

"Sure."

He led me out of the church and into the cemetery where his father was buried. We stopped at a rose-tinted headstone that read, "Vernon Dahmer Sr., March 10, 1908—January 10, 1966."

Vernon Jr. laid a hand on the headstone. He said his father knew the vote could break the stranglehold of second-class citizenship imposed on African-Americans by the state's segregationist leaders. Without that power, his father told him, "We have no control over our outcome because other people who are hostile to us are making the decisions for us."

A few years after World War II ended, he told me he had traveled to the courthouse with his father. His dad paid his property and poll taxes to the sheriff (who served then as tax collector) before taking his poll tax receipt to Circuit Clerk Luther Cox, who had blocked black Mississippians from voting for more than a decade.

When the elder Dahmer got Cox's attention, the clerk bristled. "What do you want?"

"I just paid my poll tax, and I'd like to register."

Cox pulled out a large index card with print on it and told the elder Dahmer to read this portion of the Mississippi Constitution. Cox turned his back on the black businessman and sat down.

After a few minutes of reading this excerpt, Dahmer spoke up. "Sir, I'm finished."

Cox returned and asked Dahmer to explain what the section of the constitution meant. Dahmer began to answer, only for Cox to interrupt him. "No, you don't understand it."

What upset Dahmer's son, Vernon Jr., was to see Cox speak down to his father, acting like this talented entrepreneur was all of three years old.

Afterward, father and son left the courthouse in silence. "Daddy was definitely angry, but he did not give up."

Vernon Jr. waved his hand for me to follow. After more than two dozen steps, we reached a gritty gravestone. He pointed to the name, George Dahmer, and told me that was his grandfather. "My daddy patterned his life after his father. He developed the same kind of care and concern for his fellow man by having deep compassion for those who had less and who were mistreated."

Back at his home, Vernon Jr. showed me pictures of his grandfather, George Dahmer, a distinguished-looking, light-skinned man in a dark suit and bow tie. He told me his grandfather lived with a secret many of his closest friends never knew. He was a white outcast who lived his entire life as a black man.

Vernon Jr. showed me a picture of his grandfather's mother, Laura Barnes, who was also white. She had high cheekbones and became an outcast herself after a Bavarian man named Peter Dahmer got her pregnant and left. Rejected by society in 1872 for her out-of-wedlock birth, she moved to a boardinghouse near Sullivan's Hollow, where she met Charley Craft, a former slave with piercing dark eyes who was part Creek Indian.

Working together, they fell in love and married. Other children followed. When a white mob shot into their home one night, she fired back and killed one of the attackers. They fled south to Kelly Settlement, named after slave owner John Kelly. His son, Green, had given hundreds of acres to his mixed-race descendants. The settlement became a thriving community, and there George Dahmer married Green's granddaughter, Ellen Kelly. Vernon Jr. showed me a picture of this lovely woman in a white dress.

Although born with white skin, George Dahmer lived and "passed" as African-American. He served on the Shady Grove board of deacons and on the high school's school board. The soft-spoken man and his family worked the land. When visitors stopped by, his wife served them baked sweet potatoes, cracklings, and other food. He became the community's amateur dentist, pulling out abscessed teeth.

"Here was a man born of one race who took on another race, and it never got in the way," Vernon Jr. said. "People never knew it."

Growing up, Vernon Sr. saw each of his older siblings leave home for the North, some "passing" for white. He stayed. By tenth grade, he had to drop out of school to help the family run the farm—raising corn, cotton, sugarcane, and livestock.

"My grandfather told me when you own where you stay, you are secure," Vernon Jr. said. "Nobody can starve you to death 'cause you can always make a living from the dirt."

He said the same 340 acres his family inherited remains in the family to this day. "We own every foot of it."

His father often crosses his mind. "If my dad hadn't been killed by the Klan, he would have had an opportunity to see his grandkids grow up and enjoy the life that those who killed him are still enjoying. He was killed for no reason, no valid reason other than hate."

33

In spring 1991, the Dahmer family met with District Attorney Glenn White, imploring him to reopen the case. They came away feeling cautiously optimistic, and I felt the same way after meeting with the prosecutor. He'd sounded sincere, even enthusiastic, about investigating the murder.

But then the case entered a long freeze. In the coming months, I would check in periodically on White's progress. Each time I called, however, his enthusiasm seemed to wane a little more, until he would bring up a reason why the case couldn't be prosecuted. At one point, he seemed concerned that the FBI had abused their power, which presented a hurdle to any reinvestigation. Next, he expressed doubt about the constitutionality of reinvestigating a cold case so many years later. This was while the Medgar Evers case was still moving to trial in 1991, and White saw that case as a bellwether. He wouldn't go forward until it cleared a path for him.

The wait turned from months into years. In Byron De La Beckwith's case, the gap between indictment to the final verdict was almost three years. When Beckwith was at last convicted in 1994, White seemed satisfied that all the constitutional hurdles had been cleared.

But the next time I visited with him, he told me he couldn't pursue the Vernon Dahmer case because he lacked the manpower. He had only one investigator, and he was too busy with other cases to devote any time to the Dahmer killing.

"Can you hire another investigator?" I asked. I couldn't imagine wasting the groundswell of support after the Beckwith verdict.

"No, that's set by the legislature," White replied.

I decided to write about the problem. Soon after my story ran, Mississippi House member Percy Watson pushed through legislation that funded a second investigator. White hired Michael Callahan, a recent law school graduate, and the two traveled to Tennessee, where they spoke with former FBI informant Delmar Dennis.

I was glad to see White finally interview Dennis. It had been three years since I wrote about his secret meeting with Imperial Wizard Sam Bowers.

When White returned, he told me he believed Dennis was telling the truth. He said the problem was that the list of participants that Bowers gave to Dennis was different than the one that former Klansman and prosecution witness Billy Roy Pitts had testified to.

This hardly surprised me. Bowers distrusted everybody.

When I suggested to White that Bowers may have given the wrong names on purpose, he shook his head. He remained convinced prosecutors couldn't overcome this.

"Don't Delmar Dennis and Billy Roy Pitts agree that Bowers gave the orders to kill Dahmer?"

"Yes."

"Then what does it matter?"

White gave no answer.

Back in the newsroom, I was promoted to investigative reporter after my work on the Medgar Evers case. The change meant that instead of spending my days covering courts, I could now devote my time to longer projects, giving much more time to spend on the Dahmer case.

I dove into microfilm, hoping to learn more about the charges against Bowers in the Dahmer firebombing and what followed. In his 1968 trial, two former Klansmen testified about Bowers giving the orders to kill the black businessman and farmer. The all-white jury deadlocked 11–1 in favor of Bowers's guilt.

That surprised me. In all my years of covering court, I had never seen a sole holdout juror in a noncapital trial.

I drove to the Forrest County Courthouse, where I found the list of jurors in Bowers's trial. I began tracking each of them down.

Three of the jurors—Douglas Herring, James E. Harrington, and Wayne R. Walters—talked to me about sitting around a wooden table in a small, closed room. Herring stood and said Bowers should be convicted of arson for ordering Dahmer's killing. Everyone agreed out loud with him, but when all of the jurors turned in their secret ballots, one read, "Not guilty."

"We did that four or five times," Herring said. "Every time it was the same way."

Jurors grew frustrated, Walters to the point of tears. Hours later, the man who kept voting "not guilty" fessed up, refusing to either explain his vote or to change it.

The men identified the holdout juror as Donald Carl Butler, who ran a lawn-mower repair business in Petal, Mississippi. I drove to the address, hoping to find Butler and talk to him.

I pulled my Honda into the parking lot and walked inside. He was helping a customer when I entered, and I waited until he finished.

When I brought up the subject of Bowers's trial, his anger flared. He denied being the holdout, but what he had to say made me believe he was. He spent most of our conversation lambasting the FBI and the prosecution.

District Attorney Glenn White announced he would not seek reelection in 1995, and I wondered what would happen with the Vernon Dahmer case. Would his successor pursue it? Or relegate it to the past?

In Hattiesburg, I met Democratic candidate Clifton Gaddis, who guided me to a soul food restaurant. Over lunch, he swore to me his first act in office would be to prosecute the Dahmer case. I welcomed his determination, while all the Republican candidate, Lindsay Carter, would say was that he would pursue the case if there was enough evidence.

On November 7, 1995, Gaddis lost by fewer than fifty votes. That night when I spoke to Vernon Dahmer Jr., he sounded like he had been the one defeated.

The next year brought the cruel reminder that the longer authorities delayed, the more difficult this case would be to prosecute. Klansman turned FBI informant Delmar Dennis, a likely key witness in the case, died of a heart attack.

Months later, the new district attorney sent investigator Raymond Howell to talk to me. He asked about Dahmer's murder and wanted to know what evidence was out there. I wanted to tell the investigator: "If the district attorney's office had gone forward with this case years ago, this trial would already be over, and Sam Bowers might be behind bars."

Instead, I did my best to summarize the evidence I knew. What became obvious was how little Howell knew about this case. He asked me about FBI files, which the agency had finally let White's office view. I mentioned that the previous investigator had made notes on those files, and he replied that if there were notes, he hadn't been able to find them.

When I had written my first story on Medgar Evers in 1989, the odds must have been a million to one against Byron De La Beckwith being convicted. The odds against Sam Bowers's prosecution must have now been 10 million to one. The case was going nowhere fast, and I felt weary and burned out.

Needing a break, I applied for and received a fellowship to the Kiplinger Reporting Program, where I started earning a master's degree in journalism at Ohio State University in fall 1996.

Six months later, the telephone rang. A caller with a raspy voice asked if my name was Jerry Mitchell.

"Yes."

"You were the one that got the Medgar Evers case reopened?"

"Yes."

"I just saw a movie on that."

He raved about the film, *Ghosts of Mississippi*, which starred Alec Baldwin as prosecutor Bobby DeLaughter, Whoopi Goldberg as Myrlie Evers, and James Woods as Byron De La Beckwith. After asking me questions about that prosecution, he brought up another case. "I have some information on the Vernon Dahmer murder."

"You do?"

He refused to share his name, but he did say his information involved Bowers. He said he would only share what he knew in person.

The mystery man continued. "I might need protection if I come forward."

"You sure might."

"Sam is still a dangerous man."

34

After the mystery man mentioned protection, I put him in touch with Jerry Himelstein, regional director for the Anti-Defamation League in New Orleans. They began talking and eventually laid out a plan for an April 12, 1997, meeting on the Mississippi Gulf Coast. The mystery man had also made calls to Vernon Dahmer Jr. about the case, and Vernon would be joining the meeting, too, along with his brother Dennis.

Together we sat inside a motel room in a seaside resort, the scent of chlorine from a nearby pool filling the room. Himelstein sat on a bed, while the Dahmer brothers wondered if this meeting with the mystery man was a trap. I was wondering the same thing.

At 11 a.m., there was a knock at the door, and I opened it to see a one-armed man, with a pack of cigarettes curled up in his shirt sleeve. He called himself Frank before entering with the mystery man—a huge man with a salt-and-pepper mustache and reading glasses hanging from his blue-striped sport shirt.

The mystery man straddled a wooden chair. He looked like a character in a John Wayne film, complete with a raspy voice and tough-guy posturing. He shared stories about growing up in Laurel, Mississippi, where he had worked as a teenager at Beehive News Stand and then for Sam Bowers.

Each night after work, he said, Bowers had lifted the young man's bicycle into the back of his Ford Falcon and given him a ride home. Learning the teen could use a typewriter, Bowers gave him White Knights propaganda to type and mimeograph. After he finished, he would distribute the KKK leaflets at bus stations, bowling alleys, and other public places.

Smoke drifted from his Marlboro as the man described the leader of the White Knights of the KKK. In his home, Bowers displayed a Confederate battle flag and Nazi flag, his shrine to white supremacy. Afraid of leaving fingerprints, he wouldn't touch a doorknob with his bare hands. He insisted on clandestine meetings, hundreds of white men standing in remote pastures. When he spoke to his fellow Klansmen, he paced in his seersucker suit, quoting from the Bible and George Orwell's *Animal Farm*.

He said Bowers started the secret group that became the White Knights in the back of the Beehive News Stand, where visitors could buy comic books and 6.5-ounce bottles of Coca-Cola. The mystery man had been there, and he described listening to Bowers. "Sam said that Hitler was going to have the perfect world. The communists and all were what brought him down—and the Jews."

The man waved his arm in an arc, an echo of the imperial wizard's gesture. He said the KKK leader wavered between genius and madness. "The day President Kennedy was assassinated, Bowers dressed up in an Uncle Sam suit and went and danced a jig in downtown Laurel."

Shortly before Vernon Dahmer's murder, the mystery man recalled a meeting of Klansmen in the back of John's Café, which Klansman Deavours Nix owned. Bowers commanded the room and declared, "Something needed to be done about the Dahmer nigger down South. He's causing problems." Another of the gathered Klansmen spoke up. He said that Bowers should order a "number four," the White Knights' term for killing, which only the imperial wizard could command. Bowers agreed. Then and there, the mystery man said, Bowers authorized the killing.

This revelation had the potential to breathe new life into the Dahmer case and made our mystery man a likely new witness if the KKK leader ever went on trial.

After the man finished his story, Vernon Dahmer Jr. asked what had made him decide to come forward.

"I saw you and your family on TV," the man told him. "You were saying how that you were sure that there were some people out there who knew something vital that could help get the case reopened. When you said that, I knew that I knew enough to get it reopened. I knew that if I was in your place, I'd want somebody to help me."

In the months that followed, the mystery man met with authorities and revealed his name was Bob Stringer. He explained more about why he had decided to come forward. When casinos popped up on the coast, he had become addicted to high-stakes card games. Once, he removed ten thousand dollars from a company's safe, replacing the cash with a check he signed. He believed his check would be good, but his gamble failed, and he was convicted of embezzlement—a conviction later expunged.

He had finished a twelve-step program for his gambling addiction, but he said he had relapsed. He believed it was because he failed to make amends—which included telling what he knew about the Dahmer case.

"It's been a deep, dark secret for thirty years," he said. "It bothers me. It took me so long to handle it."

35

By summer, Bob Stringer was swimming in deep water. He had agreed to renew his friendship with Sam Bowers so that the investigative team could try to gather more damning evidence.

Bill East, an investigator from the Mississippi attorney general's office, wired up Stringer with a hidden microphone to record their conversations. I trusted East, the redheaded Vietnam veteran and former cop who always pushed his investigations as far as he could. But even so, Stringer was now at a whole new level of stakes.

On July 25, 1997, Stringer pulled his pickup into a truck stop run by Bowers's business partner, Roy Wilson. Stringer slid onto a chair at the counter, where he feasted on fried eggs, hickory-smoked slab bacon, and biscuits soaked with white gravy that Wilson served him. Stringer was sipping coffee when Bowers walked in.

Bowers ordered his own breakfast, and the men began to reminisce about the old days, when the KKK met in a back room inside the Beehive News Stand. Bowers told Stringer that the militias had failed because they weren't cautious.

From behind the counter, Wilson mentioned a History Channel show in which Bowers had been featured. In the clip, the imperial wizard had blasted the US Supreme Court.

Bowers brightened. "That was probably the greatest speech I've ever given. All three news networks covered it. I talked for an hour and a half. Chief Justice Earl Warren threw out a remark. I used his same exact words and stuck 'em down his throat."

This was the first meeting of many, as Stringer and Bowers spent more and more time together. Stringer played the part of the loyal follower, and the White Knights leader called him "a good disciple" and "a great patriot." When Stringer asked the imperial wizard why he never gave him a more important role, Bowers responded that he did his best to protect him because of his age. "What you were doing was very important. You putting out propaganda caused more revolution for me to fight, and the revolution created more propaganda."

Stringer's undercover work led to an unexpected discovery—that Bowers owned illegal gambling machines at Roy Wilson's truck stop. When I learned of this, I thought of Al Capone. His gangsters had carried out dozens of killings, but in the end, he went to prison for the much less obvious crime of tax evasion. Perhaps that could be the case here.

Stringer telephoned me with updates. He shared a conversation he had with Roy Wilson, in which Wilson revealed that Bowers was still concerned about "that Dahmer deal."

"You think he did it, Roy?" Stringer had asked Wilson.

"I don't think he actually put his hands on it," Wilson responded. "But I think he had it done."

Wilson told Stringer that Bowers spent a lot of his time writing. The imperial wizard had shared an inch-thick stack of papers about his KKK days, and Wilson said that Bowers had written a book called *Rifle in the Bush*, which centered on the killings of Medgar Evers and Martin Luther King Jr. Wilson claimed the book named the real killers of the civil rights leaders.

I asked Stringer if Wilson still had a copy.

"He does. If we can get that book, we'll have all our answers."

• • •

After learning of the book and the illegal gambling machines, East believed authorities had enough evidence to prosecute Bowers for gambling. East decided to move forward, and he confronted Wilson. Caught unaware and cornered, Wilson vowed to cooperate.

"If you screw me on this thing," East told him, "you're going to have a miserable life."

East asked Wilson to bring a copy of *Rifle in the Bush* the next day. Wilson promised he would.

When East arrived the next morning at the truck stop to seize the gambling machines, they were gone. Wilson had double-crossed him.

Despite the betrayal, East decided against charging the truck stop operator. Bowers remained his target. But East could no longer use Wilson as bait. All East could do now was ask nicely. He dialed Bowers and left a message on the answering machine: "Mr. Bowers, this is Bill East from the attorney general's office. You need to call me about the machines you took out of the truck stop the other night."

The leader of the nation's most violent KKK group had been in the grasp of authorities. Once again, he had slipped away.

36

Sam Bowers's lawyer, Travis Buckley, had represented many Klansmen, including Byron De La Beckwith and Edgar Ray Killen. He gloated after Bowers avoided any kind of gambling prosecution.

The round, frog-eyed attorney had been a leader in the White Knights. Alongside Bowers, he had been indicted in the Dahmer firebombing, but not convicted. A jury, however, did convict him of kidnapping Jack Watkins, an innocent man the White Knights mistakenly believed had beaten Lawrence Byrd. But in 1969, the Mississippi Supreme Court threw out Buckley's conviction and his ten-year prison sentence because a co-defendant acknowledged during testimony that he had pleaded guilty in the case. The justices ruled that a conviction of one is not competent evidence against the other, enabling Buckley to keep his license and continue practicing law.

When I reached him by telephone, the lawyer couldn't resist taking a shot at authorities and their failed investigation of Bowers. "Most of the people they're associated with are a bunch of clowns. You can't classify them any other way." He told me the investigators in the case "couldn't find their way in from a storm."

One of Bowers's closest friends, Deavours Nix, a tall, pale, white-haired man who had owned John's Café, sounded no less cocky than Buckley. Nix was also among those accused of the Dahmer firebombing and murder. When he and other Klansmen had gone on trial in US district court in Hattiesburg, jurors deadlocked on federal conspiracy charges against him. He said the jury came within one vote of acquitting him on the charges. "Most of the people were acquitted. It was kind of a laugh."

When I reached Nix to ask about the current probe, he regarded it as a joke. "It ain't going nowhere. They got nothing."

Despite all the bad news, good news came before 1997 ended when the Mississippi Supreme Court upheld the murder conviction of Byron De La Beckwith, after he had appealed. In the court's 4–2 decision, Justice Mike Mills praised efforts "to squeeze justice out of the harm caused by a furtive explosion which erupted from dark bushes on a June night in Jackson, Mississippi."

He wrote that Beckwith's constitutional right to a speedy trial had not been denied. His "complicity with the Sovereignty Commission's involvement in the prior trials contributed to the delay."

How ironic was that? The defense's attempts to thwart justice helped ensure justice three decades later.

The decision did more than ensure that Beckwith would stay behind bars. It opened the door for other civil rights cold cases, too.

After my stories on Bowers appeared in *The Clarion-Ledger*, Hinds County sheriff Malcolm McMillin cornered me about the KKK leader. "He ain't like Beckwith. He can still reach out and touch you. You don't need to be going any places alone. It wouldn't hurt to have someone go with you. Let me know if you need help."

"Thanks, Sheriff," I responded, unsure what else to say.

"I can't emphasize that enough. I wouldn't get into too much of a routine because your face is well-known."

The sheriff was right. Bowers was no Beckwith. He was head of the Klan in Mississippi. He ordered others to carry out the violence he wanted. He was the priest who eliminated the "heretics," the leader who called on Klansmen to "counterattack" their enemies at night. That now included me.

37

Billy Roy Pitts, the lantern-jawed Klansman, had been the key witness in the trials regarding the fatal firebombing of Vernon Dahmer. He had dropped his Magnum revolver that night, got caught, pleaded guilty to murder, and received a life sentence. He had also pleaded guilty to federal conspiracy charges and received a separate five-year sentence.

Fearing the Klan might do harm to Pitts, federal authorities had shuttled him from place to place, hiding him in secret locations. His testimony helped bring four convictions in the Dahmer arson and murder. I began looking into where he had ended up, in hopes of talking to Pitts. But as I sifted through the records, I realized I couldn't find any mention of Pitts's time in state prison. Someone told me that was because he had gone into the federal witness protection program, a detail that seemed odd to me, if he was supposed to be in prison for life.

I decided to telephone the federal Bureau of Prisons. An archivist there dug up his old record and told me he had served just three and a half years in prison before being paroled on September 3, 1971.

"From what I understand," I said, "he left there and went into the federal government's witness protection program."

"That's impossible," she replied.

"Why's that?"

"The witness protection program didn't exist at the time."

"But he was supposed to serve a life sentence in Mississippi."

She explained that whenever an inmate faces additional time from another prison, that prison will place a hold on the inmate to ensure he is transferred to the new facility. "There was never a hold put on him. That's why he was released."

Pitts never served a day of his life sentence? How did that happen?

No one seemed to know, and my mind drifted to where he might be these days. Hiding underground? Living under a different name? For all I knew, he was pushing up daisies in a cemetery.

By this point, in 1998, I knew I could turn to the World Wide Web for help. It was still a place that seemed hit-and-miss when it came to information. But I went on a new website, typed in Pitts's name, and clicked the return key. His name popped up. So did his address in Denham Springs, Louisiana. So did his telephone number.

Wow. This is handy.

When I reached him, he asked, "How'd you find me? How'd you find me?"

"It's on the Internet."

"The Internet? I have an unlisted telephone number."

When the fifty-three-year-old former Klansman calmed down, we discussed the White Knights' firebombing of Vernon Dahmer and his family. Pitts confirmed that he had taken part in the raid that killed Vernon Dahmer, and he said that Imperial Wizard Sam Bowers had ordered the attack.

This meant Pitts could be a key witness if the KKK leader went on trial. The question was, would Pitts cooperate?

I tried to get a read on that, aiming to keep him talking without spooking him. In time, he talked more about the Klan violence that took place across Mississippi in the 1960s. "Bowers masterminded everything that went on in the state," he said.

I shared with Pitts what I found out about his own time behind bars—that he had served three and a half years in federal prison but that there was no record of him doing any state time.

When I asked him about this, he replied simply, "I done my federal time and come back here."

Here, he explained, was a suburb of Baton Rouge, a place he had been quietly hiding since his days in Mississippi. "My parents were getting old. I kind of built my life around this part of the country."

I brought up the life sentence again, still trying to work out what had happened, and he told me he thought that sentence ran at the same time as his federal time. I told him that authorities considered his two sentences separate, and he seemed shocked at first. Then worry spilled out. "If that's true," he said, "that means Mississippi still has a hold on me. That bothers me."

He believed he had done the right thing before, standing up against Klansmen, but he had no interest in taking the witness stand again. If Mississippi authorities dragged him back to testify, he said the Klan would kill him.

I asked him if I could drive over and chat with him tomorrow. He said no, he had done enough talking for now. But he reassured me that we would talk later.

On January 16, 1998, I learned that corrections officials, whom I had questioned about Pitts's release, had now issued a warrant for his arrest. They confirmed that Pitts had served no time on his life sentence. That meant as soon as authorities arrested Pitts, he would begin serving the life sentence he had avoided in Mississippi.

Days later, his brother, James, called me with news. His brother, the key witness against Sam Bowers, was on the lam.

Weeks after Pitts's disappearance, a secretary telephoned me to let me know I had a package at the front desk of *The Clarion-Ledger*. When I arrived, there was an envelope containing an audiocassette marked as being sent by "Billy Roy Pitts."

I played the tape, which began, "Jerry Mitchell, this first part is off the record. I want you to know that you have ruined my life."

But he said he was keeping his word in talking to me. "Back on the record, this is January 30, 1998. My name is Billy Roy Pitts. I'm considered at this time by the state of Mississippi to be a fugitive."

He said no one, not even his family, knew his whereabouts. "I'm not trying to escape justice. I am preparing myself to turn myself over to the authorities. I have a couple of things I must do."

He said he decided to flee because "my life in the hands of the Mississippi authorities probably wouldn't be worth a plug nickel. I can remember a time if a man was put in jail, that a group of men would go in the woods and hold his court for him while the sheriff would turn his head, and they would get him out of jail and hang him off the Bogue Homa Bridge."

Pitts grew up in south Mississippi, where mobs in a single week in 1942 lynched three black Mississippians, two of them only fourteen years old. Federal prosecutors tried three of the reported mob of one hundred for the lynching of Howard Wash, including a jailer who left the door unlocked. But after the defense lawyer complained of government intrusion, the all-white jury acquitted the trio.

Pitts said prosecutors in the 1960s had promised him that if he cooperated, he would never serve time in Mississippi. After his federal time, he went home, never knowing about this "breach of promise."

In a handful of FBI records I saw, Pitts made reference to a "deal" with the FBI. When he drew close to finishing his federal time, state prosecutors told federal authorities that Pitts would face "certain death" if he went to the Mississippi State Penitentiary at Parchman. Prosecutors tried unsuccessfully to get the governor to pardon Pitts.

On tape, Pitts talked about the four Klansmen convicted in Dahmer's killing. He talked of the irony that he now faced a life sentence behind bars when, thanks to governors' pardons, commutations, and the like, the convicted Klansmen did "a few years, and they're on the street now."

Pitts said he decided to join the KKK after a fellow employee told him that joining the organization "would be God's will." But then "one thing led to another—a few cross burnings, harassing people. The next thing I know, they have us out burning houses and killing people."

He spoke of Imperial Wizard Sam Bowers ordering the violence.

During one firebombing, gunshots rang out from the house the Klan was attacking, and Pitts was shot in the foot. Klansmen sped him to a hospital, where he was treated and released with no paperwork and no questions asked. In those days, he said the KKK could get away with anything, including murder.

He began to have his first doubts when the White Knights attacked a black family, not long before the Dahmer killing. "We went into this community and shot up this house and set it on fire, these women and children on their hands and knees, screaming and begging for mercy, crying out for help from God. That bothered me very bad."

He wanted out of the KKK, but he found "no way out other than the way I went. I'm very sorry for what I've done."

If he did decide to testify again, he said it would be for the family. "I owe the Dahmer family that much. I really do."

After my story ran on Pitts's taped comments, an editorial in *The Clarion-Ledger* urged him to turn himself in to authorities:

> Those days of hate in Mississippi in the '60s were written in blood and carved in the hearts of those who suffered and those who caused the suffering. The evil that was done can never be erased. But, those who committed these acts can do what they can to make amends. By coming forth and testifying against those who committed this horror, Pitts can help put the past behind him and work for the cause of justice. There is no heavier heart than one that is carrying the burden of guilt, of complicity, of assassination.

38

Two days after our February 7, 1998, editorial ran on Billy Roy Pitts, he turned himself in to Mississippi authorities. At the Forrest County jail, Pitts told the same story he had shared with me. He talked about the raids he had gone on to carry out violence for the White Knights of the Ku Klux Klan, including their attack on Vernon Dahmer and his family. He told investigators that Sam Bowers, their imperial wizard, had ordered each of these, including Dahmer's killing.

After the interview, Investigator Bill East telephoned me. He said that Pitts was cooperating, and that with him as their key witness, authorities would have enough evidence to put Bowers on trial.

East said when he first took on the Dahmer case, he thought, "Hell, this case is thirty years old." After he came to know the family and became familiar with the case, he thought, "The hell with it. It needs to be done. It should have been done a long time ago."

With the testimony of Pitts and Bob Stringer, East said that authorities had plenty of evidence against the KKK leader. "My gut feeling is we can convict Sam Bowers and not get another thing."

But more evidence against Bowers kept bubbling up. I had recently learned that, back in the mid-1980s, Bowers gave an interview with the

Mississippi Department of Archives and History. I wrote a story about the interview and how Bowers had agreed to do the interview, as long as it was sealed until after his death. Authorities subpoenaed the recordings, and East soon told me that Bowers had declared in the interview that it was okay to lynch African-Americans if they break the law. I knew these weren't idle words. In addition to the 10 known killings by the White Knights, the terrorist group carried out seemingly endless violence against black Mississippians. In the summer of 1964 alone, Klansmen beat 80 people, shot another 35, and firebombed 68 churches, synagogues, or other buildings associated with the civil rights movement.

"And here's something else," East told me. "Bowers said he didn't have anything to apologize for. Not one thing."

I continued researching Bowers and learned that he embraced the same racist Christian Identity philosophy that Byron De La Beckwith first explained to me. As I wrote up my findings on the KKK leader in *The Clarion-Ledger*, several of his supporters called to complain. One reminded me that Bowers was a fine man and a Sunday school teacher. Another confronted me: "Did you think we were going to let you go unscathed? We know where you live."

He yelled out what sounded like a war whoop. "You fucking son of a bitch. Don't think I haven't seen you a half-dozen times."

He rattled off an accurate physical description of me—something that unnerved me even more than the previous threats I'd received. I told my wife when I returned home, and she demanded I call the FBI. Soon I was sharing with an agent the details of the conversation, including the remark by the Bowers backer that "David told me not to call."

I later learned the caller had been referring to David Duke, the former grand wizard of the KKK who unsuccessfully ran for governor in Louisiana and president of the United States. Stringer had described joining Duke at the high-stakes tables at Mississippi casinos. It turned out that Duke could afford those games because he bilked $200,000 from supporters.

As the weeks passed, East kept me posted on authorities' progress. Investigators tracked down several witnesses who had testified against Bowers before, including T. Webber Rogers, a Klansman who went on a dry run before the Dahmer attack, and Klansman turned FBI informant Robert Earl Wilson, who heard Bowers brag about the attack on Dahmer. "We had a real good week," East said, "and we're on track."

On April 15, I visited East and the other investigators in their "War Room," where they had posted the names of the suspects in the Dahmer case on the wall. Bowers's name was there, and so was his right-hand man in the White Knights, Deavours Nix.

When I entered, I saw Investigator Jim Gilliland. He was the antithesis of East—soft-spoken and meticulous. Despite their differences, they worked well together, sometimes taking joint trips on their Harley-Davidson motorcycles. Gilliland grew up in Hattiesburg, and it angered him that the KKK attack had given his hometown a black eye. "Just cowardly."

East told me that he had run into Bowers's lawyer, Travis Buckley, the other day, and confronted him about long-standing allegations that Buckley himself took part in the Dahmer firebombing. He shared the conversation:

"Well, you know I wasn't there," Buckley responded to East. "I was in Washington. I've got witnesses who say I was in Washington."

"I know," East replied. "What I'm wondering about are the meetings where the Dahmer killing was planned."

"It wasn't me—uh, uh, uh. I've got a brother who looks just like me."

Red-bearded prosecutor Bob Helfrich entered. The investigators called him "Hellfire" because of his fiery disposition. He wondered aloud about all of the national press attention now coming to the case.

East said he was happy to see it. "I hope they shove a camera up Bowers's ass."

These days, he said the imperial wizard lunched three times a week at a Jitney Jungle supermarket in Laurel. "Unless a judge throws this thing out, we're gonna nail Bowers's ass."

Helfrich agreed. "We're going to get that son of a bitch."

39

I got my first glimpse of Sam Bowers at a court hearing on May 20, 1998. Prosecutors had asked a judge to open up a handful of still-sealed records on the Vernon Dahmer case in US District Court in Hattiesburg, and the judge was hearing their arguments.

When Bowers entered the courtroom, he was wearing a beige suit with a striped red-and-white tie, his scuffed saddle shoes squeaking with each step as he entered the courtroom. I studied the seventy-three-year-old man. His graying temples connected to a shock of still dark hair, and he spoke with a warm voice and impeccable manners. He resembled, I couldn't help thinking, a doting grandfather. Was this the same man a *Time* magazine photographer had captured on film a few weeks ago? The KKK leader had stepped toward the photographer, pointing his finger like a pistol, and mouthed the words, "You're dead."

During the hearing, Assistant District Attorney Bob Helfrich stood before the judge and argued that the prosecutors needed files unsealed as they finished investigating the Dahmer case. I knew, from talking with Helfrich, that he felt a strong connection to the Dahmer family and the case at hand. His own father had died in 1966, when Helfrich had been twelve years old, just like Dennis Dahmer. Helfrich's father had died of lung cancer, and that experience had been hard enough for his family. Imagining the pain of the Dahmer children, after their father's outright murder, had caused the prosecutor to empathize with this family like none before.

Helfrich's argument was efficient, clear-cut, and effective. Bowers's lawyer, Travis Buckley, tried to object, but the judge sided with prosecutors. He unsealed the files, and in doing so allowed the investigation to continue at speed. Ultimately, the files wouldn't prove that valuable, but regardless, the prosecutors were leaving no stone unturned as they moved closer to arrests. Bowers's appearance in court that day would be just a warm-up for him.

"Justice was never served the first time," Helfrich told me. "It's time justice was done."

Eight days later, Bill East and other investigators banged on the door of Sam Bowers. He answered, and they entered, telling him he was under arrest for the murder of Vernon Dahmer.

Bowers smiled. "I guess you feel real big about this."

"Mr. Bowers," East replied, "I'll feel real big about this when the jury comes back with a guilty verdict."

At 8:30 a.m., the handcuffed Bowers arrived at the Forrest County jail, where photographers snapped pictures of the KKK leader. Inside the jail, he stood in front of a wall, which measured him at six feet tall. The judge set Bowers's bond at $200,000.

I watched the news with the Dahmer family. Attorney General Mike Moore came on the television. The previous year, the *National Law Journal* had voted him "Lawyer of the Year" for his work on the tobacco litigation that led to a record $246 billion settlement with the states, and there had been talk of him running for governor. He had visited with the Dahmers, and after they shared their story with him, he tucked a picture of the family into his car's visor as a reminder of that attack.

On TV, he said, "About thirty-two years ago on a January night, eight cowards—and that's exactly what they were, eight cowards—came to this jurisdiction in the middle of the night and committed what we think is one of the most horrible and heinous crimes that's ever been committed in America. Eight people armed with big gallons of gasoline and guns and meanness in their hearts showed up in this jurisdiction for one thing—to stop people from voting. They were not only going to stop people's right to vote, but they were going to stop the man who was trying to help them."

Moore called the arrests a "historic day for this city, this county, and this state. We just think that when somebody commits a murder, whether it's this year or thirty-two years ago, they ought to not get away with murder."

As she finished watching the news report on TV, Ellie Dahmer wiped away her tears. "You go back through it, you relive it, and you ask why. You hope and pray this day will come. It's been a long time coming. These are tears of joy. The tears I'm shedding now are for Vernon because I know he is looking at us today."

Vernon Dahmer Jr., who was also watching, told me, "My father is smiling today because the system he died for is finally working for us."

Bowers was investigators' prime target, but authorities also believed they had enough evidence to charge his right-hand man, Deavours Nix, who served as the Klan's investigator, for helping to orchestrate the firebombing. At his bond hearing, the family of Deavours Nix pushed him into the courtroom in a wheelchair. The seventy-two-year-old man held a green tank as he breathed oxygen, something he told the judge he had to do all the time. He said radiation treatments had burned up his lungs—a choice of words that could only make me think of Vernon Dahmer. Nix also told the judge he was confined to a wheelchair. The judge said he did not usually release criminal defendants without bond, but he would make an exception in this case because of Nix's poor health.

Eleven days later, I telephoned Nix. I wanted to learn more about the man, and I found him surprisingly forthcoming. He talked about golf and then the White Knights. He confirmed belonging to the KKK—something few Klansmen ever did.

When I asked about the arson charge against him in the Dahmer case, he told me he was "absolutely, one hundred percent innocent. I think that was O.J.'s plea."

He chuckled. I was surprised by his reference to Simpson, whom a jury in 1995 found not guilty of murder despite powerful evidence.

"You think O. J. Simpson is innocent?" I asked.

"No, I don't think he was innocent."

He explained that if he had been on the jury, he would have acquitted Simpson. "Me and Sam was both for him a lot. We didn't agree with the way the police went over the fence without a warrant, violating the Fourth Amendment. I was pulling for him real hard, and I really wasn't surprised when he was found innocent."

Two KKK leaders pulling for O.J. to beat the rap? You can't make this stuff up.

Nix spoke of his own arrest. "It's a political move on Mike Moore's part, and of course he's calling the shots himself. You and I both know he's going after the black vote, and he might be successful at that. He better think of the white race, too."

He talked again of golf, boasting about his plan to hit the greens. "I'm going to be down at the first tee at Bear Creek Golf Club at eight thirty in the morning."

Here was a man, too sick to go to jail, or even post bond, because he was bound to a wheelchair, breathing oxygen. Now he was going to play golf?

After hanging up, I entered the office of my boss, Debbie Skipper. "You're not going to believe what Deavours Nix just told me."

"What's that?"

"He's going golfing tomorrow."

"You've got to be kidding."

"Nope. Going to the Bear Creek Golf Club at eight thirty a.m."

"How do you know?"

"He told me."

She laughed. "These Klansmen always talk to you, Jerry."

The next morning, our photographer John Severson snapped

photographs of Nix whacking his ball down the fairway of the 6,832-yard course. He carried his oxygen tank in the back of the golf cart.

My story ran with pictures in the next day's *Clarion-Ledger*, and after seeing them, the judge had Nix jailed. "If you're well enough to play golf," the judge barked, "you're well enough to post bond."

40

From the moment Sam Bowers entered the courtroom on July 13, he resembled someone caught in a time warp. He wore black shoes, white socks, and a frayed seersucker suit in need of a dry cleaning. When his lawyer, Travis Buckley, entered, the KKK leader tilted his head toward me, calling me a "chief vulture."

After the hearing began, Assistant District Attorney Bob Helfrich questioned whether Buckley could represent Bowers, since the lawyer had once been charged with arson in the Dahmer case. Buckley discounted any such conflict, and then Bowers stood to address the judge. He reassured the judge that he desired for Buckley to continue to represent him. Together, he said, they would contradict the perjured witnesses for the prosecution, just as he had decades ago, leading authorities to abandon the case.

"Let's get on with the adversarial part of this case," Bowers concluded, "and let the court fulfill its function of deciding the constitutionalities of this conflict."

"I can assure you I will do that," the judge replied.

"Yes, I felt like the court would do that."

Bowers spoke in a strange, anachronistic style, but he made his arguments calmly and pointedly, in a way that made me wonder if he would be better off representing himself than relying on the sometimes scatter-brained Buckley.

After the hearing ended, both teams of lawyers crossed the street and watched a printer spit out the names of potential jurors for the murder trial. The district attorney noticed that Bowers was wearing a Mickey Mouse belt buckle and asked Bowers about it.

The imperial wizard brightened and called the Disney mouse "the first militant."

Then Bowers broke into a bold baritone, "I don't know but it's been said: air force wings are made of lead. I don't know but I've been told: navy wings are made of gold. There's one thing that I know for sure: Mickey Mouse's wings are sky blue pure."

Until that moment, I had been puzzling over Bowers, trying to square his measured appearance in the courtroom with the violence that I knew lurked underneath. Now I believed he was insane.

A month later, Bowers went on trial in a courtroom that resembled something out of *To Kill a Mockingbird*. A carved wooden railing guarded two balconies, one with a window overlooking a Confederate monument. Jurors sat center stage in an elevated box that gave them the best view of the courtroom, and the audience, sitting behind the box, had the worst.

When jury selection began, the imperial wizard sat in one of the leather chairs on the back row of the jury box and swiveled around to face the audience of potential jurors, flashing a smile when he made eye contact. He brightened when one potential juror suggested the Ku Klux Klan was started to make sure fathers took care of their families, but his grin began to fade when another confessed that she didn't know if she could set aside her sympathy toward the Vernon Dahmer family.

By evening, jurors had been selected—six white, five African-American, and one Asian-American, ranging in occupations from a furniture salesperson to an X-ray technologist.

The next morning, August 18, the opening arguments began. Assistant District Attorney Bob Helfrich described the White Knights' attack on the Dahmer family, and the witnesses who would testify against Bowers.

The prosecutor pointed at the KKK leader. "Ladies and gentlemen, the evidence is clear and overwhelming that Sam Bowers, the imperial wizard of the White Knights of the Ku Klux Klan, ordered this cowardly attack. There will only be one choice when you deliberate, and that will be guilty."

Defense lawyer Travis Buckley put forth an argument that would have played out better decades earlier, during the days of state-sponsored segregation. "This is a media-orchestrated and politically driven prosecution— a persecution," he said. "And that is what this country is not about, a persecution—a prosecution—based on political ambition and based upon media members attempting to enhance their own positions, just as Mr. Jerry Mitchell and [TV reporter] Mark Johnson seated over there now."

Buckley stabbed his finger at me, as if in an old *Perry Mason* episode. Bowers looked on, dressed in a light blue seersucker suit and wearing a Mickey Mouse button on his lapel.

Members of the Vernon Dahmer family took the witness stand to share with jurors what happened that night. Ellie Dahmer testified that she woke at about 2 a.m. to a stuck car horn, hearing bullets pelting the house and realizing that their home was on fire. Dennis Dahmer recalled a wall of fire outside his bedroom and choked back tears as he described seeing the family grocery store, where his great-aunt lived, engulfed in flames.

The testimony of Bettie Dahmer, only ten at the time, captivated jurors as she recounted fleeing from the flames as they seared her skin. After the family escaped to a nearby barn, she said, "My father was sitting there on a bale of hay with the skin hanging off of his arms, but he never complained the whole time he was there. The only thing he was concerned about was us. . . . He wanted to know we were all right."

She held out her arms, covered with pink scars, and her fingers, still gnarled from the blaze. That night, she had rolled on the cold ground, trying to stem the throbbing pain.

In cross-examination, Buckley sought to prove that his client was nowhere near the crime. "Miz Dahmer," he said, "you, of course, didn't see anything that happened that night."

"I saw my house burn," she shot back, hot tears streaming down her face. "I saw the skin hanging off my daddy's arms. I saw that."

Buckley suggested she and her family wanted to strike back in anger.

"No, Mr. Buckley. I just want my daddy to have the same justice that everybody else in America can have. That's all I want."

Retired FBI agents testified about the evidence they found at the smoldering Dahmer house, which remained so hot that agents had to wait to search it. "We roped off the area with tape," retired agent Loren Brooks testified. After the embers cooled, he said, agents began to collect evidence, including spent shotgun shells, a charred .22-caliber revolver, and an abandoned Ford Galaxy with flat tires.

Bowers's defense attorney used this as an opportunity to pounce on the prosecution witnesses. "There's nothing on there that was found that you can identify with Mr. Bowers," Buckley said. "Is that correct?"

"That would be correct," replied retired FBI agent James Awe.

But Buckley didn't stop there. He tried to prove that FBI agents had crossed the line in their pursuit of Bowers. He alluded to mobster turned FBI informant Gregory Scarpa beating up Lawrence Byrd. Buckley asked whether the FBI was "bringing in from the Northeast, that being Mafioso-type characters" to "beat up people or to rough up or to threaten, intimidate, or whatever term you may prefer to use people to get information?"

"Not the way you describe it," Awe replied. "Absolutely not."

The defense lawyer got the name of the former mobster wrong, calling him "Frank Scarpio." "Does that name ring a bell with you?" Buckley asked.

"No, it doesn't," Awe replied.

Buckley asked about wiretaps and surveillance on the imperial wizard. "They pretty well . . . knew his whereabouts twenty-four hours a day, didn't they?"

Retired FBI agent Jim Ingram, who now served as Mississippi's public safety commissioner, told Buckley he knew of no wiretaps on Bowers. He said the FBI definitely began surveillance on Bowers after the killing of Vernon Dahmer.

Then Buckley brought up journalist Jack Nelson's book *Terror in the Night,* which detailed how the White Knights in the mid-1960s began to bomb Jewish homes and synagogues in Mississippi. Many bombings had been the work of Bowers's best disciple, Tommy Tarrants, and eventually police in Meridian, Mississippi, had set up an ambush to kill him. While Tarrants was attempting to blow up a Jewish leader's home, police opened fire on him. He somehow survived, but his KKK accomplice that night, Kathy Ainsworth, a married schoolteacher by day in Jackson, died. Nelson had exposed the FBI's role in the ambush.

"Do you remember him [Nelson] saying anything about the FBI engaging in extralegal activities in Mississippi?" Buckley asked.

Ingram replied yes, saying he disagreed with Nelson.

Buckley claimed that Bowers was the ambush's real target. "Are you denying on personal knowledge that the FBI tried to set it up for Sam Bowers to come there and kill him?"

Ingram replied that wasn't true.

In the end, the defense lawyer's questions backfired. Instead of creating a picture of a sympathetic client harassed by the FBI, he succeeded in giving jurors—many of whom weren't even born when Dahmer was killed—a glimpse into the KKK's brutality and violence in Mississippi.

"The White Knights were a very secretive, close-knit organization with one man who made all the decisions," Ingram told jurors. "That was Sam Bowers."

41

Former Klansman T. Webber Rogers told jurors that discussion of this "Dahmer project" went back to October 1965, when Klansmen gathered in an abandoned tenant house on Lawrence Byrd's farm off US 84 near Laurel. The sixty-one-year-old former barber said he remembered the meeting took place in October because not long after, he suffered a chain saw injury that led to his leg's amputation.

At the meeting, Imperial Wizard Sam Bowers became upset that nothing had been done about Dahmer, Rogers testified. "He wanted to know why . . . the job down south hadn't been took care of. He wanted it done right."

Rogers said that Bowers and Klan leader Deavours Nix debated whether the job should be a "three" (a firebombing) or a "four."

"What is a four?" prosecutor Bob Helfrich asked.

"Abolishment," Rogers replied.

Only Bowers had the authority to order a three or four, he said.

When the White Knights met again in December 1965, he said Bowers was angry. Pounding his fist on the witness stand, Rogers imitated the imperial wizard, quoting Bowers as saying, "Something has got to be done about this damn nigger down south." He said the KKK leader wanted to know why the Dahmers still hadn't been attacked. "It should have been done. It's two weeks behind."

Rogers said he and other Klansmen went on a dry run to check out where Dahmer lived. He said they pulled up into the family's driveway, making a mental note of both the grocery store and Dahmer home.

Inside the White Knights, "were there consequences for disobeying orders of superiors?" Helfrich asked.

"Yes, sir, there are."

"And what are those consequences?"

"Whatever Mr. Sam recommends is what you get."

Back in 1967, he had testified that after he refused to follow White Knights' orders, three Klansmen abducted him. He tried to run away—only for them to shoot him in his good leg.

Under cross-examination from defense lawyer Travis Buckley, Rogers admitted he had been convicted in 1965 of two felonies, including carrying a concealed weapon, and had received a suspended sentence. He denied Buckley's suggestion that he was shot because he jumped bond.

The trip into Mississippi's past rekindled familiar fears in Rogers and the other witnesses. At one point, Buckley asked Rogers if he was still living over near Seminary, Mississippi. Prosecutors objected, and the jury went out. Rogers still refused to say where he lived.

"Have you received any threats?" the judge asked.

"Hell, yeah—before and now," Rogers replied.

When Billy Roy Pitts stepped to the witness stand, he looked more like a Sunday school teacher than a scary Klansman. In his dawdling drawl, the fifty-eight-year-old former Klansman testified that when he was sworn into the White Knights, Klansmen placed a sword and pistol on top of a Bible, calling themselves Christian soldiers.

A month before Dahmer's January 10, 1966, killing, Pitts said Klansmen gathered at a vacant house with wooden church pews, listening to Bowers. Pitts testified that Bowers spoke of "projects" that needed to be done "to show these people in Washington that the people in the South meant business. That he was tired of carpetbaggers coming out of the North down here stirring up our niggers and . . . giving us problems."

Pitts began listing the people present, including Bowers, Deavours Nix, Cecil Sessum, and Travis Buckley. When a court reporter asked Pitts to repeat the names, Buckley's name rang out a second time. This time the lawyer shot up like a cannon. "Your honor, if it may please the court, I have a matter to take up with the court that's of utmost importance."

With the jury out, Buckley complained, "He is accusing me of a felony here in this court. I think that is grounds for mistrial, your honor."

Buckley sputtered, insisting he was in Washington, D.C., at the time. "It's kind of like throwing a skunk in the jury box and telling them to ignore the odor."

Although Buckley had once been arrested and charged with arson in the Dahmer firebombing, he maintained he had never seen his name before in any FBI records regarding the Dahmer case, except for a mention of him at John's Café. Helfrich replied that Buckley had been provided a 1968 statement in which Pitts identified Buckley at the December 1965 meeting.

The judge denied Buckley's request for a mistrial, but asked jurors, when they returned, to ignore the testimony regarding the lawyer.

Under resumed questioning by the prosecutor, Pitts said the one project Bowers wanted done right away was "this nigger in Forrest County, this job down south. I later learned that the project name was the Vernon Dahmer job."

He testified that, on the night of the attack, when Exalted Cyclops Cecil Sessum picked him up at his home in a red Volkswagen, Sessum gave no explanation. A group of men gathered at Sessum's father's store, where they checked shotguns and handguns to make sure they worked. Then they pumped gasoline into a dozen jugs. Before hitting the Dahmer home, they stopped at a black cemetery and urinated on graves, where one Klansman joked, "The only good nigger is a dead one."

They left the cemetery in two cars, a Pontiac and a Ford Galaxy, and kept their lights off as they drove into the darkness. After arriving at the Dahmer home, Pitts said he and Sessum dashed across the lawn, and Sessum took out his pocketknife, jabbed holes in one jug, and used a forked stick with a rag as a fuse. The firebomb smashed through the Dahmers' living room window. Pitts crouched on the corner of the house, his quick-draw holster on his hip, ready to pull out his .22-caliber Magnum and kill anyone who came. No one did, but before Pitts left, "I heard a man's voice. Sounded like someone in distress."

His words swept over the Dahmer family, watching from the balcony. Ellie Dahmer removed her glasses and wiped away tears.

During the raid, Pitts said the driver of the Ford Galaxy turned on his headlights, prompting Klansmen in the Pontiac to get confused and open fire, shooting out two tires on the Ford. As a result, all the Klansmen had to cram into the Pontiac and leave together.

Back from the raid, Pitts said, Bowers became furious when he learned that Klansmen had to ditch the Ford. He also raged at Pitts for dropping his gun. Pitts recalled Bowers jabbing his finger in his face, saying, "I hand-picked you myself as a replacement on this job, and you let me down."

After hearing that FBI agents were after him in the aftermath of the raid, Pitts said he shared the information with Bowers, who urged him to stay silent and not to worry. Pitts quoted Bowers as saying, "It's all going to be all right. There ain't no jury in the state of Mississippi gonna convict a white man for killing a nigger."

Pitts fled Mississippi and wound up talking with his brother, James, a preacher in Louisiana. "It was my decision after talking to him to go to the FBI, come clean, tell the whole truth, pay whatever price I had to pay, do whatever I had to do, and then start my life again."

Now, thirty-two years later, Pitts talked of the guilt. "My Lord, a man's life was taken, and I was a part of it. That's something I could not get out of my mind," he said. "I'm sorry for being a part of this. I wish to God I had never been a part of it, but it's something I can't forget."

Under cross-examination, Buckley questioned Pitts's claim that he had received any threats. "Has anybody that you can point a finger at tried to bother you in any way that you know of?"

Pitts said he didn't know identities of those who threatened him, explaining that his fellow Klansmen "don't come out in the open where you can visually see them. They held the trial of Vernon Dahmer in his absence. Then went to his home while he was there at his house with his family and destroyed him, destroyed his family's life."

Buckley did his best to portray the former Klansman as a paid liar. Pitts admitted he received more than $8,000 over a several-year period ($100 a week) as an informant, saying that the money went to help pay for relocating his wife and two children to ensure their safety.

Buckley then turned to a game plan that had worked so well for the defense three decades earlier, painting Pitts as a philandering husband on the federal dole. Back then, jurors were presented with photographs of Pitts lounging by the swimming pool with his girlfriend while federal marshals watched. The effect was to discredit Pitts, piercing his image as a trustworthy family man. Hoping to replicate that strategy, Buckley began to cross-examine Pitts about the visits of a woman besides his wife.

"I'll just save you a lot of time," Pitts said. "I admit she was my girlfriend. I had an affair with her."

It wasn't the dramatic revelation the defense lawyer was hoping for, but Buckley pressed forward. He asked Pitts about which days his wife visited and which days his girlfriend visited.

"If you want to know if they both visited, yeah, they did," Pitts replied. "But not at the same time."

Jurors and the audience howled in laughter.

Bob Stringer took the witness stand and talked about the White Knights' fliers he typed, produced, and distributed to public places for Bowers. The fifty-two-year-old businessman said he met the KKK leader while working at the Beehive News Stand in the early 1960s. Asked who was running it at the time, he replied that it was Carl Ford, another lawyer sitting by Bowers at his defense table.

Stringer told jurors about overhearing Bowers say "something about the Forrest County boys wasn't doing their job. Something had to be done about the Dahmer nigger down south."

He told jurors about how he became addicted to gambling and went through a twelve-step program in recent years. He said he came forward to make amends as part of the ninth step, in order to clear his conscience. "I knew what I knew could help the Dahmer family, but I also knew that it could possibly harm other people. I had to do a lot of soul searching and studying on this step to weigh it out and decide which was the best way to go with it. And I decided that helping the Dahmer family was the best way to go."

Lee Martin, a dark-haired special assistant attorney general whose calm demeanor contrasted with Helfrich, asked Stringer why he waited so long.

"You have to understand 1966 in Jones County, which was the center of a lot of evil," Stringer replied. "You just didn't stick your neck out. It was a dangerous situation."

Buckley did his best to discredit Stringer, saying he tried to entrap Bowers in the investigation of payoffs on video poker machines. Stringer acknowledged he had indeed talked with Bowers as a part of that undercover probe but denied trying to entrap him.

Before the day ended, the terror of the past came hurtling into the present when the judge halted the trial and called the attorneys into his chambers. "I have just been informed by the sheriff there has been a bomb threat called in to the attorney general's office in Jackson," the judge said. "They are vacating the building."

After returning to the motel from the Bowers trial, I checked my voice mail at work. Someone had left a message: "The news media and Mike Moore have done something that no one else has been able to do in the past thirty years—resurrect the White Knights of the Ku Klux Klan—and the new one will make the old one look like Mickey Mouse."

42

When Deavours Nix took the witness stand for the defense, it seemed like old times: Bowers's trusted lieutenant vouching for the imperial wizard, the Klansmen seeking to cheat justice again.

Since their last trial, time had done what authorities failed to do. Nix sat with his oxygen tank, and Bowers gripped a document inches from his eyes to read it. In some ways, this resembled a trial for a Nazi war criminal, tracked down from some secret lair in South America, but the truth was that Bowers had never had to hide.

Nix smiled at his old friend. He had been the only Klansman willing to stand up for the leader of the nation's most violent KKK organization. He tried to do his part, attacking the credibility of the prosecution's witnesses and calling Bowers "one of the best men I've ever known." Nix said he had accepted the position of statewide investigator for the White Knights because "I didn't want to hurt nobody's feelings."

Under cross-examination, Nix claimed that he didn't know if Bowers belonged to the KKK or not. Then prosecutor Bob Helfrich asked Nix if he remembered testifying in federal court that Bowers was the imperial wizard of the White Knights of the Ku Klux Klan.

"No, sir," Nix replied.

"What color robe did you have, Mr. Nix?"

"I didn't have no robe."

"You didn't have a robe."

"No, sir."

The prosecutor handed Nix two photographs and asked, "What does that person in the two photographs have on?"

"It looks like it might be a robe."

"Got a hood on it?"

"Uh-huh."

"Holding a gun?"

"Yes, sir."

"And that's you in the robe?"

"No, sir, that ain't me."

"That ain't you?"

Nix began to back up. "I don't believe that's me."

Helfrich showed Nix the printing that accompanied the photos. "What does it say?"

"Photograph."

"How many?"

"Two photographs . . ."

"Uh-huh . . ."

". . . of Deavours Nix."

Failing to realize how absurd this all sounded, Nix continued to dodge and deny, distancing himself from the Klan he admitted he belonged to. He insisted the group's real goal was benevolence, delivering "baskets of fruit at Christmastime to people that was needy."

The prosecutor asked Nix how many fruit baskets he had delivered for the Klan.

Nix paused, then answered. "I haven't delivered any."

The jury and audience erupted in laughter.

I have never covered a trial involving a more serious matter than the KKK's killing of Vernon Dahmer. I have also never covered a trial filled with as many laughs.

If there was a court jester at the trial, it was Circuit Judge Dickie McKenzie. While potential jurors waited for attorneys, the judge told lawyer jokes. When a courtroom artist sketched his profile, he flipped the combed-over strands away to reveal his bald head and said, "Bad hair day."

But the jovial judge became testy when pagers and cell phones sounded off during testimony. When one too many phones beeped, he told spectators they could no longer bring in their cell phones, and he threatened to find the next offender in contempt. Later during testimony, one cell phone kept ringing and ringing. Discovering it was his own, he joked, "I'll have to hold myself in contempt."

Before Deavours Nix took the witness stand, I overheard him talking to his lawyer, Lawrence Arrington, the same one who had represented him in the 1960s. Arrington advised him that he would signal him with a raised hand if Nix needed to claim his Fifth Amendment rights against self-incrimination.

Nix began testifying, and several minutes later, I glanced back at Arrington, who was fast asleep. So much for the signaling.

During cross-examination, the defense lawyer pressed Cathy Dunn, then-wife of Klansman Burris Dunn, about how she knew for sure that her husband was in the KKK.

"He told me—and he also had a white robe."

Spectators laughed so loud that Judge McKenzie had to gavel the courtroom quiet.

But beyond the punch lines, what Cathy Dunn had to say about Bowers proved quite damning. She testified that just days after the attack on the Dahmer family, Bowers had visited her home. Bowers usually stayed with the Dunns when he was in the Jackson, Mississippi, area. Dressed neatly in a white suit with a red tie, the Klan leader had strode in that day clutching a folded-up newspaper that contained a headline and story about the killing of Dahmer. When he unfolded the paper for the Dunns, he'd pointed to the headline and smiled. "Did you see what a good job my boys did?"

The testimony seemed to send a chill through the courtroom, the cold reality of a Klan leader beaming over his bloodshed. After Cathy Dunn left the witness stand, she told me that her then-husband, Burris, bragged about jobs the White Knights carried out, including bombings, cross burnings, and other violence. Just as terrorists have cells, she told me, "The Klan had groups that would go and pick up somebody, kill them, and bury their body."

She said her husband, Bowers, and other Klansmen regularly listened to tapes of the sermons of Christian Identity preacher Wesley Swift, whose racist teachings included that Adam and Eve were white, that nonwhites have no souls, and that Jews were the offspring of Satan. Before 1967 ended, the White Knights began bombing Jewish homes and synagogues.

Bowers's murder trial prompted many white supremacists to slither out of the woodwork, supporting him and Nix, calling in threats. But the trial had the opposite effect as well, inspiring a reunion of civil rights pioneers. Hollis Watkins, who had stayed with the Dahmer family while he worked on registering black voters, came to hear the testimony. He recalled Dahmer paying others' poll taxes so they could cast their ballots. "He wanted to help make Mississippi a better place for everybody."

Victoria Gray Adams, who once ran for Congress and joined Dahmer in the push for voting rights in Hattiesburg, came, too. Like Dahmer, she had been turned away from registering to vote at this courthouse. On January 22, 1964, she and other civil rights activists, joined by dozens of clergymen from the North, came to the courthouse to protest Circuit Clerk Theron Lynd's refusal to register black voters. "That day was so cold, and it never stopped raining," she said. "Those that didn't have rain gear bought it and kept on marching." Holding a sign that read "Freedom Now," Fannie Lou Hamer sang, "Which Side Are You On?" By the time darkness fell, civil rights activists had defeated both Lynd and the weather, registering large numbers of voters.

Longtime civil rights leader C. C. Bryant wore an NAACP symbol to the trial to honor his friend. Both his name and Dahmer's had appeared with Medgar Evers's on a KKK "death list" shortly before Evers's 1963 assassination. The next year, night riders firebombed Bryant's barbershop and his church in McComb, Mississippi. "We can move forward," Bryant said now, "if we can learn and if we can come together [and] lay aside every sin."

43

Special Assistant Attorney General Lee Martin stepped up to the jury box, sounding somber as he began his closing statement. He recounted the prosecution's argument and pushed back against the defense lawyer's assertion that this was nothing but an emotional prosecution, where "you wouldn't hear the facts about the case." Martin conceded that the case had been emotional—it couldn't be otherwise—"but we presented facts to you."

He recounted the testimony of former Klansman T. Webber Rogers, who said Imperial Wizard Sam Bowers beat on the table and said that "something had to be done about this damn nigger down south, [that] it should have already been done." And, the prosecutor said, Billy Roy Pitts talked of how a KKK project down south needed to be taken care of—a "nigger who was causing a lot of problems between the blacks and whites with the voter registration drive."

Defense lawyer Travis Buckley ambled to the podium after Martin. He suggested that the real reason for this trial had nothing to do with the evidence and everything to do with the press. "This is a case where Mr. Bowers is being offered up on their altar to be sacrificed to the media for political expediency and to promote political ambition."

He accused Mississippi attorney general Mike Moore of pursuing the murder because he "seeks political advancement. And he decides he has to offer up something to the crowd like throwing a bone to hungry lions."

Buckley called Bowers "a model citizen," remaining a recluse "so that he would not draw attention" for the Dahmer case, Buckley said. He called for sympathy for his seventy-three-year-old client, almost blind and deaf. What he never said was that Bowers was innocent.

Instead, the lawyer shifted the focus toward the Dahmer family, suggesting they had pursued the case because of revenge in their hearts. "That's not justice," Buckley said. "That's persecution."

Then, in one of the trial's more surreal moments, the defense lawyer regaled jurors with the life story of Adolf Hitler. Buckley talked of the Nazi leader mesmerizing listeners and rising "to prominence through his oratorical ability, through his ability to appeal to the masses—mass psychology."

He compared publicity against his client to the propaganda spread by Hitler, who "understood mass hypnotism. He was a genius. But he abused it. He was an evil genius." Authorities were now trying to "use propaganda in such a way as to try to sway the public opinion and to try to sway the jury's opinion because they are not interested in competent, credible, believable evidence," Buckley said. "Return a verdict of not guilty."

I glanced into the audience, noticing several puzzled faces. Bringing up the name of this infamous Nazi leader in the trial of a KKK leader who admired Hitler made me wonder if Bowers had been the one who asked him to say it.

Assistant District Attorney Bob Helfrich made his way to the podium next. The judge let him know he had twenty minutes to speak.

"I'm not gonna use all my time," the prosecutor replied. "It's been a long week. It's been an even longer thirty-two years."

He glanced at the Dahmer family in the balcony and then back at the jury box, where two rows of jurors faced him. "Mr. Buckley wants to talk about Hitler, great orator, evil genius, able to make people do things through propaganda, and if he tells it over and over and over, they do it. And what did they do? They killed thousands and thousands of Jews. Did Hitler do it? No, his henchmen did it. Was Hitler responsible? Yes. And what do we have here? Sam Bowers. Meeting after meeting after meeting, initiations, oaths, secrecy, robes, Bibles with guns and knives and crosses, propaganda over and over and over. And what do they do? Exactly what he wants. Let's talk about Hitler."

He pointed his finger at Bowers, dressed in his white seersucker suit. "Let's talk about an evil genius sitting right there."

Helfrich reminded jurors there was no statute of limitations on murder. "If Hitler did the things he did in this county and if we can prove it, by God we would. And I don't care how long ago that was. What is right, ladies and gentlemen, is right."

The prosecutor recounted Billy Roy Pitts's testimony that he had heard the voice of Dahmer in distress. "His voice is still in distress because Sam Bowers is still walking the streets."

At 10:01 a.m., the dozen jurors in the Sam Bowers murder trial left the courtroom to begin their deliberations. Three and a half hours later, news rumbled through the courtroom that there was a verdict. Bowers didn't bother to wait for the jury to confirm what he already knew—he was guilty. In preparation for prison, he emptied his pockets, took off his watch, and removed his Mickey Mouse pin.

After the judge received the verdict and said it was in proper form, he called Bowers and his lawyer before him.

The clerk stood and read the verdict aloud. "We, the jury, find the defendant, Sam Bowers, guilty of murder."

Bowers hardly blinked as he listened, seemingly unbothered by the thought of spending his last days behind bars.

The judge told him, "I do hereby sentence you to serve a term of life imprisonment in the Mississippi State Penitentiary. And I will remand you to the custody of the sheriff to begin implementation of that sentence. Take him away, Mr. Sheriff."

When he heard the word "guilty," Vernon Dahmer Jr. covered his face with his fingers, tears streaming behind his calloused hands. He finally had time to cry.

Ellie Dahmer wept, too. As she and her family exited the courthouse, the crowd outside applauded them. "Oh, this is a happy moment for us," she said, surrounded by her children. "It is a moment we have been waiting for for about thirty years."

The more tears she wiped away, the more followed. "These are tears of joy. I am shedding them for Vernon because I know he is looking at us today."

Dahmer's son Dennis said, "Thirty-two years ago, Mr. Bowers and his fellow Klansmen started something. Thirty-two years later, we hope to bring closure to this matter with the results of this jury today. Our father gave his life for a system that he believed in, even though that system wasn't fair to him in his lifetime. We hope today's verdict reflects the fact that we're living in a new South and, more particularly, a new Mississippi."

The family thanked the district attorney's office, the attorney general's office, local leaders, supporters, and even the group that Buckley blamed—the press. Afterward, the family hugged authorities and thanked them again.

Back at their home, the family gathered on the front lawn beneath the shade of the towering oaks. Friends drove by. They honked their horns and yelled out in victory.

Before darkness fell, Vernon Jr. drove to a quiet cemetery and stared at a familiar rose-tinted headstone that read, "Vernon Dahmer Sr. Husband, Father, Community Leader, Voting Rights Activist." The retired air force master sergeant fell to his knees, telling his daddy that he could rest in peace now because justice had finally come.

44

Days after Bowers was sentenced to life in prison, Bob Stringer telephoned. He said he had been walking toward his pickup when he heard tires squeal. He looked up and saw a truck racing toward him. He reached inside his pickup and whipped out his nickel-plated .357 Magnum.

The truck screeched to a halt and the driver asked, "Were you going to kill us?"

"You're goddamned right I was."

He said that he believed the truck was a threat because it had a license tag from Bowers's home of Jones County. "I got plumb weak kneed after that deal," he told me. "You know, I'm going to have to keep looking over my shoulder. It's not right now that I'm worried about it. It's next year or the year after that because time is on their side."

I saw Sam Bowers one last time. He was inside the Forrest County jail, locked in cell #1. A deputy told me, "He's so cool. He hasn't said two words since he's been here."

On the black-and-white television monitor, I saw Bowers resting on his jail bunk, thumbing through a magazine. I had permission now to interview Billy Roy Pitts, who was in the same jail.

When Pitts walked up to me, we both gazed at Bowers on the monitor. He wondered aloud if Bowers's inept defense had been a ploy. "Something ain't right."

He said the imperial wizard had walked by earlier. "He looked straight at me and give me this big grin. When he passed by me, he laughed all the way to his cell."

Pitts believed the laughter signified that Bowers was already plotting to get even. "It was like, 'I got your number, buddy.'"

Days after Bowers was transferred to the Central Mississippi Correctional Facility, Pitts got his life back when Governor Kirk Fordice suspended the rest of his sentence. After the former Klansman returned home to Denham Springs, Louisiana, I visited. He talked of the guilt he still suffered, nightmares invading his sleep.

Months later, he returned to Mississippi to testify in a hearing. When he was done, he stepped to the back of the courtroom, where he came face-to-face with Vernon Dahmer's widow, Ellie, and her children, Dennis and Bettie.

Pitts told her, "I've been wanting to do this for a long time. I don't miss a day praying for your family and asking God to forgive me for what I've done. I hope your family can forgive me."

She dabbed her eyes with a tissue, her voice creaking, "I forgive you."

He nodded, thanking her. "The main thing I wanted to do before I died was to get straight with God."

With those words, he could no longer hold back the tears, and neither could the children of Vernon Dahmer.

PART IV

ADDIE MAE COLLINS

DENISE MCNAIR

CAROLE ROBERTSON

CYNTHIA WESLEY

45

Minutes after Imperial Wizard Sam Bowers left the courtroom in hand-cuffs, reporters asked me, "Who's next, Jerry?"

I mumbled something optimistic, but the truth was I had no clue. Watching Byron De La Beckwith get convicted of Medgar Evers's murder was something I never dreamed I would see. And the odds of Sam Bowers going to prison had seemed so impossible that I'd half-joked with my wife that I would retire if it happened.

Back at *The Clarion-Ledger* newsroom, I sat down with my boss, Assistant Managing Editor Debbie Skipper, and Managing Editor Shawn McIntosh. We decided to do a package of stories examining unpunished civil rights killings, especially those that authorities were already investigating across the country.

One was the Sixteenth Street Baptist Church bombing in Birmingham, Alabama, which I began reading about in the books I had. On September 15, 1963, an explosion had ripped through the church. Four young girls were killed in an instant. It was a grievous, despicable crime, even for the KKK in Alabama in the 1960s. Yet for years, no one had been charged.

When the bombing had occurred, Bill Baxley had been a student at the University of Alabama. He vowed that if he could ever do something about it, he would. In 1971, Baxley took office as attorney general and wrote the names of the four girls on the card the state of Alabama had given him to make long-distance telephone calls. He said their names reminded him daily that their killings by the Ku Klux Klan had gone unpunished. "It baffled me then, and it baffles me now how people can say how when you try to bring justice to the people who killed four little girls that you should let sleeping dogs lie."

Baxley worked doggedly on the case, and in 1977, he won the lone conviction of Bob Chambliss, the man who had made the bomb. When I interviewed Baxley for my article, he told me he had lacked the evidence to pursue the prosecution of several other suspects in the bombing.

Weeks later, I headed for Birmingham. Smoke drifted sideways from a steel mill as I pulled into the city of more than 200,000. This was the place where the Dixiecrats, who had bolted from the Democratic Party, nominated South Carolina senator Strom Thurmond for president in 1948. This was the place known as "Bombingham," where the Ku Klux Klan blew up more than fifty African-Americans' homes, churches, businesses, and other targets between World War II and the 1960s. Explosions hit one black neighborhood so often it was called "Dynamite Hill."

I learned that the brutal wave of bombings peaked in 1963 in response to Martin Luther King Jr.'s agreement that year to help with a major campaign combatting segregation in Birmingham. The local civil rights effort hinged in large part on Reverend Fred Shuttlesworth, who had helped King start the Southern Christian Leadership Conference and had already been a repeated victim of the violence by the time King arrived. In 1956, Shuttlesworth and his family survived the Christmas night bombing of the parsonage where they were sleeping, next to the Bethel Baptist Church he pastored.

Shuttlesworth told me that minutes after that attack, a Birmingham police officer said to him, "Reverend, I tell you what I'd do if I were you. I'd get out of town just as quick as I could." Shuttlesworth replied, "Officer, you're not me, and you go back and tell your Klan brethren that if God could deliver me through all of this, I'm here for the duration, and the war is just beginning." Months later, Shuttlesworth survived a mob's attack when he tried to enroll his two daughters in an all-white Birmingham school.

Through it all, Shuttlesworth kept fighting. He continued to challenge segregation over the years that followed, culminating in King's arrival in spring 1963. It was on Good Friday of 1963 that police threw the pastors behind bars, leading King to write his famous "Letter from a Birmingham Jail" in response to eight white clergy who called him an extremist. "Was not Jesus an extremist in love?—'Love your enemies, bless them that curse you, pray for them that despitefully use you.' . . . Was not Thomas Jefferson an extremist?—'We hold these truths to be self-evident, that all men are created equal.' So the question is not whether we will be extremist, but what kind of extremists we will be. Will we be extremists for hate, or will we be extremists for love?"

Birmingham police packed the jails with protesters, but civil rights leaders continued, turning out more than one thousand young people to push the campaign forward, marching from the Sixteenth Street Baptist Church into downtown Birmingham. Led by Public Safety Commissioner "Bull" Connor, police sprayed fire hoses, smashing students against walls and sidewalks. Police clubbed the young people and trotted out German shepherds to attack. Television broadcast the images, prompting international outrage, and Birmingham leaders negotiated an agreement with civil rights leaders to formally end segregation.

Over the next several months, the University of Alabama opened its doors to two African-American students, and public schools followed suit, letting in a handful of minority students. Despite these small steps, the bombings continued.

The worst came on the morning of September 15, 1963. Addie Mae Collins, Carole Robertson, and Cynthia Wesley, all fourteen, and eleven-year-old Denise McNair, along with Collins's younger sister, Sarah, gathered in the girls' bathroom in the basement of the Sixteenth Street Baptist Church, getting ready for the youth service after a Sunday school lesson titled, "A Love That Forgives." When the clock struck 10:22 a.m., a bomb hidden beneath the church's outside stairs exploded, killing four of the girls and injuring dozens of others.

Shock waves from the explosion could be felt not only across town, but across the nation, horrified by the hate. The bombing became a rallying cry for civil rights activists, and FBI agents swarmed to the city to solve the crime.

When I visited the rebuilt Sixteenth Street Baptist Church, I spoke with Reverend John Cross, the church's pastor at the time of the bombing. He recalled the scarring scene. After hearing the explosion, he smelled gunpowder and gasoline. Dashing downstairs, he crawled into the crater the bomb had created. He dug down into the debris, and one by one, he found the bodies of the missing girls. When he heard a groan, he found Sarah Collins alive.

Outside the church, a crowd had swelled, growing angrier. Cross grabbed a megaphone and spoke. "Yea, though I walk through the valley of the shadow of death, I will fear no evil: for Thou art with me." But he could not stop the day's death and destruction.

Rage over the church bombing resounded, meeting a white mob eager for more violence. Before that Birmingham Sunday ended, five black businesses burned, and two more black youths were killed. A police officer blasted sixteen-year-old Johnny Robinson in the back with a shotgun after someone threw rocks at a car from which white teens were hurling racial slurs. A white teenager shot thirteen-year-old Virgil Ware in the face and chest, believing he had thrown rocks. The teen who killed Ware received probation, and the officer went unpunished after he claimed his gun had gone off accidentally.

In the wake of the tragedy, change slowly came to Birmingham, and the church was rebuilt. Sixteen years later, Richard Arrington Jr. became the city's first African-American mayor. Kelly Ingram Park, where police had sprayed fire hoses on the young people in 1963, became a tourist attraction. When I arrived in 1997, the city had just embraced the Birmingham Pledge, aimed at improving relations and eliminating racism.

But, as with many things involving race in America, for every two steps the city made forward, there seemed to be three steps back. White flight, a declining tax base, and poverty continued to plague the city. And the crimes of the civil rights era, in many cases—like the Sixteenth Street Church bombing—had never been addressed head-on.

Reverend Cross told me that September 15, 1963, continues to haunt him. "It gets on my nerves, so I can't go to sleep. I have some restless nights."

Inside a downtown federal building, I met US attorney Doug Jones. Dressed in a dark suit, this son of a steelworker seemed to have a boundless enthusiasm. He kept tugging at his collar, as if permanently uncomfortable in a tie. Like me, Jones had grown up in a white suburb in the segregated South. Like me, he had grown up unaware of some of the key events in the civil rights movement, even as they played out in the society surrounding him. He was nine and busy pretending to be Joe Namath, the quarterback for the Crimson Tide, when the bomb exploded that would change the lives of so many.

In the immediate aftermath, FBI agents investigated the bombing and came to the conclusion the attack had been carried out by the Klansmen of Eastview Klavern 13, who called themselves the Cahaba River Group. Witnesses had placed the KKK's longtime bombmaker, "Dynamite Bob" Chambliss, outside the church. Other Klansmen identified as there that night included Tommy Blanton Jr., who was supposedly driving the car, and Bobby Frank Cherry, a Klansman who had received demolitions training. The FBI also learned about a fourth suspect, Herman Frank Cash, who helped his brother run a whites-only barbecue joint that became a KKK hangout.

The FBI wiretapped suspects, developed informants within the Klan, and found witnesses in the case, leading agents to write a May 13, 1965, memo outlining the evidence that they had collected. Six days later, FBI director J. Edgar Hoover deep-sixed the investigation, calling the chance of any conviction "remote." In addition, he refused to let agents share their evidence with local authorities.

Seven years later, Alabama attorney general Bill Baxley resurrected the case, but the FBI remained reluctant to cooperate. With the help of the four girls' families, Baxley pressured the FBI to share enough information to help get a jury in 1977 to convict Chambliss, who spent the rest of his days in prison before dying in 1985. Eight years later, Cash died, and the other men went unpunished.

Jones told me he cut law school classes to watch Chambliss's murder trial, drawn to the history unfolding at the Jefferson County Courthouse. Chambliss's niece testified that her uncle, while watching reports of the bombing, declared aloud, "It wasn't meant to hurt anybody. It didn't go off when it was supposed to." When closing arguments took place, Jones leaned over the balcony rail for a better view as Baxley placed a picture of each one of the girls in front of jurors. "It was," he told me, "the high drama that movies are made of."

Twenty years later, President Bill Clinton nominated Jones to serve as US attorney for the Northern District of Alabama. Just before the Senate confirmed him, he read in the newspaper that the FBI was now reinvestigating the church bombing case. "I just about dropped my coffee. I thought, 'That will be my case.'"

Despite the passage of time, he said Birmingham had yet to shake its past. He believed the time was right to change that because this new generation could see "the unfairness in the criminal justice system that was supposed to protect people, but failed."

46

I decided to dive deeper into the case, reaching out to the two still living suspects in hopes of getting them to talk. Tommy Blanton lived in a ten-by-five-foot trailer in the area. He wouldn't speak, but he wrote that he "had nothing whatsoever to do with the crime, but the fact that government and media have told the same lies over and over again, it tends to cause people to believe those lies."

The last suspect, Bobby Cherry, lived in the Texas town of Mabank, less than an hour southeast of Dallas. When I reached him by telephone, he denied any role in the church bombing. He did, however, admit to joining the KKK.

He talked about being friends with the other three suspects and insisted they were innocent. Suspect Bob Chambliss "was covering up for people." As for suspect Herman Cash, "all he done wrong was drank whiskey."

Although Cherry said he was no longer with the KKK when the killings took place, he insisted the group had nothing to do with the bombing of the Sixteenth Street Church. "You couldn't have gotten within twenty miles of it. Hell, there were cars all around the place."

When I mentioned the ongoing FBI investigation, he called it "a bunch of baloney. I wasn't even involved, didn't know anything about the mess until I heard it on TV."

He was even more critical of Spike Lee's documentary, which included interviews with the victims' families. "A bunch of those people were lying. You could tell by looking at them."

He campaigned for George Wallace and was appointed an honorary lieutenant, later serving as Wallace's bodyguard. He blamed the killings on Birmingham policemen, the FBI, and members of Wallace's staff. "Hell, all of his officials belonged to the Klan."

"How do you know that?"

"I figured it out in archives. I'm smarter than they are."

On June 16, 1999, the telephone rang. It was Rick Journey, a talented TV reporter I had met before in Birmingham. He had been reporting on the case and had promised to keep me informed. He told me that the granddaughter of Bobby Cherry had just testified before the federal grand jury investigating the Birmingham church bombing. Journey shared her telephone number.

Hours later, I caught up with Teresa Stacy, a twenty-three-year-old mother from Fort Worth, Texas. She told me her grandfather had said outright that he "helped bomb a church back in the sixties and killed a bunch of black folks." She had also heard other relatives boasting about his role in dynamiting the Sixteenth Street Baptist Church, saying "stuff like how Grandpa helped to blow up a bunch of niggers in Birmingham."

Back in 1997, Cherry had held a press conference in Texas, insisting he was innocent of the bombing. "Them feds won't leave me alone," he declared. "They've been harassing me for 30 years. I'm innocent. I ain't done nothin'."

Stacy said that the sight of her grandfather saying those words had angered her. "When you're young, you don't know it's wrong. You look back on it now, and it's pretty sick."

After hearing her claims, I telephoned Bobby Cherry again. He denied everything: "I never said nothing like that in my life. I didn't talk about that during that time. I didn't talk about it after."

He also assured me he had a solid alibi. "There ain't nobody alive or dead who can say I had anything to do with it."

More than a week later, an email arrived from Cherry's wife, Myrtle, saying her husband wanted to speak with me in person. The offer surprised me, given my work on the previous cases, but I was more than happy to tell her yes. The next thing I knew, I was talking on the telephone with Cherry, working out the details for an in-person interview.

When I had interviewed Byron De La Beckwith, I felt confident because I knew the details surrounding the case. But I felt horribly inadequate as I prepared to interview Cherry because I knew so little about the case. I decided to call US Attorney Doug Jones, hoping to learn more information from him.

"Cherry's going to talk to you?" Jones asked.

"Yes. He said he really wanted to."

I explained to Jones that I knew little about Cherry's alleged role in the church bombing and would like to know more. Jones promised to get back to me with more information.

More than an hour later, he and the two leading FBI agents on the case, Bill Fleming and Ben Herren, spoke to me on the telephone. Over the past several years, the pair had pored through more than nine thousand pages of FBI records in "BAPBOMB" and tracked down potential witnesses across the United States. They mentioned Cherry's July 9, 1997, interview with diminutive detective Bob Eddy, who had a knack for getting Klansmen to talk. In that conversation with Eddy and Herren, Cherry described the KKK as a "Christian organization."

One FBI report put Cherry in the alley that night outside the Sixteenth Street Baptist Church. The report suggested he was the one who planted the bomb that blew up the morning of September 15, 1963.

"You should ask Cherry where he was when the bomb exploded the next morning," Fleming said.

"What's his story?" I asked.

Fleming said Cherry told investigators he went that morning to Modern Sign Company, a Klan hangout several blocks from the church, and that the bomb exploded before he got there. "He said he'd never been to the church, but he told a neighbor he'd seen the hole."

As for the four girls killed, he said Cherry referred to them as "those niggers." Fleming also encouraged me to ask Cherry about the civil rights leader, Fred Shuttlesworth. "He bragged about whipping Shuttlesworth."

Fleming asked me if Teresa Stacy had explained her relationship with her grandfather.

"No."

"Her granddaddy molested her, and he also did it to other cousins, some of whom are still in Alabama."

"That's awful."

Jones said, "That's what we're dealing with here."

These allegations meant that if Cherry somehow dodged an arrest in the bombing, the former Klansman might still wind up behind bars. Molestation was a charge that few people would wink at, no matter how much time had passed.

Bobby Cherry and his wife ate from plates brimming with barbecue in Gun Barrel City, Texas. Rib bones stacked up, and Cherry licked remnants of sauce from his fingers. "Before I die, I want my name cleared. I didn't have nothing to do with that bombing."

Back at his home, the tall man with the bulbous nose and the wavy gray hair said he joined the Klan in 1957 because "I didn't like the communistic way things were going." Soon after, his chapter of the KKK joined with several other chapters to form the United Klans of America, Alabama's equivalent of the White Knights, led by Imperial Wizard Robert Shelton. "We figured if we all got together, we'd have a stronger voters' league." Cherry worked as a security guard for the KKK, guarding both Shelton and Alabama governor George Wallace, who "called all the shots." He said he quit the group a year before the bombing, but acknowledged he continued to keep company with these Klansmen. Then he began to rail against the FBI, saying they started harassing him after the 1963 church bombing.

"Tell me about it," I replied.

"The day before that, I was up there at Snow's Modern Sign Company," just a few blocks from the Sixteenth Street Baptist Church. While inside the company, he said he ran a silk machine to make Confederate battle flags and signs for white protesters outside an all-white Birmingham school "to keep their kids from going to integrated schools."

That night, about six men walked inside Modern Sign Company, including Bob Chambliss, Thomas Blanton, and several others, Cherry told me. "They had some new Klansmen there, but I didn't know who they were."

Later, the men "hollered at me and told me they were going to eat. They asked me to go with 'em."

Cherry declined. "I was getting tired."

He told me he didn't believe Chambliss, Blanton, and others had anything to do with the bombing. "If I thought anybody would blow up a church, I'd have gotten a club and gone after them."

He said he left the sign shop that night at a quarter till ten, because he was heading home to watch live *Studio Wrestling* on local TV. This was part of his Saturday routine, he said. He also mentioned another reason for heading home that night—doctors had recently diagnosed his wife with cancer—in 1961, or maybe 1962—giving her six months to live. "They sent her home to die four or five times, but she straightened back up. She lived till March 1968."

Cherry said that on the night before the bombing, a friend of the family, Flora Thomas, came over to help take care of his wife. He handed me her March 15, 1980, sworn statement in which she said Cherry "was at home at 10 o'clock Saturday night because he never missed wrestling on TV. I stayed up most of the night due to sickness in the family. Bobby never left the house."

When I asked Cherry about an FBI report that said he was seen hours before the bombing, planting a bomb outside the church, he shot back that it was a lie. "Shit, I was home before wrestling. I always made sure I was home for wrestling."

The next morning, he said he woke up about nine and returned to the

Modern Sign Company. "I went up there to get them signs. That's when I found out about the bombing. I left [at] about fifteen to ten to go up there."

Cherry said the bomb exploded before he ever got to the sign shop. He saw a "fire wagon go down there," and when he arrived he could hear "the sirens all settling down." When the owner of the sign shop, Merle Snow, returned, Snow told them people outside the church were saying "some of these white folks done blowed the church up down yonder and the Ku Klux done it."

In the days following the bombing, agents began to tail him. "We'd go to church, and the FBI would be there. When we got back, everywhere we went, the FBI was standing there waiting, wanting to talk. It got as aggravating as hell."

He eventually agreed to a lie detector test. "I said, 'Hell, yes. I haven't done anything.' I thought they were honest, but they weren't."

Cherry said he passed two lie detector tests for the FBI but failed a third because the technician bumped the needle. He shared a copy of the test, in which he was asked, "Have you ever been present when a bombing was planned?" The polygraph examiner concluded Cherry showed "evidence of deception." The examiner reported that Cherry showed a "strong reaction" to the question: "On Friday night, was Tommy Blanton with you making a bomb?" Cherry also reacted to the question, "Did you bomb the Sixteenth Street Baptist Church?"

During the six hours we talked, Cherry spent most of his time trashing relatives. One was serving a twenty-eight-year prison sentence for car theft. Another died in a 1992 shoot-out with police. Cherry lambasted his son, Tom, saying he shouldn't be trusted because all he wanted was money for a book about his father and leniency for his son, Tom Jr., who was doing hard time in a Texas prison for robbery.

Cherry insisted he never committed any violence against anyone black, but he peppered his denial with contradictions and racial epithets. "I knocked one of 'em in the head one night, but the nigger called me a son of a bitch," he said. "I knocked him in the head, got in the car, drove off, and left him. That's the only thing I've ever done." He snickered. "He's still living. He's walking around."

• • •

After the interview, I chatted with the son he castigated, Tom, a dark-haired truck driver whose cackle, like his father's, lasted too long for comfort. When I asked about his father's alibi, he said, "I can remember we used to watch wrestling, but I can't remember that night." He didn't recall his mother being diagnosed with cancer until years after that.

He said he and his father were inside the sign shop when the church exploded, and they could feel the shock waves. "We didn't know what it was at the time. We'd been there for a while fixing signs."

He said his father was wrong in saying the bomb exploded before they arrived. "That's an event you remember like JFK."

On the way back from Texas, an idea crossed my mind. I remembered growing up that my hometown newspaper printed the entire schedule for the three TV channels we could watch. Perhaps *The Birmingham News* did the same thing.

When I arrived in *The Clarion-Ledger* newsroom the next morning, I visited our librarian, Susan Garcia, and brought up the idea to her. Would she mind checking to see if the *News* ran a TV schedule on September 14, 1963, and if so, get a copy of it and see what was on television? I wanted to find out exactly when the wrestling had aired. She said she would be happy to check.

The following day, she emailed me, "There was NO wrestling."

I could hardly believe it.

I telephoned WBRC, and I was soon speaking to a forty-year veteran of the Birmingham television station, Mary Davis. I asked her about WBRC airing live studio wrestling.

She said the station never aired such wrestling but that the two other stations had. In the late 1950s, WAPI aired *Studio Wrestling* at 10:30 p.m. each Saturday but replaced it in fall 1962 with the popular *Route 66*. The other station, WBMG-Channel 42, aired *Studio Wrestling* at 10 p.m. each Saturday but didn't go on the air until 1965—two years after the bombing.

In other words, there was no wrestling for Cherry to watch. It was, as

best I could tell, an alibi he concocted when the FBI briefly reexamined
the case in 1980. I telephoned Cherry again and finished writing my story:

> MABANK, Texas—For 35 years, Bobby Frank Cherry
> has been an FBI suspect in the 1963 Birmingham church
> bombing that killed four girls.
>
> For 35 years, he has gone uncharged, and his alibi has
> gone unchallenged. The 69-year-old retired truck driver
> maintains he was home the night the bomb was planted
> because he was watching wrestling on TV—and shares a
> sworn affidavit to prove it.
>
> There's at least one problem with that alibi. There was
> no televised wrestling for Cherry to watch.
>
> Instead, the programs that took place at 10 that night
> were *Route 66* on WAPI-Channel 13 and *Films of the Fifties*
> on WBRC-Channel 6, according to schedules in the Sept.
> 14, 1963, Birmingham News.
>
> Asked about television schedules that poke holes in
> his alibi, Cherry responded, "There was no damn *Films of
> the Fifties* on. Son of a bitch, something's wrong. Wrestling
> was on."

47

My story exposing Cherry's lack of an alibi prompted FBI agents to subpoena television logs from Birmingham stations for that night. This case was now in high gear.

Two weeks later, television reporter Rick Journey called to let me know that Cherry's relatives were testifying in front of the federal grand jury investigating the Birmingham church bombing. I made it there by lunchtime.

Upon arriving, I found Cherry's forty-seven-year-old son, Tom, sitting in a courtyard. I walked outside and watched him puff on his cigarette, sliding the smoke out his nostrils. He told me the grand jury questioned him about his father's whereabouts the morning the church exploded.

When his family gathered a few years back, he said his father told them authorities were "going to try and tear this family apart." He shook his head. "That's exactly what has happened."

I also spoke with Cherry's second wife, Willadean Brogdon, who looked much older than her age of fifty-nine. After reading an Associated Press version of my 1998 story about a federal grand jury investigating the church bombing, she had driven more than two hundred miles to an FBI office in Montana. I asked her why she hadn't come forward sooner.

"He threatened me if I ever said anything."

A feisty former truck driver who once hauled explosives, she had met Cherry in 1969. The couple dreamed of their children becoming one big family. But the dream wound up being a nightmare when Cherry beat and brutalized her. "He would never let me go anywhere. He would say, 'I saw you talking to this person and that person.'" He would falsely accuse her of having an affair. "With eleven kids there to take care of, I didn't have time to do things."

She believed Cherry had mental issues. At one point, he had threatened to blow up Birmingham City Hall, and she signed papers to have him committed to a state mental institution, Bryce Hospital. He was committed, but he went free after a few weeks.

But she also had heard him speak about the church bombing. She said that Cherry's vehicle had once broken down near the Sixteenth Street Baptist Church. "I had to help him get his car. And he told me, 'That's the church we bombed.'" She said Cherry explained that he didn't "put the bomb together. He said, 'I lit it.'"

As Cherry grew more violent and abusive, Brogdon fled the Klansman, only to have him track her down. "My sister tried to run him off. We got in the truck and left." Several months later, she said her home burned to the ground, killing her nine-year-old daughter, Rebecca.

She told me her fears have never gone away. "The day he's arrested, that's the day I'm ready to move."

With the emergence of new witnesses such as Teresa Stacy and Willadean Brogdon, combined with tape recordings and other evidence the FBI had saved from its original investigation, the Justice Department believed it had enough to bring a case against Bobby Cherry and Tommy Blanton.

On May 16, 2000, an Alabama grand jury indicted each of the two former Klansmen on four counts of murder for the 1963 killings of Addie Mae Collins, Denise McNair, Carole Robertson, and Cynthia Wesley.

Cherry insisted on his innocence, saying, "Hell, I ain't never wanted to bomb nothing."

He told me once again that he was watching wrestling on TV the night the bomb was planted at the Sixteenth Street Baptist Church. "This whole thing was a lie that they didn't have wrestling. I called *The Birmingham News* and found where it was on that Saturday night."

The fact that he continued to claim that there was wrestling on television baffled me. And the fact he was claiming the newspaper backed his claim made even less sense. *The Birmingham News* hadn't published anything that would back Cherry's claim.

He also lamented the state of law enforcement in Alabama. Cherry shared that his son, Tom, had nearly killed a man at a wrestling match decades ago, but he convinced the district attorney to reduce his son's charges to misdemeanors. "I was pretty popular back then."

Popular? Because they believed you blew up a church and killed four girls?

A judge released Cherry and Blanton on bond, awaiting their trial. Defense lawyers challenged the charges, and Cherry's attorneys suggested their client was mentally incompetent to stand trial.

The world had reacted with outrage to the bombing, and now the world began to weigh in on the arrests. Spike Lee, who directed the moving documentary on the girls' killings, sounded bittersweet—happy for the families, but upset the arrests had taken so long. "Bob Chambliss, his nickname was 'Dynamite Bob.' It's not like he's got the athletic prowess, you know, on the gridiron or the baseball diamond. This guy was responsible for numerous bombings."

Still, Lee praised the changing climate that made it possible to imagine Cherry and Blanton behind bars. "Back in those days, you weren't going to get an all-white jury to convict. Everybody was in cahoots. Morality at the time was that black people—niggers—were regarded as subhuman. It was the same thing as killing a dog."

He said Americans should seek prosecution of those responsible for these heinous crimes. "It's the same as Jewish people hunting down Nazi criminals. They don't care if someone is ninety-five years old. They don't care if Nazi criminals are on their last breath. We have to be just as vigilant. We have to do the same."

48

After the arrests, a thick book arrived in my mailbox—*A Fire You Can't Put Out: The Civil Rights Life of Birmingham's Reverend Fred Shuttlesworth*. I flipped through the pages, noticing black-and-white photographs. I saw an Associated Press photograph of his 1957 beating, which had occurred after he tried to enroll his daughters at the all-white high school. This was the assault that the FBI agents had told me that Bobby Cherry had taken part in. Cherry had denied it when we spoke, but even if he hadn't, the statute of limitations had long passed on the crime. But there was no question that evidence of his role in the attack could aid the current case. It was, after all, proof that he had a motive to blow up the church—his hatred of African-Americans.

In the photograph of Shuttlesworth's beating, I counted more than a dozen men, but the picture was so distant, there was no way to make out any faces. I contacted the author, Andrew Manis, and asked if there were any other pictures of this beating.

"Pictures? There's footage of it."

He pointed me to the 1961 CBS documentary *Who Speaks for Birmingham?* But as I watched it, I realized I had a problem. I had no idea what Bobby Cherry looked like back in 1957.

I telephoned Cherry's son, Tom, who drove big rigs. He said he would be coming in the next week to Jackson. I asked if he would be willing to drop by and look at the footage. He said sure.

In the meantime, I telephoned Reverend Shuttlesworth himself, to hear his story of the beating. Now working as a pastor at the Greater New Light Baptist Church in Cincinnati, Shuttlesworth was candid about the terrifying experience.

On September 9, 1957, he arrived at the all-white Phillips High School with his wife, two daughters, two other students, and Reverend J. S. Phifer, who drove the car. There was a white mob outside the school, and as soon as Shuttlesworth and his wife stepped out of their 1957 Plymouth, the mob converged on them. One attacker shouted: "Let's get this son of a bitch and get it over with. We missed him last time."

As the blows rained down on him, Shuttlesworth tried to flee. He told me, "I realized if I didn't get away, I would die right there."

He and his family made it back inside the car, and Phifer sped away, with Shuttlesworth's leg still hanging out. But Shuttlesworth had taken multiple blows to the head and face. His wife, Ruby, received a stab wound to her upper buttocks. His daughter, Ricky, suffered an injury to her right ankle when the door was shut on her leg.

When the physician saw Shuttlesworth's facial injuries, he was surprised the civil rights leader hadn't suffered worse injuries. The pastor told the doctor, "The Lord knew I lived in a hard town, so he gave me a hard skull."

One week later, Tom Cherry came to *The Clarion-Ledger* newsroom, where I showed him the footage of Shuttlesworth's beating. A white mob grew, pressing the civil rights leader and his wife up against the car. Tom pointed at a tall, thin, sandy-haired man in a white shirt with a cigarette dangling from his mouth. "That's him."

Mob members took turns punching the civil rights leader. As the crowd surged again toward Shuttlesworth, the man with the cigarette stuck his hand in his pants pocket.

"He's reaching for them brass knucks," Tom said. "He used to carry a pair of brass knucks and a gun all the time."

The civil rights leader tried to escape the onslaught—only to get his jacket twisted over his head. The man with the cigarette uncorked an uppercut, and Shuttlesworth reeled.

"Knocked him down, didn't he?" Tom chuckled, sharing the same raspy laugh as his father.

He said that his father had bragged about beating Shuttlesworth. No one was ever prosecuted in the case, despite police charging Jack Cash, I. F. Gauldin, and J. E. Breckenridge with intent to murder.

Shuttlesworth emerged from the hospital with his right arm in a sling. In the documentary, he showed scars from the blows and said, "What you don't understand is why men, otherwise calm and peaceable men, whether they be white or otherwise, could act like raving beasts and want blood. Their hopes were to kill me."

49

Piecing together the Birmingham church bombing case involved years of work, mainly by two FBI agents, Bill Fleming and Ben Herren. In addition to combing through all the FBI records on the case, they had found long-secret tape recordings the FBI had collected on suspects. The pair had also tracked down witnesses across the United States, including new witnesses who came forward after seeing news stories.

Despite all that hard work, US Attorney Doug Jones telephoned me with the news that suspect Bobby Cherry wouldn't go on trial. The trial judge had found the former Klansman mentally incompetent. This surprised me. I hadn't sensed anything like that in my conversations with Cherry.

In the meantime, the case against suspect Tommy Blanton went forward. On April 16, 2001, his murder trial began, just blocks from the Sixteenth Street Baptist Church, in the same courtroom where Jones had seen suspect Bob Chambliss convicted in the bombing.

Blanton had a night-school law degree, but he didn't represent himself. That task fell to Jones's former law partner, John Robbins, who didn't wait for prosecutors to insult his client. He did it for them, calling Blanton a loud-mouthed former Klansman. "He was as annoying as hell, but it doesn't mean he planted the bomb," Robbins said to the jury. "Just because you don't like him and the views he espoused doesn't make him responsible for this tragedy. He's not the same man he was."

Robbins expressed his sympathy to the girls' families filling the front row of the courtroom. "We can't imagine the pain these folks have gone through."

That pain echoed in the photographs that Jones showed jurors. The church basement had been turned into rubble, where rescuers found the four girls' bodies. A car hood folded like an accordion, and a Chevy had a door blown off. Across the street, the blast took out windows, and a clock on the wall read 10:24. "When the bomb went off, the clock stopped," Jones told jurors. "Time for Birmingham stood still."

Blanton looked the part of a once-tough bully, and testimony from his then-girlfriend, Waylene Vaughn, reinforced that view. She recalled that he had attended KKK meetings and terrorized African-Americans, pouring acid onto their car seats while they were inside a grocery store. Vaughn also testified that Blanton had swerved his car toward black pedestrians as they walked down the streets. "All I want is a chance to kill one of those black bastards," she quoted him as saying.

Her relationship with Blanton played a role in one of the most important pieces of evidence in the case, the so-called Kitchen Sink Tape. Its survival seemed a miracle. FBI agent Bill Fleming had rescued the tape from being thrown out, and a blind stenographer had deciphered the hard-to-hear words before technology enhanced the audio.

The FBI recorded the tape on June 28, 1964, the night after agents had questioned Blanton's wife, Jean. Blanton might have been dating Waylene Vaughn at the time, but he was two-timing his soon-to-be wife to do so. And agents used the relationship to pry information loose. Agents suggested to Jean that Blanton had lied about his whereabouts on the Friday night before the bombing. Blanton had broken off their date that night, and the agents made Jean wonder if he had done so to cheat on her with Vaughn.

By this time, an undercover FBI agent had already rented an apartment from the Blantons and installed a microphone in the wall that the apartment shared with the home.

When Blanton returned home that night, the FBI recorded the conversation that took place. Jean confronted him in the kitchen, and Blanton pushed back, asking what she told the agents. After she recounted their questions, he reassured her that agents were only asking about that Friday night because they were interested in the meeting he attended, "the Big One . . . where we planned the bomb."

"Tommy, what meeting are you talking about now?"

"We had that meeting to make the bomb."

Blanton switched the subject to his wardrobe, wondering aloud what shirt to wear.

Jean, however, remained suspicious. "It's what you were doing that Friday night when you stood me up."

"Oh, we were making the bomb," Blanton said, trying to reassure her.

She continued to press forward. "I didn't know whether to think you stood me up to go out with somebody else. That's the first thing that hit me. You stood me up to go out with Waylene."

Blanton said that it was impossible that he was two-timing her that night. But what amounted to an alibi in a conversation with his wife proved—for the purposes of the murder trial—an outright confession. He had just admitted to helping make the bomb that killed four girls.

Before prosecutors rested their case, Klansman-turned-FBI-informant Mitch Burns took the witness stand. Wearing a white shirt and bolo tie, Burns talked of four decades ago when he worked as a meatpacker and truck driver by day and attended KKK meetings at night.

By 1964, he had decided to leave the group when an FBI agent showed him pictures of the four girls killed in the church bombing. He agreed to go back into the Klan, and the FBI paid him two hundred dollars a month for expenses to spend time with suspects in the church bombing. Agents rigged the spare tire in his 1956 Chevy with a reel-to-reel recorder and hid a microphone, which taped conversations of him and Klansmen inside the car.

He spent much of his time with Blanton, and the FBI recorded more than thirty hours of conversations. "We hit just about every honky-tonk between here and Blount County. When we got tired of that, we hit every one between here and Bessemer."

Prosecutors played excerpts of the recordings in which Blanton said, "They ain't gonna catch me when I bomb my next church." Another time, he reeled off his favorite things to do—fishing, hunting, sex, and bombing. On their trips, Burns said Blanton often drove by the Sixteenth Street Church, and Blanton also threatened to bomb the FBI building in Birmingham.

Under cross-examination, the defense confronted Burns about this threatened bombing, seeking to prove it was nothing more than idle talk. "Did you blow up the FBI building?"

"I didn't hear nothing pop," Burns replied. "Mr. Blanton and me never bombed nothing."

The defense asked whether all this talk between him and Blanton was really a lot of joking.

"I was acting," Burns said. "I don't know what he was doing."

The former Klansman denied being a racist, but admitted he helped burn crosses outside the homes of two black families. "I didn't get no joy out of it."

When the defense questioned the large amount of money Burns received from the FBI, he responded that it barely covered expenses. "How far do you think fifty dollars a week will go when you go honky-tonking?"

After the testimony ended, the defense lawyer told reporters that Blanton's words proved nothing. "All the tapes show are two drunks driving around Birmingham, running their mouths off."

Jones believed the recordings did prove something. "The tapes show the obsession the defendant had with 'the bomb,' dynamite and his total contempt for the church."

The jury deliberated for two hours before convicting Blanton. "They say that justice delayed is justice denied," Jones said. "I don't believe it. Justice delayed is still justice, and we've got it here in Birmingham, Alabama."

But there was still one suspect on the loose.

50

Justice, it seemed, would never come for Bobby Cherry. In spring 2001, defense experts visited Cherry, whom the judge had committed to stay at the Taylor Hardin Secure Medical Facility. During their examination, they said Cherry couldn't recall two of his five marriages. They said it was obvious he suffered from dementia, scoring below 75 in IQ. Prosecution experts countered that Cherry suffered only mild cognitive problems and was competent to stand trial. As proof, the experts pointed to his extensive collection of videotapes of TV newscasts about the bombing.

While these experts clashed, Doug Jones called me with the update, and I registered my surprise.

"Cherry seemed plenty sane when I talked to him," I said. "Well, no more crazy than any other Klansmen I've interviewed."

"I know," he replied. "It's disappointing. We're still working on it."

He shared news that he was contemplating a run for the US Senate. He had started his career as staff counsel to the Senate Judiciary Committee for then–US senator Howell Heflin, the last Democratic senator to serve Alabama before it turned Republican red.

Jones said if he ran for the Senate, he could no longer be a part of any prosecution team. When I asked him why, he said if there was a trial, it would be viewed as benefiting him politically.

"Yeah, they should talk to Bobby DeLaughter about all those political benefits he reaped," I said. "Voters kicked him in the butt after he won Byron De La Beckwith's conviction."

"What was he running for?"

"Mississippi Court of Appeals."

"How bad did he lose?"

"Wasn't close. I even heard Imperial Wizard Sam Bowers campaigned against him."

"Figures."

"That's what you're going up against, Doug."

"Somebody needs to stand up, Jerry."

Three weeks before Christmas in 2001, a hearing took place. Defense lawyers told the judge to stick to his decision that Cherry was incompetent, saying it was obvious he suffered from dementia and lacked the memory to assist his lawyers.

Prosecutors suggested Cherry was "crazy" all right—crazy like a fox. When experts questioned the former Klansman at the Taylor Hardin facility, he appeared dull. There wasn't much he could recall.

But new video recordings that prosecutors obtained from the facility revealed a different side of Cherry that came out only after the experts had left. Described before as lethargic, he could now be seen speed walking. Now when he spoke to other patients, he appeared logical and affable. As long as he wasn't being tested, Cherry had excellent recall of specific details from 1963—just as he had when I interviewed him a few years back.

The staff at the facility came to a new conclusion—Cherry was faking.

After the new year began, Doug Jones telephoned me with the news. The judge had ruled Cherry competent to stand trial.

51

In early 2002, Doug Jones called with the news that he had dropped out of the Senate race and would be prosecuting the Bobby Cherry murder trial. "I'm back in the saddle again. Who knows, maybe you'll be a witness?"

But before Jones could make the decision, the Cherry trial wound up being postponed again. In April 2002, Roy Moore, chief justice of the Alabama Supreme Court—who would later lose to Jones in a historic 2017 Senate race—halted all trials, citing a lack of funding. The shutdown stemmed from a dispute between him and the legislature, which gave the courts $2.7 million (about 1.8 percent) less than requested.

Jones worried what another delay would mean to this thirty-nine-year-old case. So far, fifty possible witnesses had already died, and others were in poor health. Reverend John Cross, former pastor of the Sixteenth Street Baptist Church, had just suffered a stroke. Jones said another crucial witness had one foot in the grave. "I just hope he survives long enough to testify."

He decided to approach Jefferson County commissioners to see if they would be willing to pay for the trial instead. They approved $272,000 in funding. The Cherry trial was now back on schedule.

• • •

On May 6, 2002, prosecutors and defense lawyers took turns questioning 114 potential jurors about how much they knew about the church bombing. Most had been too young to remember.

That was one reason the prosecution turned to jury consultant Andrew Sheldon, who had worked the murder trials for Byron De La Beckwith and Sam Bowers before handling the Tommy Blanton case. A son of the South, the consultant resembled a dapper professor with his gray suit, wire-frame glasses, and kind blue eyes. He had started his legal career in 1968, representing poor people who couldn't afford lawyers. Eight years later, he went back to college, obtained a doctorate in clinical psychology, and counseled patients. In 1985, he married the two professions, becoming a new breed of jury consultant.

The Medgar Evers and Vernon Dahmer trials enabled Sheldon and other consultants to refine their jury questionnaire, aimed at uncovering prejudices. He liked the open-ended questions, such as, "If your son or daughter were to bring home for dinner a person of another race, how would you feel?" One potential juror answered that would be fine. Another? "That would *never* happen. Not in my house."

In the church bombing trial, Sheldon and prosecutors hit upon a unique strategy of focusing not so much on the KKK, but on the fact that children were killed inside a house of worship. Their ideal jurors? Parents that were churchgoers. While the press focused on white jurors outnumbering black jurors two to one, Sheldon smiled when he wound up with a jury packed with mothers. They made up all but one of the jurors hearing the case against Blanton, and they convicted him in less than two hours.

As the Cherry trial readied to begin on May 14, families of the four little girls filled the front row. Alpha Robertson sat in her wheelchair at the end of the row. The KKK had killed her youngest child, Carole, that fateful Birmingham Sunday. I couldn't imagine what she had gone through, back then and in all these years since. When a *New York Times* reporter suggested this trial might bring her closure, she scoffed. "Closure? I have often wondered why they associate that word with this affair. For those who are not involved, it is easy to say that."

I thought of my own children, Katherine and Sam. If hate had stolen them away, how would I have responded? Rage, for sure, followed by bitterness.

But what I saw in this mother was her enduring grace. "You can't waste a life hating people because all they do is live their life, laughing, doing more evil."

As she began to testify from her wheelchair, she leaned forward, her words transporting jurors back to a morning almost four decades ago. On that Sunday morning, she had marveled at how grown-up Carole looked at fourteen, wearing her first pair of black pumps. With her small Bible inside her purse, she walked with her father to Sunday school at the Sixteenth Street Baptist Church. While getting ready to join them, Mrs. Robertson said that she heard "an awful sound, like something shaking the world."

Her powerful testimony hushed the courtroom, as did other witnesses who had survived the explosion that rocked the church on the morning of September 15, 1963.

Reverend John Cross's daughter, Barbara, had been inside the church. She spoke of the sudden darkness and the sound of screams. "I thought Russia had bombed Alabama." When light peeked through, she fumbled until she found a door. She dashed outside, screaming. She couldn't find her four friends, buried in the rubble. When she finished speaking, a few jurors wiped away tears.

Prosecutors shifted to witnesses who could implicate Cherry, starting with Bobby Jerome Birdwell, who came to the FBI after reading in the newspaper that the case had been reopened. He told jurors that he and Cherry's oldest son, Tom, had been friends growing up. Days prior to the bombing, the two of them had been playing outside. The temperature hit 90 degrees that afternoon, and the boys rushed inside Cherry's home for water.

Birdwell, then eleven, spotted something on the couch. A white robe. With holes for eyes. A KKK robe. Tom told him it was his father's.

As the boys passed by a room, they could hear a group of men talking. One of them was Cherry.

The subject of their conversation was familiar: Birdwell had already heard Cherry say that his children would never go to school with "niggers." Now he heard Cherry and several other men criticizing school integration but with even more extreme language. Birdwell was unable to make out much of the conversation, but he did make out the words "bomb" and "Sixteenth Street." When the church blew up less than a week later, Birdwell recalled the words, but he was too scared to share what he heard.

Prosecutors also portrayed Cherry as a furious Klansman, enraged by school integration, by showing footage of the 1957 beating of Fred Shuttlesworth. Cameraman Jimmy Parker identified the footage he shot that day. Birdwell identified Cherry as one of Shuttlesworth's attackers.

Under cross-examination, defense lawyer Mickey Johnson asked Parker what he did with the footage. He said he sold it.

Johnson asked why he didn't give it to police.

Parker pointed at the screen. "It looks like a lot of people committing a crime—with several policemen watching."

Several jurors laughed.

Prosecutors called Mitch Burns, the same Klansman turned FBI informant who had testified in Tommy Blanton's trial about the FBI recording his numerous conversations with Blanton. Bobby Cherry joined them sometimes and could be heard on the tape, saying, "[Alabama governor] George Wallace said on TV to use whatever force is necessary." Cherry also admitted on tape to lying when the FBI gave him a polygraph test.

The judge allowed jurors to hear the "Kitchen Sink Tape," in which Blanton talked about making the bomb at the Modern Sign Company on the Friday night before the bombing. Prosecutors had successfully argued the tape was admissible because Cherry was a part of this conspiracy.

Prosecutors then called a series of witnesses who discussed Cherry bragging about his involvement in the church bombing, months and years after the fact. His granddaughter, Teresa Stacy, testified that when she was a child, Cherry had shared that he "helped blow up a bunch of niggers back in Birmingham."

Michael Wayne Gowins, who was dying of asbestosis, testified that he met Cherry in 1982 in Dallas, where they both worked at an apartment complex. One day, he said Cherry came in to help clean carpets, and the two Alabama natives began to converse. "He said he had to get out of Birmingham because the niggers were taking over." Gowins said that Cherry had talked of being a KKK member, before adding, "You know, I bombed the church."

Gowins said he never reported the matter, thinking the bombing had already been prosecuted. When he read in the newspaper in 1997 about the case being reinvestigated, he telephoned the FBI.

Prosecutors also called Cherry's ex-wife, Willadean Brogdon, who said her then-husband admitted to lighting the bomb's fuse. When their car broke down near the Sixteenth Street Baptist Church, he pointed at his handiwork. She said he voiced few regrets about what he had done. "He said, 'I'm sorry I killed those four girls, but at least they can't grow up to have more niggers.'"

Defense lawyer Mickey Johnson questioned the credibility of these witnesses. Johnson tried to poke holes in Brogdon's statement to the FBI, in which she claimed to have had an audiotape at one time of Cherry admitting to the crime. *Why wasn't it in evidence?* Johnson wanted to know.

Still, it was difficult to combat the full choir of voices assembled. There were too many examples, too many similar stories, for Johnson to beat them all back.

Prosecutors turned Cherry's own words against him, and the concocted alibi he had shared with me came back to haunt him. He had told me he was watching wrestling the night before the September 15, 1963, church bombing. Now prosecutors introduced the television logs that showed there was no wrestling on TV, not only that night, but any time in 1963.

Cherry had also told me he headed home that night because his wife was diagnosed with cancer in 1961 or 1962 and given only six months to live. Now prosecutors introduced medical records that showed his wife wasn't diagnosed with cancer until August 1965—almost two years after the bombing.

Back in 1963, Cherry gave a series of statements to the FBI. He never mentioned his wife's cancer or watching wrestling, but he did tell the FBI in writing that he spent all evening with Tommy Blanton, Bob Chambliss, and other Klansmen at the Modern Sign Company on the Friday night before the bombing.

Then–FBI agent John Downey, who had interviewed Cherry during the original investigation, said he denied a role in the crime. But Downey testified that the Klansman didn't stop there. Cherry went on to say that "the only reason I didn't do the church bombing was maybe because somebody beat me to it."

When the defense suggested Cherry's remark could have been tongue-in-cheek, Downey rejected that conclusion. "If somebody asked me whether I robbed a bank, I would just say no, I wouldn't say somebody beat me to it. The impression I got was this possibly could be the guilty man."

Prosecutors, who had begun their case with a description of the horror that day at the Sixteenth Street Baptist Church, ended their case by underscoring the deadly results of the bombing, sharing photographs of the four slain girls in the morgue. Denise McNair's father, Chris, identified her body in the photo and shared a piece of the deadly rubble that the jurors studied.

Cherry's alibi had fallen apart, footage had shown him beating a civil rights leader, and witnesses had recalled him bragging about the bombing on numerous occasions. The big question was whether the jury would believe those witnesses, or whether the defense could poke enough holes for Cherry to wriggle free.

52

To combat accusations against Bobby Cherry, the defense tried to prove that a lie planted years ago had bloomed into the presumption that he helped bomb the Sixteenth Street Baptist Church.

The defense called Mary Frances Cunningham to the witness stand. A December 7, 1964, FBI document quoted her as telling agents she saw her brother-in-law, Bob Chambliss, along with three other men, Cherry, Tommy Blanton, and Herman Cash, outside the Sixteenth Street Baptist Church the night before the bombing.

Cunningham acknowledged meeting in 1964 with the agents investigating the bombing. She denied, however, making that statement to them or anyone else.

Through her testimony, the defense hoped to show her 1964 statement had sparked the FBI's interest in Cherry—and if that statement was later recanted or shown to be a lie, then the case against him was founded on nothing at all.

I glanced at the jurors. Some looked puzzled, some bored. Some faces I couldn't read. Were they buying the defense's gamble?

During a break, the defense lawyer cornered me and other reporters.

"The story told has taken on a life of its own, despite the fact that the person said the story is false."

He insisted Cherry was not a prime suspect until this statement surfaced.

If that was the case, I asked, then why did FBI agents interview Cherry more than a dozen times before this document?

"He was the only one who would talk."

That weekend, I telephoned Doug Jones, checking a few details about the trial and the church bombing.

"There's something you've missed, Jerry, and so has the defense."

"What's that, Doug?"

"I can't tell you."

"I won't print it."

"No, I can't."

"I promise I won't print it."

"Believe me, if I tell you, you'll want to print it."

"Can't you give me a hint?"

"I'll let you know this much—there are two pieces of evidence that connect, but the defense has no idea they connect."

"Sounds clever."

"Yes, but it's a bit of a gamble, too. How will the jury react?"

"What are the pieces of evidence?"

"Just pay attention in closing arguments."

The defense did its best to portray Cherry as an open-minded man who loved people of all races, but their witnesses did him no favors.

Cherry's two grandsons told jurors they had never heard their grandfather use any racial slurs or brag about the church bombing. When Jones asked one grandson if Cherry had ever used derogatory remarks toward African-Americans, he shook his head no. "Only the use of the word *nigger*."

A preacher for an integrated church in Texas, Robert High Sr., told jurors that in his twenties he had been a man "full of hate," but Cherry dissuaded him from joining the KKK. "He told me the worst thing I could do was get tied up with that."

Under cross-examination, Jones asked the preacher if Cherry had mentioned violence he took part in. "Did he ever tell you that in 1957 he was among a group of white men that beat up a black preacher?"

"No, sir."

"Did he ever tell you he split a black man's head open with a pistol?"

"No, sir."

Asked if he had ever heard Cherry say "nigger," High responded that Cherry had used it often. "And I've used it."

Closing arguments began, and the prosecutors' secret strategy came to light. In preparing for the case, Assistant US Attorney Don Cochran had caught an important connection between the Kitchen Sink Tape and Cherry's 1963 written statement to the FBI, in which he said nothing about watching wrestling. Rather than revealing this connection in the normal course of testimony, prosecutors waited until the end to reveal it—too late for the defense to challenge the evidence.

In a PowerPoint presentation, Cochran shared the text of Tommy Blanton's conversation with his wife, Jean, about "making the bomb" at the Modern Sign Company the Friday night before the bombing. In his early statement to the FBI, Cherry acknowledged being at the Modern Sign Company that same night, and he identified Blanton and the KKK's best bomb maker, Bob Chambliss, as being present. In other words, Cherry's own story put himself in the same place as the other convicted bombers, right at the moment the bomb was being made.

It was, Cochran felt, as close to a confession as authorities needed.

"The time for justice is here," Cochran said, after connecting the dots for the jury. "In fact, it's way overdue, and that's what I ask for—justice for Addie, justice for Carole, justice for Cynthia, and justice for Denise."

Cherry's lawyer, Mickey Johnson of Birmingham, told jurors that prosecutors had turned Cherry into "the human equivalent of a cockroach. Even the animal rights people don't get upset with killing a cockroach."

He conceded that statements attributed to his client might show racism, but they hardly showed guilt. "More time has been spent here throwing the N-word around instead of talking about the proof of what happened in 1963."

He told jurors that Cherry had changed in the decades since, joining an interracial church. He then launched into a discussion of racism, suggesting, "Most people of all races have that in them."

After Johnson concluded, Doug Jones stood in front of the jurors to conclude the prosecution's case. He called Cherry's supposed change "a sham." He described Cherry and his fellow bombers as "cowards that cower underneath their hoods." With the horrors of 9/11 still fresh on the nation's mind, the prosecutor called the Klansmen "the forefathers of terrorism."

The McNair family held hands as Jones showed jurors a picture of Denise McNair hugging her white, blond-haired doll. He said the photograph conveyed "an image of hope" for all Americans to move beyond race. He urged jurors to return a guilty verdict and let justice "roll down like a mighty river."

The nine white and three black jurors deliberated for three hours before the judge halted them at 6 p.m. The next morning, May 22, the jury continued, and before 1 p.m., it reached a verdict.

Jurors returned to the courtroom, and their foreman, a short white woman, rose. The families of the four girls clutched hands and mouthed silent prayers. They had been disappointed so many times before, they had come to expect despair. When the word *guilty* rang out—four times, once for each of the girls—tears fell like rain.

The judge delivered four life sentences.

As bailiffs moved toward Cherry, he crooked his finger at Jones and other prosecutors. "This whole bunch have lied all the way through this thing. I've told the truth. I don't know why I'm going to jail for nothing."

Sarah Collins Rudolph, who lost an eye and her sister in the blast, nodded as bailiffs handcuffed Cherry. "His time has come," she said. "Now it's time for him to pay."

Family members and friends took turns hugging Jones. He looked back at me, moisture welling in his eyes.

"Beats running for the Senate, doesn't it, Doug?"

He nodded yes, the tears slipping down.

Days later, Doug Jones telephoned, recalling the countless obstacles that he, fellow prosecutors, FBI agents, his staff, and many others had overcome to convict the last two living suspects. They had built on the work of Bill Baxley, who had made it his mission to solve this case. Baxley had been able to put Chambliss behind bars, and Jones had picked up where Baxley had left off. Now justice had come for Blanton and Cherry. The killers of Addie Mae Collins, Denise McNair, Carole Robertson, and Cynthia Wesley were finally behind bars. "Nobody," Jones said, "can ever take that away from me."

Less than three months later, Alpha Robertson died, and three months after that, Mitch Burns followed her. Within a year of the verdict, Michael Gowins had breathed his last.

"If we had gone to trial even six months later," Jones told me, "we wouldn't have been able to convict Bobby Cherry. That's how close we came to losing."

PART V

JAMES CHANEY

ANDREW GOODMAN

MICHAEL SCHWERNER

53

Back in Mississippi, my wife, Karen, welcomed me home and welcomed Bobby Cherry's conviction. I was grateful to be back and to settle into the flow of life in Jackson, though I was uncertain about what would come next. I told Karen that I thought the Cherry case might be my last, and by now, she didn't believe me. But I wasn't sure I had much of a choice. I wanted to keep reopening cold cases, but when I looked around, time appeared to have run out. Too many witnesses had died. Too much evidence had been lost. Too few prosecutors were willing to tackle these tough cases.

Back in 1998, after the conviction of longtime imperial wizard Sam Bowers, my editors and I had worked on a package of stories about unpunished civil rights killings. The Birmingham church bombing had been the most promising, and now it was closed. When I went back to the short list, the prospects for the remaining cases looked grim.

Still, there was one that stood out. The case that had sparked all my work over the past decade: Mississippi Burning. In 1964, James Chaney, Andy Goodman, and Mickey Schwerner were brutally murdered by the White Knights of the Ku Klux Klan—a crime meant to send shock waves around the nation. It continued to gnaw at me that the Burning murders were never reckoned with.

When I first looked into the case in 1989, it had been a complete long shot—one that had fallen short. More than a decade later, the hurdles to success were even higher. There was now precedent for a case, if prosecutors needed it. But each passing year had reduced the pool of witnesses and evidence, raising the bar over and over again. Doubts abounded, but I knew I would at least have to try to ferret out—or rule out—any leads in the Burning case before I'd be able to move on.

My first thought went to Imperial Wizard Sam Bowers. He was behind bars for life now, due to his role in the Vernon Dahmer murder. But, before that, the only time Bowers had served in prison was his six-year federal sentence for civil rights violations in the Mississippi Burning case.

After his release, Bowers had given a long interview that was still sealed at the Mississippi Department of Archives and History. Authorities had subpoenaed the interview in the Dahmer case. Now I wondered if he might have said anything about Mississippi Burning.

Weeks after Bowers's conviction, I telephoned Bill East, an investigator for the Mississippi attorney general's office, who had obtained a copy of that interview during the Dahmer investigation. I asked him if I could read Bowers's interview, and he promised to see what he could do.

Days later, he suggested I visit him at his office on North State Street. There he led me to a room where three bound transcripts sat on a table. They were all part of an extended interview with Bowers. East told me I could take notes, but I couldn't make copies.

The reclusive Bowers, who never spoke with the press, referred to himself as "a criminal and a lunatic" in the transcripts. He tried to justify lynchings and killings as ways of preserving the southern way of life: "Citizens not only have a right but a duty to preserve their culture."

"By taking someone's life, though?" he was asked.

"If that person wants to put his life on the line in order to destroy that culture, yes."

Just as I'd been hoping, Bowers didn't hold back on the subject of the Mississippi Burning case. He bragged that his 1967 conviction on federal conspiracy charges had "embarrassed" the government because he forced them to use "illegal and unorthodox investigative and judicial efforts."

He denied involvement in the killings; there was no surprise confession waiting on these tapes. But he did say that authorities "could have gotten me for obstruction of justice." He talked of throwing his might into frustrating the investigation. "I was up there doing everything I could to keep those people from talking and everything else."

When the jury convicted him, he said he felt no anger. "I was quite delighted to be convicted and have the main instigator of the entire affair walk out of the courtroom a free man. Everybody—including the trial judge and the prosecutors and everybody else—knows that that happened. This hurts the imperial authority when they have to stoop to conquer, and I think that I did make them stoop to conquer."

He expressed pride that these killings and many others carried out by "semiliterate rednecks" had gone unpunished. "Every stone in the Watergate conspiracy has been uncovered, exposed to the light of day. Yet in the Philadelphia case and dozens of other cases in Mississippi, very, very little is known; much of what they think they know is inaccurate. The case has never really been solved in the sense that Watergate has been solved."

The imperial wizard's words banged around in my brain as I thanked Bill East and left. Bowers was taunting the federal authorities, bragging that "the main instigator" in the killings of the three civil rights workers had walked free. Who was he talking about?

I telephoned Joe Sullivan, the six-foot-two retired agent who headed the FBI investigation into the killings. He answered, and I could hear the traces of the upper midwestern accent in his voice, both kind and no-nonsense. No matter when I called, he was willing to talk.

I mentioned that Bowers had done a series of interviews and spoke about the Mississippi Burning case. I read aloud the portion where the KKK leader discussed "the main instigator" and asked, "Who is Bowers referring to?"

"Edgar Ray Killen," Sullivan said. "He was the moving force."

54

The first time I saw Edgar Ray Killen, he was waiting to testify before the grand jury that indicted Byron De La Beckwith. As Killen, wearing a cowboy hat, crouched in his chair, he looked more like a vulture than a witness.

A descendant of some of Neshoba County's first settlers, Killen made his living from east Mississippi's plentiful pine trees, running what some locals called a "peckerwood sawmill." He would pay landowners for the right to chop wood on their property, hoping the logs he cut between sunup and sundown would fetch a high enough price to cover expenses, leaving him a little bit to spare.

In addition to his logging, Killen worked for some local lawyers as an "investigator," proclaiming his prowess inside the courtroom. "When I walk in with my briefcase, it's over," he liked to tell people in town. When I asked the local judge, Marcus Gordon, about this, he explained that what Killen was doing was visiting jurors at night to get them to return favorable verdicts. That constituted jury tampering, which was illegal, he said. "He had no character. None."

Despite those views, many Neshoba County locals regarded him as a hardworking man and a godly one. On Sundays, he preached at rural

Baptist churches. He had once been so popular that he delivered sermons on the local radio. That is, until he was spotted leaving town with a female parishioner, causing whispers of sin to race around the county. When he returned days later, the married preacher faced a divided church—one group willing to forgive, the other ready to hurl him out the sanctuary doors.

One member recalled, "There's an old story about the two wolves inside of us, one good and one evil. The one you feed is the one you become." Many of Killen's parishioners saw Killen feeding the wrong part of himself. The dispute grew rancorous, ending with the preacher's ousting.

Through it all, no one raised much of a fuss about Killen belonging to the KKK.

I wondered if Sam Bowers's "main instigator" comment might provide the spark needed to reopen the Mississippi Burning case. If so, what evidence existed against Edgar Ray Killen?

Since 1989, I had been collecting Mississippi Burning files, and now I dove back into them afresh. FBI investigators had assembled an almost embarrassing wealth of accounts, and among the most revealing documents were two 1964 confessions from Klansmen James Jordan and Horace Doyle Barnette, who had opened up and told the FBI the up-close story of the Mississippi Burning murders:

At about 6:30 p.m. on summer's first day, June 21, 1964, James Jordan and a small group of men sat inside the Longhorn Drive-In in Meridian, Mississippi, taking drags on their cigarettes. Long a teen hangout, it had become a gathering place for the KKK—hardly surprising since the owner, Frank Herndon, was an exalted cyclops for the White Knights in Lauderdale County.

As the men talked and killed time, Preacher Killen pulled up in a fellow Klansman's 1959 gray-and-white Chevy. He was agitated. He told Herndon, James Jordan, and others gathered that three civil rights workers had been arrested, that they were being held in jail in Philadelphia, and that they needed their "asses tore up." He needed four or five Klansmen to team up with others from Neshoba County.

Jordan helped gather recruits, grabbing fellow Klansman Wayne

Roberts. They went together to buy gloves. Killen had suggested they buy a box of rubber surgical gloves for the night's events, but when they couldn't find any, they grabbed brown cloth gloves from the grocery store of Dick Warner, another Klansman. The group met back up with Killen at Akin Mobile Homes, where Jordan worked as a salesman.

Killen spoke to the gathered Klansmen and outlined a plan of attack. He reiterated that the trio had been arrested on a traffic charge and that they could not be held long. He asked if everyone had their guns. They did.

One carload of Klansmen headed out for Philadelphia, and the second car followed. After arriving in town, not far from the Neshoba County jail, where the civil rights workers were being held, Killen got out of his vehicle. He strolled up to Klansman Horace Doyle Barnette and said, "We have a place to bury them, and a man to run the dozer to cover them up."

Killen showed the Klansmen where to watch for the civil rights workers, who would soon be released from the jail. When every detail was set, he had Klansmen drop him off at a local funeral home, to make sure he had an alibi.

It was about 10:30 p.m. when Cecil Price released James Chaney, Andy Goodman, and Mickey Schwerner. The deputy walked them to the parking lot, where their station wagon was still sitting, and told them: "See how quick you can get out of Neshoba County."

Killen had promised that Mississippi troopers would stop the station wagon once it was on the road, but when they failed to, Price pursued. So did other Klansmen. Soon, they were all speeding down the two-lane road, hitting 100 miles per hour.

The station wagon took a hard right, and the pursuers followed. After red lights began flashing, the wagon came to a halt. Price got out of his patrol car. He walked over to the wagon and told the three men, "I thought you were going back to Meridian if we let you out of jail."

The deputy ordered the young men into his patrol car and started driving again. The other vehicles followed until the convoy reached a remote road called Rock Cut. They stopped, and Klansmen poured out of their cars.

Holding a .38-caliber pistol, Wayne Roberts opened the rear driver's-side door of Price's cruiser and jerked Schwerner out of the backseat. He dragged the civil rights worker to a nearby ditch, put his finger in Schwerner's face, and barked, "Are you that nigger lover?"

Schwerner tried his best to stay calm, even to connect with the Klansman. "Sir, I know just how you feel."

Roberts jammed his pistol into Schwerner's ribs. He pulled the trigger.

The civil rights worker collapsed, blood streaming from his chest.

Roberts returned to Price's car and grabbed Goodman from the backseat. This time the Klansman said nothing.

He fired his pistol a second time, and Goodman crumpled beside Schwerner in the same ditch.

Hearing the blasts, Jordan ran up and yelled, "Save one for me."

James Chaney took several bullets—one in the abdomen, one in the back, and one in the skull—from both Roberts and Jordan.

"You didn't leave me nothing but a nigger," Jordan said, "but at least I killed me a nigger." This part of the *Mississippi Burning* movie had been word for word.

Klansmen loaded the bodies into the station wagon, and Barnette followed a 1957 Chevy to the dam site, where property owner Olen Burrage told him, "It is just a little ways over there." Roberts walked toward the dam, and so did the six-foot-two bulldozer driver, wearing khaki clothes.

Now past 1 a.m., Burrage handed Klansmen a jug full of gasoline to burn the station wagon. He told them he would come back and pick them up in a larger vehicle, saying, "No one will suspect a truck on the road this time of night."

Flames had begun to shoot up from the station wagon by the time the Klansmen returned to town. Sheriff Lawrence Rainey barked to them, "I'll kill anyone who talks, even if it was my own brother."

Jurors in the 1967 US district court trial never heard the full statements by Jordan and Barnette. While some of these details emerged during Jordan's testimony against his fellow Klansmen, jurors never saw Barnette's statement because Judge Harold Cox stripped the Klansman's confession of every name except Barnette's and Jordan's.

Prosecutors presented plenty of other evidence, leading the jury to convict seven Klansmen, including Barnette, Deputy Price, and Sam Bowers, of conspiracy to deprive James Chaney, Andy Goodman, and Mickey Schwerner of their civil rights. But the rest of the eighteen charged walked free, including Sheriff Rainey and Preacher Killen. No one was ever charged with murder.

Killen still lived about a mile from where Klansmen had executed the three men on Rock Cut Road. On his front lawn, he kept a sign featuring the Ten Commandments, one of which read, "Thou shalt not kill."

I decided to telephone Killen, hoping to get him to talk.

He answered the telephone and told me he had just come in from chopping wood. After I introduced myself as a reporter from *The Clarion-Ledger*, he told me he used to know somebody who worked at the newspaper. "There's somebody in Jackson who keeps stirring things up and stirring things up and stirring things up."

I stayed silent for a moment. The last thing I wanted to tell him was it was me. Then I asked him if he was still preaching. He spent the next ten minutes discussing the subject.

"Were you preaching back in 1964?" I finally asked.

That was all it took for him to begin to discuss the events of that fateful summer. He launched into a diatribe against the FBI, saying agents continually harassed him. "You name it, they did it. I never understood why they could lie and it not be against the law." Those agents, he said, "would threaten you if you didn't tell them what they wanted to know. They did things you'd shoot your neighbor for."

When I brought up the confessions from James Jordan and Horace Doyle Barnette, Killen told me Jordan "fabricated more than ninety percent of what he told. He was not a close associate of mine." He failed to address Barnette's statement, which was more damning. It placed Killen at the head of the operation, quoting him as saying that the KKK had a bulldozer and a place to bury the three civil rights workers' bodies.

Killen told me that before I could fully understand what happened on the night of June 21, 1964, I needed to understand communism. He said that Schwerner and Goodman were "underground agents with the Communist Party. The CIA had them under constant surveillance."

He seemed comfortable talking now, so I brought up Bowers's statement. I read what the KKK leader said about the "main instigator" walking away a free man, asking Killen what he thought.

Killen hesitated and then spoke. "I don't know what main instigator he's talking about." He insisted he didn't even know Bowers until they met at the 1967 trial. "According to the news media, he was my boss," he said in denial.

Actually, I knew, the press had merely reported the trial testimony. The transcript revealed that Killen received orders from Bowers to kill Schwerner.

When it came time for Killen's defense, his lawyer had put witnesses on the stand who insisted the preacher had spent his night at the funeral home, where there were two wakes, including one for a young child. I wondered if his alibi might trip him up all these years later, just as it had Bobby Cherry.

"Now, I understand you had an alibi," I said.

He launched into a description of being at the funeral home that night. "It wasn't a setup alibi. It was something unplanned," he said. "Country folks, if we set up, we'd set up with family."

Nothing like a Klansman to explain the right way to set up an alibi.

All the same, I was grateful that he was eager to talk. So I asked Killen a question I had been waiting to ask, about how he saw things decades later: "What do you think should happen to the people who killed these three men?"

He paused and answered, "I'm not going to say they were wrong."

He continued. "I don't believe in murder. I believe in self-defense."

It sounded like a line he had been repeating to himself for years.

55

Prying open a cold case often relies on proving that justice failed to be done the first time. In the days after my call with Killen, Sam Bowers's statement stayed in my mind, now mixing with the preacher's quick, cool response when I brought it up. I hoped that Bowers's boast might provide the evidence needed to show that the case still had life in it.

I shared the Klan leader's remarks with the families whose loved ones had been killed. James Chaney's brother, Ben, the one that Mickey Schwerner had called "Cub," thought Bowers's admission showed that true justice never took place.

Both he and Schwerner's widow, Rita Bender, told me they wanted to see a grand jury investigation into the case. She asked, "Isn't it time for the state of Mississippi to really inquire into the role it played, instead of continuing to duck responsibility?"

I reached Andy Goodman's mother, Carolyn, in her Upper West Side home in Manhattan, where she kept a sketch of her son hanging over her desk. She noted that while Mississippi would never hear a murder charge back then, "Now in 1998, it's a different matter. People are prepared to look back."

I shared what I had found with my editors, and the story became part of a package titled, "Crimes of the Past." Bowers's remarks became the lead story: *The man who once headed the nation's most violent Ku Klux Klan organization admitted he thwarted justice in the 1964 killings of three civil rights workers and said he didn't mind going to prison because a fellow Klansman got away with murder.*

Nearly thirty-five years after Klansmen killed James Chaney, Andy Goodman, and Mickey Schwerner, a *Clarion-Ledger* editorial called for the prosecution of the 1964 slayings. Momentum seemed to be swinging that way, too, with Rita Bender writing District Attorney Ken Turner, "Too many years have passed without a serious attempt by the state of Mississippi to apply its resources to the attainment of justice in this case."

Bender, a successful lawyer in Seattle with her husband, Bill, called on the district attorney to pursue the case, just as Mississippi authorities had done in the killings of Medgar Evers and Vernon Dahmer. "It certainly shows that it can be done, and it shows that it should be done."

When I caught up with Turner, a staunch Methodist and Sunday school teacher, he wouldn't say anything. He explained that he doesn't comment on anything pending, which seemed like a comment in itself. Was the case indeed pending?

While in Philadelphia, Mississippi, I visited Stanley Dearman, the soft-spoken editor of *The Neshoba Democrat*, which occupied the same brick building that McClain-Hays Funeral Home had in 1964. As a journalist, he was fearless and passionate about ferreting out facts. Since 1989, Dearman had called for the prosecution of the killers, and he had even traveled to New York City to interview Andy Goodman's mother, Carolyn, upset that justice had yet to be done. His perspective was clear-minded and uncompromising about what Neshoba County needed to do.

"People need to realize," he said, that "no matter how remote, the thing doesn't go away. It stays on your hand like a stain."

Fellow citizens told him to leave the case alone, but "there's no statute of limitations for a damn good reason," he said. "You can't say, 'You can have a free murder every twenty or thirty years.' It doesn't work this way."

• • •

I spoke with Edgar Ray Killen a half dozen times more on the telephone. He seemed unaware of my stories, and that was fine with me. If the investigation heated up or he hired a lawyer, I knew our conversations would end. In the meantime, I wanted to get as much information from him as I could about the Mississippi Burning case.

When I mentioned the possibility of interviewing him in person, he suggested I visit his home near Union, Mississippi, at about 9 p.m. I shuddered a little. That meant I would be driving in the dark on the same remote road where Chaney, Goodman, and Schwerner met their deaths.

For years, I had interviewed Klansmen in their homes, but this seemed too risky, even foolish. I asked if he could meet at an earlier time, and he said no, because he worked all day, except on Sundays. That was when he preached.

He mentioned cutting timber on land many miles west of Union, and I suggested a compromise. I asked him if I could treat him and his wife, Betty Jo, to dinner. "Do you like catfish?"

"Oh, I love catfish."

My watch showed I was late when I pulled my Honda into the parking lot and walked inside the restaurant that served all-you-can-eat catfish, hush puppies, french fries, slaw, and sweet tea for just $8.95. Edgar Ray Killen greeted me, wearing his cowboy hat.

I sipped water from a red plastic glass while Killen devoured catfish like the room was on fire. The waitress served him four whole fish before whisking away the bones.

I asked him about District Attorney Ken Turner possibly reopening the case.

Killen shook his head. "Turner really doesn't have a lot of evidence. That's what's been his reluctance."

The preacher denounced the FBI again, saying agents harassed him, threatened him, and locked him in a room for most of a day, telling him if he didn't talk he was "a dead SOB."

He denied belonging to the KKK, but that didn't surprise me. Few Klansmen admit that.

"I would even say I was for" the Klan, he said, wiping his mouth with his napkin, "if I had control."

If he had control?

He leaned forward, tilting his hat. "Say I did have a Klan, and something blew up twenty miles away." He shook his head. "Even if I knew nothing about it, I'd be blamed."

His main complaint about the Klan, it seemed, was that one couldn't be an open member without dealing with the hassle of suspicious authorities all the time. I hadn't heard that one before.

But since he had no trouble discussing the Klan, I brought up Delmar Dennis, who testified that Killen told Klansmen in spring 1964 that Mickey Schwerner's killing had already been approved by Imperial Wizard Sam Bowers.

Dennis "was lying," Killen spat.

The preacher said he had no motive for killing the three civil rights workers. It wasn't until later, he explained, that he learned Schwerner and Andy Goodman "were both communists."

When I asked how he learned this, he replied that he had access to US intelligence. "It wasn't illegal, but I did have a source of information."

He wouldn't say who, but he talked about his close relationship with Jim Eastland from Mississippi, one of the nation's most powerful senators. I had listened to the tape of Eastland talking to Lyndon Johnson after the trio's disappearance. The senator told the president, "I don't believe they're missing. I believe it's a publicity stunt. I don't think there's a damn thing to it. There's not a Ku Klux Klan in that area. . . . Who could possibly harm them?"

Killen brought up Martin Luther King Jr., insisting he was a communist, too. After King's assassination, FBI agents knocked on Killen's door, wanting to know his whereabouts on April 4, 1968. "They asked me to make a statement, and I told them the only statement I'd make was in front of twelve of my peers."

He told me he did have an alibi for King's killing. But he said that if he had shared it at the time, agents would have harassed the person vouching for him. Even so, days later Killen couldn't resist picking up the business card the FBI agent had left. The preacher dialed the number, and when the agent answered, Killen asked who killed King.

"Why do you want to know?" the agent asked.

"Man," Killen replied, "I want to shake his hand."

After paying the bill and tip, I waved good-bye to Killen and his wife. I headed toward my Honda, and I had already unlocked the door when I noticed Killen heading toward me.

I waited, expecting him to speak. Instead, he strolled past me and stepped behind my car. I saw his eyes darting in a straight line, realizing too late that he had just read my license plate number.

In a flash, I knew what this meant. He could contact the clerk's office in Jackson, get my address, and pay me a personal visit. Or more likely, send his friends.

On my long drive back to Jackson, all I could think about was what a terrible mistake I had made.

56

After four years in prison, Cecil Price, the Neshoba County deputy who had run down the station wagon of the civil rights workers, had sought to put his violent past behind him. He returned to town, joined the Philadelphia Country Club, and spent his days as a jeweler before working for a trucking company. For more than three decades, he had lived in Philadelphia undisturbed, in a brown clapboard house a block off the town square.

Price might have been welcomed back to town after his stint in prison, but James Jordan and Horace Doyle Barnette, who had given confessions to their involvement in the murderous mob, became pariahs because they spoke to the FBI. After the 1967 trial, the federal government relocated Jordan to a small town outside Jacksonville, Florida, where he worked at a funeral home until his death.

After time in prison, Barnette returned to his native Louisiana, where he worked in the auto parts business. Family members told me he received threats almost to the day he took his last breath.

In contrast, the other killers, like Price, drew handshakes and greetings on the sidewalks of Philadelphia.

Dearman told me that such support had finally begun to fade. While I trusted his judgment, I wondered what a jury might do.

Beyond Killen, I had been seeking out the other Klansmen who had helped commit the Mississippi Burning murders. A dozen of those who went on trial in 1967 were still alive, but most wouldn't talk to me.

Some who did only wanted to discuss their health. Jerry McGrew Sharpe, a fifty-eight-year-old onetime used car salesman whom the jury failed to convict, told me, "I've had numerous strokes. Went blind on top of that."

Lawrence Rainey, the seventy-seven-year-old former sheriff, said he suffered from "cancer of the throat. I've had open-heart surgery. I have a stainless-steel valve in my heart. I'm doing a little piddling around. I ain't able to do very much."

He insisted he had nothing to do with the killings and that he supported prosecution. He blamed the lack of a murder indictment on the FBI. "Circuit Judge O. H. Barnett sent J. Edgar Hoover a telegram to turn over their conspiracy evidence. He never did answer."

What Rainey didn't mention was that Judge Barnett, who would have overseen that grand jury, had reportedly been spotted at a KKK rally. The FBI had balked because it didn't want to deliver its evidence and informants right into the hands of Klansmen.

The few men who did talk to me insisted on their innocence, including James T. "Pete" Harris, who had served as investigator for the White Knights' Klan Bureau of Investigation in Meridian. Confessions from the FBI informants had fingered Harris as the one who began dialing from the pay phone at the Longhorn Drive-In, recruiting Klansmen for the job that night.

"I was found not guilty," Harris said, "and there was a lot of 'em that was falsely charged."

When I reached Olen Burrage, who owned the property where the bodies of the three civil rights workers were buried, he hung up as soon as I brought up the killings. When I called back, the seventy-one-year-old man barked, "Look, buddy, find somebody else to talk to. You're wasting my time."

Jimmie Snowden, a sixty-six-year-old man convicted of being a part of the murderous mob, had a more chilling message when I talked about reopening the case. "You know what? You're about to kill the cat."

But for all my curiosity, none of the perpetrators I called revealed anything worthwhile. I would need to find another way in.

Killen had avoided time behind bars in the Mississippi Burning case, but I knew he had wound up going to prison for five months in 1975 for threatening a woman. The Baptist preacher had been charged with making a threat on a telephone call to the woman, after her husband had caught Killen having an affair.

I obtained an audiotape of the call and heard Killen's voice, livid. He yelled at the woman about her husband: "That son of a bitch will be dead at eight o'clock, you hear. Folks die for things he did. You understand that? I don't make any mistakes and get the wrong man." He urged her to get him to turn himself in "to the local law and get them to bring him to me, and I might then consider talking to him, right after I stomp him."

The circumstances were different, but that last detail caught me. Killen was talking about law enforcement officials delivering people to him for violent purposes—just like they did in the Mississippi Burning case.

A prosecutor in the Birmingham church bombing told me that he believed the tape could be evidence against Killen, but Mississippi authorities seemed less bullish.

I telephoned Killen all the same. He had begun to feel the heat from the Mississippi Burning case, saying he was going to have to hire a lawyer.

He grumbled, "I have no rights."

Then he delivered a dig. "I have to be a newspaper reporter or a nigger if I want to have rights."

Calls to reopen the case reverberated around Mississippi. After my cold-case story ran, a woman called my line at *The Clarion-Ledger* to criticize my article and the idea of reopening the Mississippi Burning investigation. She heaped praises on Cecil Price and his wife, saying they "couldn't be finer people."

As the conversation continued, she told me her daughter had been killed some years back.

"How terrible," I said.

She told me her heart went out to the trio's families, suggesting their children and grandchildren are the ones suffering from new interest in the case. "I can let mine go. Why can't others let theirs go?"

"Was your daughter's killer ever prosecuted?" I asked.

"Yes," she said, "but the jury acquitted him," which meant the killer could never be retried for murder.

She talked again about the Mississippi Burning case. "It hurts me to see them bringing more charges, but there's not a thing I can do in my daughter's case. There's nothing I can do because twelve men and women let him go away."

"What if he could be tried again? What if that was possible? Would you want that?"

"I'm sure I would, and I would right now."

After a pause, I spoke. "Don't you think these families feel the same way?"

57

In one Freedom Summer photograph, Rita Schwerner leaned back in her dark sunglasses, waiting for word about the disappearances of her husband and the others. She did her best to conceal her feelings, wishing her grief could be anywhere but in public.

She was one of the strongest people I have ever known and also one of the most private. When we first started speaking in 1989, she remained wary. Some reporters had burned her.

As the years passed, she had begun to trust me a little more. She had long resented the label of "Mickey Schwerner's widow." She felt that ignored her current husband, Bill Bender, a talented and affable lawyer she had been married to since 1967, and with whom she had had two wonderful children.

For her, prosecution of the killings of Mickey and others had nothing to do with retribution or even closure. Instead, it had everything to do with acknowledging what happened. "These murders, other murders and church burnings didn't happen in a vacuum. There was an atmosphere of frenzy created. I believe strongly that history has to be understood because if it isn't understood, it gets repeated."

• • •

It was past midnight on June 22, 1964, when someone knocked on the dorm room door where she was staying at Miami University in Oxford, Ohio, and told her she needed to come to the office. When she arrived, a caller said her husband, Mickey, and the others, James Chaney and Andy Goodman, were missing. They had failed to check in at 4 p.m. as planned.

She knew the drill. If anyone failed to check in, a flurry of phone calls followed. Activists would call the hospitals. Then the jails. Then law enforcement officials. Then the Justice Department.

Those calls turned up nothing. She sat by the phone, waiting and wondering. She finally stretched out on a couch, closing her eyes, but never finding sleep.

After dawn broke, fellow activist Ivanhoe Donaldson came by and invited her to join him on a walk.

Mickey had developed a bit of a friendship with Donaldson, but she hardly knew him. They strolled together on a sidewalk that snaked across the green campus, and he spoke up. "Rita, you know he's dead."

Days later, she flew with fellow civil rights activist Bob Zellner, a white Alabama native, to Mississippi, where they met Neshoba County sheriff Lawrence Rainey in his patrol car. Rainey sat in the driver's seat, next to a top Mississippi Highway Patrol official. She stood there, gazing at the charred remnant of what she and Mickey had driven across Mississippi roads. Mickey really was dead.

Rainey whirled around, pushing his beefy right arm over the back of the front seat. He said he knew nothing about the missing men.

"You're lying," she shot back. "I'm not going to go away. I'm not going to give up until I find out what happened. And if you don't want me to find out, you'll have to kill me, too."

Rainey became red-faced, clenching his fingers into a fist, ready, it seemed, to smack her in the face. He told her he had no idea why she would think he might lie.

She started to speak again. The sheriff told her to shut up.

"I'm not going to shut up. I'm not going to leave until you tell me what happened to my husband."

Her bravery eventually convinced officers to show her the remains of Mickey's station wagon. In the garage, the couple's station wagon looked anything but familiar. Set on blocks, the soot-covered vehicle had no tires, no windows, and no seats—the victim of a vicious fire set to destroy any remaining evidence. She stood there, gazing at the charred remnant of what she and Mickey had driven across Mississippi roads, and in that moment the realization finally washed over her. Mickey was dead.

58

The Mississippi Burning case received an unexpected push in late 1998 when a federal grand jury indicted Cecil Price, accusing the sixty-year-old former Neshoba County deputy of falsifying tests for commercial driver's licenses. If convicted, he could face up to ten years in prison.

Not long after, Assistant US Attorney Jack Lacy invited me to his office. For more than a decade, I had known the white-bearded former English professor, fond of quoting poetry to jurors. He had witnessed the riot on the University of Mississippi campus when James Meredith enrolled in the fall of 1962 and had been among the few white students who dined in the cafeteria with the lone black student.

The prosecutor said he believed the federal charge against Price represented significant leverage. If the former deputy wanted a light sentence, he would have to testify in the Mississippi Burning case.

"I would love to prosecute this case if I could," Lacy said. "And Cecil Price would obviously be just the kind of witness you want to transport the jury back to the scene of the crime."

Lacy had been working for Mississippi attorney general Mike Moore back in 1989, when the office considered pursuing the murders of Chaney, Goodman, and Schwerner. Moore had told me that the case went nowhere back then because they had lacked enough evidence and enough living witnesses.

Lacy now shared with me that he had been pushing for Edgar Ray Killen's prosecution in 1989, and that he and fellow Mississippi special assistant attorney general John Henry had concluded that—even though some physical evidence had been destroyed—enough vital evidence was available to prosecute, including an autopsy report, dental records, and the 1967 federal court transcript.

Lacy handed me a copy of his original report, which identified Killen as the number one suspect to prosecute. The 177-page report concluded that the transcript alone proved that the Klan leader "actively planned the events of June 21, 1964, put together a group of men to execute the plan, and instructed that group on the execution of the plan."

The federal prosecutor believed it wasn't too late to prosecute. There were still enough witnesses, enough evidence, and enough time, as long as authorities hurried, he said. "How are we going to live with ourselves in the next century if we are unable to correct the glaring errors of the past?"

The stories I had written, along with Rita Bender's letter, soon paid off. Neshoba County district attorney Ken Turner was starting to move. He told me he had spoken to the Justice Department's Civil Rights Division, seeking the FBI files in the case.

The news surprised the agent who once led the investigation, Joe Sullivan. "That is quite a change of pace. The bureau, I'm sure, can dredge up all the evidence."

When I telephoned Killen, I pressed him for more details about the statements the FBI had gathered against him.

He sounded wary, making me wonder how much longer he would take my calls.

He finally spoke. "I'm concerned when people give false information. There are not any witnesses to give truthful information on it."

"Are you concerned what the district attorney is doing?"

"No. It concerns me some you're questioning me."

• • •

I called the Jackson office of the FBI about District Attorney Ken Turner's request for the Mississippi Burning case files. Julian Gonzales, supervisor for the civil rights squad for the FBI in Jackson, confirmed he had indeed spoken to Turner, but he said the district attorney had yet to request the files.

"He didn't request the files?"

"Ken's comment to me was that right after the first of the year, he'd be getting caught up and that once he was caught up, if he needed help, he'd call us. We're just waiting to hear from him."

I telephoned Turner, who said, "This is not something I can make weekly reports on."

He insisted he was reviewing materials, but he wouldn't say what they were. "I'm just kind of taking one step at a time."

News that the district attorney had yet to request the FBI files upset Rita Bender, and it upset me, too. She said authorities still had the opportunity to right this wrong. "If not now, when?"

As I continued to push Turner's office, Mississippi attorney general Mike Moore called me to his office. He had also received a letter from Bender, urging him to get involved in the renewed Mississippi Burning investigation. When Moore mentioned visiting with Neshoba County's district attorney about the case, I replied, "I have to be honest, Mike. He doesn't seem very enthusiastic about the case. He still hasn't requested the FBI files."

He smiled. "You're a good reporter, Jerry."

He told me he had been promised the entire FBI case file by the US attorney general's office in Washington, DC, just as he had in the Vernon Dahmer case. "Jerry, I don't want to say anything publicly, but I promise we're working on this."

He reminisced about the Sam Bowers trial, saying how happy he had been to see members of his staff get recognized. "That meant a lot to me."

I brought up the fact that the former sheriff's deputy was now cooperating with them: "Mike, you're great in front of a jury. I can just envision you standing there one day, questioning Cecil Price as a witness."

He smiled again. "I'd like that."

• • •

The last time Price had been before a judge, he had received six years in prison on federal conspiracy charges in connection with the 1964 killings of the three civil rights workers. This time, he entered the courtroom wearing khaki western pants and cowboy boots, pleading guilty to a single count that he had made false statements on a commercial driver's test score sheet, allowing drivers to pay money for passing grades.

Prosecutors shared that Price had told authorities the names of thirty people who never took the tests, but whom he had given passing scores anyway. The former deputy expressed sorrow for what he had done, and the judge sentenced him to one hundred hours of community service. The twice-convicted felon walked free, just like that. There was no mention of the Mississippi Burning case, which shocked me. But it turned out that the judge could only consider crimes from the past decade in punishing Price. That failed to include the KKK conspiracy to kill the three young men.

The good news for Mississippi authorities, though, was that his federal probation required Price's continued cooperation in the murders of Chaney, Goodman, and Schwerner. Bill East, the Harley-loving investigator for Moore, could hardly contain his glee when he called me. Price, he said, was going to tell them everything he knew.

Price told authorities that he had arrested the three civil rights workers on the afternoon of June 21, 1964. He then reached out to Billy Wayne Posey, who ran a service station, and told him "to contact Killen to get the boys beat up." When Killen called him later, Price said he advised the preacher that the civil rights workers were in jail, mentioning Schwerner by name, and Killen replied, "Oh, good, we have been looking for Schwerner."

He said Killen asked him to keep the men locked up "until he could get a group together, and he would take care of it from there." Hours later, Price said Killen called back, urging him to continue to keep the men in jail. Killen said it was taking longer to get a group together. Price responded that he could not hold the three men much longer.

After he hung up, Price said he drove to Old Jolly's Car Lot, where he met Killen and others, including a half dozen men from Meridian he didn't know. Price said Killen told the group that when Price released the men, Mississippi Highway Patrol officers would stop the station wagon and turn the men over to the Meridian Klansmen. Price said he assumed "the boys were going to be beaten," rather than killed. Before Price left, he said he heard Killen announce he was going to the funeral home to establish his alibi.

Price released the men from jail at about 10:30 p.m., and when the highway patrolmen didn't stop the trio's station wagon, Price volunteered and caught up with them. He said he hit Chaney and put the three men in the backseat of his patrol car.

The Klansmen all drove to Rock Cut Road, a place that seemed secluded to Price. He said Alton Wayne Roberts shot Schwerner and Goodman, and James Jordan shot Chaney. Afterward, the group loaded the bodies into the station wagon.

Price, who passed a lie detector test, said Killen later told him that he hoped the FBI "don't look in any pond dam." He said that "he did not know what happened to the guns used to kill the 3 boys, but he heard that they were melted down by someone in Meridian."

Price's statement against Killen was damning. Investigators now had someone who was a part of the conspiracy ready to testify against Killen. They had someone who could get up on the stand and walk jurors through the night's fateful event.

But, still, the attorney general's office worried that they lacked a "smoking gun." And so they waited, rather than going forward with a trial—a decision that would risk the whole case.

59

As investigators second-guessed themselves, I began to pore through the testimony of the 1967 federal conspiracy trial. A federal source had recently shared a copy of the 2,802-page transcript with me. The more I read, the more I realized Sam Bowers had been right about one thing—testimony had been convincing that Edgar Ray Killen was guilty. Two different police officers testified that soon after the three civil rights workers disappeared, Killen was sharing details of how the KKK killed them. So how did he walk free?

I thought back to the Vernon Dahmer case, where I had reported about evidence of jury tampering in the 1968 trial of Imperial Wizard Sam Bowers. The story revealed that justice had never been done and had also aided the push for prosecuting Bowers. So what happened behind closed doors in the Mississippi Burning case?

I dug through the court file until I found the jurors' names. One by one, I tracked down them or their families.

Langdon Anderson, who had since died, was the first whose family I reached. I spoke with his daughter, Martha Willoughby, sharing with her that Bowers had said the "main instigator" of the three civil rights workers' killings had gotten away with murder.

"That was 'Preacher' Killen," she said, filling in my next line for me. "My dad was disgusted they failed to convict him. My dad's attitude was 'murder is murder,' and if someone did it, they're guilty."

I asked her if she knew what happened inside the jury room.

"A woman on the jury refused to convict Killen. She said she could never convict a preacher."

It was an 11–1 verdict, then—just like Sam Bowers received in the Vernon Dahmer case, where jury tampering was involved.

Armed with this new information, I telephoned other jurors. J. P. Hollingsworth, an eighty-two-year-old former juror who lived on the Mississippi Gulf Coast, confirmed what Willoughby had told me.

Harmon Raspberry, even older at eighty-six, still lived in the tiny town of Stonewall. He said that it didn't matter to him what Killen's occupation was. "I felt like because he was a preacher, he ought to know better than the rest of 'em."

Jurors and their families confirmed the jury had deadlocked 11–1 in favor of convicting Killen on federal conspiracy charges.

Unable to reach Willie Arnesen, now living in a nursing home, I telephoned her son, Donald Vance. He confirmed that his mother had been the one that voted "not guilty" on Killen.

When I asked why, he told me she'd said that Killen "could look you in the eye. None of the rest of 'em could look at you."

Later on, though, he said that his mother had changed her mind. "Mama found out he was a scoundrel and said she was sorry she let him go."

I pored through old newspapers and books I could find at the Mississippi Department of Archives and History building, a few blocks from *The Clarion-Ledger.* It turned out Arnesen grew up in Neshoba County. I wondered if she and Killen knew each other.

After exploring for clues in Philadelphia, I stopped by *The Neshoba Democrat* office to speak with editor Stanley Dearman again. He remembered the trial well. He had covered it. After the trial, he said Killen had boasted that he wasn't convicted because he had gotten to one of the jurors. If so, that would constitute jury tampering.

I located one of the remaining jurors near Poplarville, the same southwest

Mississippi town where Senator Theodore Bilbo had lived and the KKK had run wild. Retired nurse Nell Dedeaux invited me inside and shared details from the Mississippi Burning trial as if they had happened several weeks ago instead of several decades. She talked of federal marshals guarding her family. She talked of burning crosses nearby. She talked, too, of threatening calls to jurors, warning what would happen if they failed to vote "not guilty."

After eleven days of testimony, jurors began deliberations. Dedeaux said that she and several other jurors had immediately declared that Killen was guilty. "He helped them do it. It was just dirty the way they did those boys."

One juror worried aloud that the KKK would firebomb her family if she voted guilty.

Dedeaux told her, "You ought not to have got on here then."

After several votes on Killen, she said the jury deadlocked 10–2 in favor of his guilt.

That angered her. "I just can't understand people who won't vote guilty when the evidence is there, and the facts are there."

US district judge Harold Cox read jurors a charge that urged them to reach a unanimous verdict, if possible. The female juror who had expressed fears changed her vote to guilty on Killen. The lone holdout, however, continued to vote not guilty.

I showed her a photograph of Willie Arnesen and asked her if this was the holdout juror.

"That's the one."

She said the holdout juror kept telling them, "I'm not going to find Brother Killen guilty. I don't believe it. He wouldn't do such a thing. I'll stay here till Christmas."

She was still angry at the holdout juror. "Damn her. I know the preacher was guilty. He got away with it."

This was a crucial piece of the puzzle: I knew the identity of the holdout juror—a juror who had violated her oath, basing her verdict on something besides the testimony. While this wasn't enough evidence to get the case prosecuted, it was enough evidence to prove that the trial of Edgar Ray Killen had been far from fair. And that, I knew, was enough to kick the case wide open.

60

After my story appeared in *The Clarion-Ledger*, I got a call from an old source, Bob Stringer, whose appearance had prompted the reopening of the Vernon Dahmer murder. He told me that Edgar Ray Killen was lying when he said he hadn't met Sam Bowers.

"How do you know, Bob?"

"I was there."

He said that Bowers had driven him one day in spring 1964—before the killings—to a remote rural church. "I was his boy. I always felt Sam was grooming me for something."

The first time he and Bowers went there, armed guards protected the KKK gathering.

"Did Bowers speak that day?" I asked.

"He sure did."

I remembered the book, *Attack on Terror*, which described a meeting of the White Knights of the KKK in spring 1964 where Bowers spoke before a crowd. The gathering was at the Boykin Methodist Church, located near Raleigh. Klansmen were asked the names of their counties and their KKK numbers.

Stringer confirmed that this was the very same meeting, and we both drove to the old wooden church, less than an hour southeast of Jackson. As I stepped inside the dim church, I marveled at its construction. The logs formed perfect walls, and I saw no signs of rotting. Sunlight peeked through a portion of the wall that rose no higher than my waist, constructed in the days before air-conditioning. All the opening did was stir the steamy heat.

Stringer showed me where Bowers had stood, railing against the upcoming "nigger-communist invasion of Mississippi." His speech was a call to arms as Freedom Summer neared. He called their "Christian" organization "the physical spear upon which the enemy will either impale himself and perish, or sweep aside, then to proceed almost unhindered in his evil work of destroying civilization."

Stringer sat on one of the wooden pews, where about one hundred Klansmen had been that day. Bowers had told them their first contact with civil rights activists should be as "legally deputized law enforcement officers." Klansmen must "roll with the mass punch which they will deliver in the streets during the day, and we must counterattack the individual leaders at night. Any personal attacks on the enemy should be carefully planned to include only the leaders and prime white collaborators of the enemy forces."

The prime white collaborator the White Knights had their eyes on, even at that very meeting, was Mickey Schwerner. He had been working in the Council of Federated Organizations (COFO) office with his wife, Rita, in Meridian, since January 1964. Schwerner had already drawn lots of local attention for inspiring local African-Americans to protest and register to vote, drawing the nickname "Goatee" because of the beard he wore. Within two months of his arrival, he became a target of Mississippi Sovereignty Commission spying. The commission had then shared its report on the couple with Meridian police, many of whom belonged to the White Knights.

A few weeks after Bowers's speech, Stringer said that he and Bowers returned to this same church. While there, they met Killen and another man whose name he didn't know. Schwerner's name monopolized the conversation that day. Stringer said he heard Bowers tell Killen, "Goatee is like the queen bee in the beehive. You eliminate the queen bee, and all the workers go away."

As soon as Stringer finished speaking, I realized that he represented a potential new witness against Killen, tying Killen to the task of carrying out the imperial wizard's orders to kill Schwerner. I had a new story, another piece of the puzzle falling into place, and authorities had the new evidence they were looking for.

By 2000, momentum had shifted toward prosecuting the Mississippi Burning case. Former Neshoba County deputy Cecil Price was cooperating with authorities, and they now had another new witness in Bob Stringer. They also had the federal court transcript, preserving the testimony of key Klansmen.

Once timid about the case, Mississippi attorney general Mike Moore now sounded bold. "It's our belief at this point that Preacher Killen was one of the masterminds in the Neshoba County killings. We're making progress in the case. All the troops are excited."

While he believed a prosecution could help erase the dark stains of Mississippi's past, he emphasized a lot of work was needed before the case went before a jury. He said it bothered him that the state of Mississippi had never prosecuted anyone in the case. "These three kids believed in what they were doing, and they were brutally murdered."

When I asked which suspects he was looking at, he replied, "All of them. The way the kids were killed is as mean a crime as I know about—killing for no other purpose than to kill them."

As I continued to ferret out new information and write more stories, reminders of the brutal killings began to find me—rather than the reverse. I had received threats in each of the other cases I had helped reopen, but the experience never became less jarring.

In 1999, our family had moved to a small, suburban neighborhood outside Jackson, and within months we learned that both of our next-door neighbors knew suspects in the killings of Chaney, Goodman, and Schwerner.

When I walked out one morning to get my newspaper, my neighbor stopped me. "I was in Philadelphia this past weekend," he said. "You know, the Klan wants to kill you."

He chuckled. "I told 'em if they wanted to know where you lived it would cost them big bucks."

He laughed again. I did my best to fake a smile.

61

In early 2000, Moore continued to assemble the case, but there was still no clear timeline. Meanwhile, as I was looking into a different civil rights cold case, I stumbled across a new potential witness against Killen and other killers in the Mississippi Burning case. I visited with an FBI informant named Ernest Gilbert, who had headed recruitment for the White Knights of the KKK. At his home just across the Louisiana line, he told me that while he knew little about the Mississippi Burning case itself, he did know some of the chief players, including then-sheriff Lawrence Rainey and then-deputy Cecil Price.

Gilbert met me in his golf cap and shook my hand. He was ghostly pale, age seventy-five, with a mole on his left cheek. We sat down on his couch, he with some difficulty. Then he began his story, leading by saying that he wished he had never joined the Klan, because of all the violence. "I couldn't live with it. It messed my life up."

One of his biggest regrets, he told me, came when he helped kidnap a black teen jailed for flirting with a white girl. That night, authorities released the teen into the hands of waiting Klansmen—just as in the Mississippi Burning case, weeks before Chaney, Goodman, and Schwerner were killed.

The story he was beginning to tell sounded familiar, and I asked him to wait a minute. I went outside to my car, where I had stuffed my books on the Mississippi Burning case. I found *Attack on Terror* and brought it inside. I flipped through the pages until I located the story he was talking about—the KKK's abduction of Wilmer Faye Jones.

After graduating from Carver High School in Pascagoula, Jones had returned to live with his mother and stepfather in Philadelphia. He stood out among teens in town because he was wearing a goatee.

On June 2, 1964, he wound up in the hands of the infamous sheriff Rainey and deputy Price, because he'd been accused of asking a white female worker at Thompson's Drug Store for a date. When Jones denied the accusation, Rainey backhanded him.

The sheriff asked what he learned at high school, and he replied history, economics, and other subjects.

"Hell, nigger, I'm not talking about stuff like that. I'm talking about integration, segregation, and what they taught you about that kind of stuff in school."

Deputy Price asked what was on his chin, and Jones said many like him were growing whiskers. The deputy asked if he belonged to the Black Muslims, COFO, NAACP, or anything like that. After Jones said no, Price pulled out his pocketknife and sliced off some of the beard.

After Price locked him up in jail, the deputy returned six hours later with the sheriff. The sheriff told him it was a quarter to 1 a.m., that he only had fifteen minutes to get off the streets, that he'd better get rid of that beard and better not call any white girls.

When Jones stepped outside, he spotted two white men near a light post. One had a shotgun and the other had an automatic pistol.

In his FBI statement, Jones described the men: "Number One—the white man with the automatic pistol was about 35 to 40 years of age, about 6 feet, 2 inches, weighed about 180 pounds, and had dark hair which was thick and hanging over his forehead a little. He had a flesh-colored mole or wart about the size of an eraser on a pencil, just below his cheekbone on his left cheek."

I handed the book to Gilbert. When he read the description of Number

One, he said, "That's me. I put a gun in his back and told him to get in the car."

Jones described five armed men in the car, one of them called "Preacher." He described the Preacher as five-foot-eight, 180 pounds, who had a snub-nosed revolver he held in his back when he got in the car after the men handcuffed him.

Gilbert told me this was Edgar Ray Killen, the man who had invited Gilbert to come. They drove down dirt roads until they reached a gate. After driving inside, Klansmen yanked Jones out of the car, and headlights shone in his face as they interrogated him.

Had he been with the NAACP? Been involved in civil rights? Tried to date a white girl?

Jones kept answering no.

Gilbert told Jones he had been sent from Alabama to kill him, not wanting the teen to know he was from Mississippi. "I didn't have no intention of killing him," Gilbert explained to me. "I fought in the war, but I ain't no murderer."

He shoved a gun in Jones's face, threatening to hurl him in the well. "You're fixing to die, and I want to know the truth."

"I did not call that girl. She called me."

When Killen demanded that Gilbert kill Jones, Gilbert said he refused. "You got a gun," he responded to Killen, "and you got me into a damn mess. I tell you what you do, you kill him."

Killen backed down.

The Klansmen drove Jones to his mother's house, where Gilbert told him, "You go in the house. You get your clothes. If you try to run, I'm going to go in, and I ain't gonna leave nobody alive."

Jones complied, and the Klansmen then dropped the teen at a bus station. Gilbert warned him that if he returned to Neshoba County, he would be killed. Killen dipped his hand into his pocket and pulled out a wad of bills. He handed seven dollars to Jones.

When Gilbert finished his story about what happened that night, he told me, "I certainly didn't believe in killing him because he was scared to death. That's why he's alive today."

. . .

When I returned to Jackson, I told Investigator Bill East about my trip to Louisiana. He slipped me the FBI files that revealed what happened before Jones was abducted.

On the evening of June 2, 1964, Gilbert spoke to fellow Klansmen at an abandoned school building—the same place Klansmen gathered two weeks later when they met to beat members of the Mount Zion Methodist Church and burn it down. Sheriff Lawrence Rainey "was in charge of the meeting, and he and Killen were in Klan regalia," the FBI memo read. "Numerous police officers were in attendance."

The purpose for the meeting? To "dispose of a subversive."

The Klansmen present discussed Jones's arrest and decided to form an action squad of Killen and four others, including Gilbert.

After the FBI began investigating the three men's disappearances, agents learned of Jones's abduction. They brought him back to Mississippi. He identified Klansmen involved in the crime and led agents to a remote farm with a deep well, where Klansmen threatened to hurl him to his death.

When I talked with him, former FBI inspector Joe Sullivan recalled going to the farm with Jones. "We could hear the rattlesnakes in the well."

He said that Jones's abduction gave the FBI insight into the disappearances of the three civil rights workers. He also said it was notable that the two cases shared the same modus operandi—jailing people, then releasing them at night into the hands of waiting Klansmen.

Those similarities made Gilbert a potential new witness in the case. A judge could permit him to testify about Killen's involvement in Jones's abduction, cementing proof that the Klan had carried out a similar scheme three weeks earlier.

62

Not long after interviewing one-time Klansman Ernest Gilbert, I stepped into the "War Room" of the Mississippi attorney general's office. FBI photographs in the Mississippi Burning case papered the walls. There were pictures of the burned-out station wagon, the dam, and civil rights workers James Chaney, Andy Goodman, and Mickey Schwerner. I saw a list of "potential defendants"—Edgar Ray Killen, Sam Bowers, Cecil Price, Billy Wayne Posey, Lawrence Rainey, Jimmy Arledge, Jimmie Snowden, Richard Andrew Willis, James "Pete" Harris, Olen Burrage, Herman Tucker, and Jerry McGrew Sharpe. Killen and Price had separate photographs and biographies.

Stacks of FBI documents from the Mississippi Burning case had been indexed. Investigator Bill East told me they had interviewed about one hundred people. The latest had been Gilbert, who shared with them all about his involvement with Killen in abducting Wilmer Faye Jones.

The next time I spoke with East, he told me the Neshoba County grand jury planned to meet in October 2000 and that Killen would be indicted.

I could hardly believe the news. After thirty-six years, the Mississippi Burning case would have the state's first indictment.

• • •

When October neared, I telephoned District Attorney Ken Turner to see if the grand jury was still slated to meet and consider a case against Edgar Ray Killen. He told me that was unlikely to happen unless something miraculous took place. The next grand jury wouldn't meet until April, but he said if there was a case to present before then, he would call a special grand jury.

This surprised and confused me. I telephoned East. He sounded miffed that the case hadn't been presented to the grand jury. When I pressed the investigator to explain what had happened, he wouldn't say anything further.

I reached out to Special Assistant Attorney General Lee Martin, who was overseeing the case. "We're making progress," he told me. "We're optimistic we'll be able to pursue charges."

He struck a much different tone than East, a sure thing reduced to a mere possibility. When I asked him about authorities' time frame, he shrugged. "As long as we're satisfied that we're making progress, why make a deadline on ourselves?"

I knew of plenty of reasons they needed to hurry. The longer they waited, the more suspects and witnesses could die. The other day, former Klansman turned FBI informant Ernest Gilbert had reeled off a long list of health woes he suffered from. This was indeed a race against time.

At first, the new year of 2001 brought good news. The attorney general's office found a witness who could implicate Sharpe, a Klansman who had reportedly been part of the mob that killed the three civil rights workers. Investigator Jim Gilliland telephoned me, looking for a photograph of Sharpe from back then. I pointed him to *Life* magazine, which featured pictures of all the suspects after their December 1964 arrests.

But bad news soon followed. Sharpe died, and so did Herman Tucker. The FBI had identified him as the bulldozer driver who buried the bodies; he was another Klansman whom the jury had acquitted in the 1967 federal trial.

April came and went, still with no grand jury for Killen. Then the worst news hit, on May 6, 2001. Former deputy Cecil Price died at the University of Mississippi Medical Center after fracturing his skull.

The sixty-three-year-old man had been working for Olen Burrage, who operated a trucking company and still owned the property where the trio's bodies were buried. Authorities said Price had been in a cherry picker when he fell about twenty feet, hitting his head on a trailer. Authorities described what happened as an accident, but that didn't stop rumors that foul play was involved.

Price had been cooperating with authorities, but they had been in no rush to bring the case to trial. Now their key witness was dead.

When I telephoned Attorney General Moore at home, it sounded like he had the air knocked out of him. "Unbelievable."

The next morning, he told me, "Even though this is a major setback, we're going to forge ahead with our investigation. Hopefully we have a couple of things that will pan out. If they do, we'll be in good shape."

He called Price's death "a tragic blow."

"Is this a death knell to the case?"

"We don't want it to be."

63

The only way I knew to keep the Mississippi Burning case alive was to keep writing about it. One mystery surrounding the case had never been solved: an intermediary known as "Mr. X" supposedly received $30,000 after telling the FBI where the bodies of James Chaney, Andy Goodman, and Mickey Schwerner were buried. But no one had ever found out who Mr. X was.

If he was still alive, he represented a potential new witness in the case. Even if he was dead, discovering his identity could bring additional attention to the case and perhaps put more pressure on authorities to press charges. I had long believed that working the edges of the case can sometimes lead back to the middle. I hoped that would be true if I could dredge up the identity of Mr. X.

According to the book *Attack on Terror*, the shadowy Mr. X had slipped into FBI inspector Joe Sullivan's motel room to talk on July 31, 1964, to reveal where the bodies were buried. I telephoned Sullivan and was surprised to find that he was helpful in giving me clues about Mr. X's identity, even if he was unwilling to give me his name.

He described Mr. X as "a person I encountered almost immediately on arriving down there. He stayed friendly."

When I brought up Olen Burrage, who owned the property where the trio were buried, he laughed. "I'm not going to let you screen out a person. I'm not going to tell. If it was Burrage, your guess isn't all that bad because it was on his property. I don't mind telling you it's not Burrage. We had to serve a search warrant on him."

He talked about the promise he made to Mr. X, to keep his identity hidden. "That's something I'm obliged to do. If I ever found another occasion, I'd like to have a reputation for integrity. I told him it was secure with me."

"Is Mr. X still alive?"

"I'm not going to go any further with you."

I ran down clues on different possibilities for Mr. X, but I kept striking out. I telephoned Sullivan again, and our conversations became a game. I pumped him for details, and he shared what he could, all the while keeping Mr. X's identity a secret.

He said he met Mr. X for the first time at the Neshoba County Courthouse, where about one hundred state police, local police, and "just plain volunteers" showed up to assist FBI agents in the search for the missing trio. That same day, June 23, 1964, the FBI discovered the civil rights workers' station wagon near Bogue Chitto Creek. The wagon had been torched, and agents found Mickey Schwerner's charred watch inside. There were no bodies, however.

That night, Sullivan spoke briefly to Mr. X. "It was a busy meeting."

By the next day, the mostly law enforcement crowd, minus Mr. X, showed up to assist Sullivan and the FBI. "Most of the people at the meeting showed up the next day and then they started to fall off. It was at that point that we knew we had to have some more people."

Sullivan explained that Mr. X had learned the location of the dam where the trio's bodies were buried from an unnamed Neshoba County citizen. I reread *We Are Not Afraid*, which discussed Sullivan's interaction with Mr. X. A former FBI agent told the authors Seth Cagin and Philip Dray that Mr. X was "an officer of the law in Neshoba County."

If true, that reduced the list considerably. Sullivan had already told me Mr. X wasn't one of the twenty-one suspects. That eliminated Neshoba

County sheriff Lawrence Rainey, Deputy Cecil Price, and Philadelphia police officer Richard Willis.

The only other law enforcement officers in Neshoba County that I knew were the Mississippi Highway Patrol officers stationed in that area, Earl Poe and Harry Wiggs. Wiggs, who was still alive, told me he didn't know anything about the now-deceased Poe being Mr. X. He said he certainly wasn't. He mentioned that their boss, Maynard King, who worked for the highway patrol in Meridian, lived in Neshoba County.

Sullivan described the Mississippi Highway Patrol as cordial but not that helpful. When I asked if Poe or any of the other highway patrolmen were Mr. X, Sullivan replied no. "They were not our answer to the problem."

When I brought up King, Sullivan confirmed that the highway patrol supervisor had shared a list of Klansmen with him but downplayed this deed, saying King never attended a Klan meeting. "He might have thought he knew Klansmen. He was not able to document it by confession or observation."

He called King "a good police officer, an up-front legitimate police officer. He was neighborly with all of Neshoba Countians. He was not a klucker."

Hundreds of navy sailors assisted agents in scouring the swamp and other areas. When that search failed to find the bodies, Sullivan turned to Mr. X. "I'd touch base with him, or he'd touch base with me. I'd give him questions, and if he had answers, we'd meet."

On several occasions, the two men met in a remote place. Sullivan said they even dared to talk on the street corner "somewhere where we weren't under observation by the Philadelphians."

Mr. X shared details about the KKK and which neighbors were friendly. Sullivan urged him to "probe where he thought he had the confidence of the people and he was not suspected of being an enemy spy by the denizens of Neshoba County."

Their friendship grew, and they met on July 30 at the Holiday Inn North in Meridian. "We were in the dining room, and we just had a friendly conversation. I'm sure he was ready to tell me more, and that was why he came." The two began dining about 6 p.m. "He was a steak man," Sullivan said.

During the dinner, Mr. X told Sullivan the men's bodies were buried on the Old Jolly Farm. The next day, Sullivan had an FBI agent meet with Mr. X "just to let him know what we were going to do so that he didn't have any surprises. That gave him a chance to know his meeting was becoming fruitful and that we were being conscientious about protecting him."

The retired inspector called Mr. X a "gutsy guy," instrumental in helping the FBI solve the murders. "He didn't think it was good for Mississippi."

I told Sullivan that reporter Bob Woodward had told me that he planned to reveal the name of his Watergate source, "Deep Throat," after he was dead.

Sullivan laughed, refusing to budge on Mr. X. "I told him the secret was secure with me."

Maynard King was the last candidate left on my list. I drove to Philadelphia, Mississippi, and met with his family. They asked me what I knew.

I laid out the clues: Mr. X had been a law enforcement officer in Neshoba County. Mr. X had met Sullivan on June 23, 1964—the same day Sullivan admitted he met King. And Sullivan had admitted that King shared a list of Klansmen with him. I also recalled Sullivan's story about first meeting King. Sullivan said: "He asked me if I wanted a drink and pulled out a bottle of moonshine."

When I told this story to King's family, his son, Joe, laughed. He said his father was close friends with Sullivan and that his dad called the FBI inspector "the smartest guy he ever met in his life."

I asked if his father liked steaks.

"He loved them."

In fact, he said his father grilled them outside the highway patrol office. His father knew almost everyone in Philadelphia and said he was "probably the most likely candidate" for telling Sullivan where the bodies were buried. "He had a knack for what to say and when to keep his mouth shut."

I asked the family if King could have gotten a $25,000 or $30,000 reward from the FBI. They shook their heads.

King's son suggested his father was a real lawman who never would have done it for the money. "Come hell or high water, he was going to do his job."

People pushed his father to run and replace Lawrence Rainey as Neshoba County sheriff, but on September 8, 1966, the fifty-five-year-old lawman suffered pain in one of his legs. After rushing to the hospital, doctors sent him home, where he suffered a fatal heart attack. His family received a letter from J. Edgar Hoover, saying he was sad to hear of the loss of such an outstanding officer as King.

The fact that the FBI director wrote a letter of sympathy made me confident of my hunch—that King was indeed Mr. X. The more I learned, the more it all made sense.

The day after Sullivan learned where the bodies were buried, FBI agents interviewed Sheriff Lawrence Rainey, Deputy Cecil Price, and other suspects, offering them rewards of $25,000 or more.

So why would FBI agents offer rewards when they already knew where the bodies were buried? That question spun in my mind all night.

By morning, I felt I had the answer. Offering a huge reward, just days before the bodies were found, could sow seeds of distrust. Klansmen would believe someone in their midst had blabbed for money.

The story got even stranger when I saw the FBI records, which detailed two agents delivering $30,000 in cash. Retired FBI agent Jay Cochran told me the $30,000 went to Sullivan, whom he presumed was giving it to King. My suspicion was that Sullivan used the cash to help pay for the excavation of the trio's bodies and kept the rest as a cash fund for agents to pay off KKK informants.

The whole thing sounded like a brilliant disinformation strategy, something a spy might cook up. And what was Joe Sullivan doing during World War II? Spying on the Nazis in Venezuela.

My pursuit of the Mr. X story led to an unexpected new witness in the case, Wallace Miller's widow, Nell. She recalled her husband meeting in the back bedroom with Killen after the June 21, 1964, disappearances of the three civil rights workers. Her statement corroborated her late husband's testimony that Killen had shared details of how the Klan had killed the men.

The Mississippi Burning case was now back in the news, a spotlight on the killings that had never really gone away.

On August 28, 2001, I telephoned Special Assistant Attorney General Lee Martin. He told me they were close to making a decision in the Mississippi Burning case. From the tone of his voice, it sounded like authorities had changed their minds and were now leaning against it. Martin seemed resigned, or optimistic only distantly. He mentioned a *20/20* program on the Mississippi Burning case that had just aired on ABC and said he hoped some people might come forward after seeing it.

I brought up the name of Bob Stringer, who had told me days earlier that he had never been interviewed by the attorney general's office. That had stunned me.

I knew authorities had been upset with him after Sam Bowers's 1998 conviction in the Vernon Dahmer case: they heard Stringer knew a man who might have information against another possible defendant, but Stringer had refused to give up the name. I didn't see why that would warrant ignoring Stringer, though, when he was ready to testify in a separate case.

When I asked about Stringer being a possible witness—right now, not in the distant future—Martin snapped at me: "He ain't hitting the stand. We're still waiting for his help on the other case." I understood Martin's anger, but thought he and other authorities were making a mistake in refusing to talk to Stringer.

Meanwhile, Stringer was starting to feel heat for coming forward. When I heard that the old wooden church, where Stringer and I had met, had been torched, I telephoned Stringer to tell him the news.

"It's kind of scary that it would burn," he said. "They might be sending a message."

He then shared that someone had broken into his business the night before, cutting phone and burglar alarm lines.

"Do you think it was a regular burglary, Bob?"

"I did till I heard this."

64

The next year, 2002, brought only more bad news. Retired FBI inspector Joe Sullivan died of prostate cancer on August 2 of that year. Sadness swept over me. I would miss my conversations with the agent that author Tom Clancy called "the greatest lawman America ever produced." As impressive as his investigative skills had been, I was more impressed with the way he had spent his retirement, serving the poor in a soup kitchen, where he had been thrown a surprise eighty-fifth birthday party.

Sullivan would have been a likely witness in the Mississippi Burning case. While other agents could testify in his place, no one else had his encyclopedic knowledge of the case or his gravitas.

On November 8, another former lawman died, this time former sheriff Lawrence Rainey. He had been suffering from throat and tongue cancer.

Defense lawyer Bill Kirksey, representing one of the few still-living Mississippi Burning suspects, told me that ever since the case was reopened in 1999, Killen began going to a different church every Sunday, standing outside, greeting people, and telling them he needed their help. "A Neshoba County jury will never convict Killen."

Authorities had missed their window in the Mississippi Burning case. They had failed, and so had I.

In November 2002, Attorney General Mike Moore told the Associated Press, "The chances of our bringing that prosecution are very, very slim, and I hate it. But at some point, you have to face reality."

Wondering if I was overlooking something, I reached out to former US attorney Doug Jones of Birmingham and Andy Sheldon, the jury consultant in many of these cases. I emailed them the full run-down of the potential testimony against Killen:

Weeks before the killings of Chaney, Goodman, and Schwerner, Bob Stringer said Imperial Wizard Sam Bowers had given Killen the order to carry out Schwerner's elimination. In an eerie parallel of the trio's abduction, Ernest Gilbert said he, Killen, and other Klansmen had abducted a black teen and that Killen wanted him dead. According to Delmar Dennis's testimony, Killen told Klansmen that Bowers had approved Schwerner's "elimination." One of the killing party, James Jordan, testified that Killen recruited him and other Klansmen to intercept the trio after they were released from jail. Days after the trio disappeared, Killen shared the details of the murder plot, including his own involvement, with Meridian police officer Wallace Miller.

After reading all this possible evidence, Jones said, "That's more than we had in the Bobby Cherry case to start with."

On January 3, 2003, Sheldon asked me to join him in meeting with Attorney General Mike Moore. In that session, Sheldon told Moore that Jones had authorized him to "tell you that we're willing to come over and spend the day looking at what you have, telling you what we think."

Moore thanked Sheldon, saying he didn't need the help because the problem was all the dead witnesses and suspects. "There's no one left we can bring a case against."

"Edgar Ray Killen is alive," I said.

"Everyone knows he was involved. It's just a matter of proving it."

Moore rattled off the names of all who had died, including Cecil Price. "I think you called me about his death, Jerry."

I nodded.

"I wanted to try this one myself," Moore said. He believed the case was too difficult to bring, and that Sheldon or anyone else examining it would be wasting their time.

I sympathized, but I also told him what happened in the Birmingham case. "Doug Jones didn't think they would be able to go forward with the Cherry case, and then a new prosecutor came in and helped them piece it all together."

Moore said that was well and good, but there was no proof against Killen.

"You have the transcript," I said.

"Yes, but you can't have a trial reading the transcript. This is not Jackson or Hattiesburg; this is Neshoba County. We've got to have a rock-solid case before we go forward."

By the end, Moore softened. "I don't want to seem so arrogant that we don't want the help."

Sheldon spoke up. "Perhaps I'm being arrogant in thinking that this case is like the other ones, which came together despite impossible odds."

Our push did not amount to enough, though. Weeks later, Moore told me he was leaving office for private practice so that he could afford to send his son to college. Sheldon emailed me: "Not much hope, I think, with the Philadelphia case."

65

The new year represented a possible new start for the Mississippi Burning case. It would usher in a new attorney general, Jim Hood, and a new district attorney, Mark Duncan. But would they mean new hope, or more of the same?

On February 9, 2004, I received a call from Chicago-area history teacher Barry Bradford, who was working with his students on the case. He mentioned that he had just had a positive conversation with Mississippi special assistant attorney general Jonathan Compretta, a new voice in the loop.

Ten days later I telephoned Compretta, hoping his influence could help jump-start the case. I showed him a list of eight potential witnesses, those still alive and those whose testimony was preserved by the transcript of the 1967 federal trial. I also shared that the feds and the state of Alabama had teamed up to prosecute the Birmingham church bombing, leading to two convictions.

He sounded intrigued. "It would be great if we could get this case done."

I told him the feds could help state authorities by reviewing their file.

If the feds concluded there wasn't enough to prosecute, they could all hold a joint press conference and share that conclusion.

"That's a great idea," he replied. "We need to resolve this case, one way or another."

Days after that conversation, an email arrived from Special Assistant Attorney General Lee Martin. He asked for a copy of the list of eight potential witnesses and their possible testimony—something I had published before in *The Clarion-Ledger.*

A week later, I heard from potential witness Bob Stringer that an investigator from the attorney general's office was going to interview him, finally. "I asked him if they're fixing to do something on it," Stringer told me. "He said they don't know."

But Stringer said he would probably meet with the investigator. "Tuesday or Wednesday of next week. I'll give you a call afterwards."

About a week later, I heard from Jerry Himelstein, regional director for the Anti-Defamation League in New Orleans. "You know about Bob?"

"No," I said, confused.

"Bob Stringer committed suicide Sunday night. He apparently had been gambling again very heavily and had gotten into a lot of financial trouble."

He said Stringer had killed himself with the .357 Magnum he kept tucked in the side panel of his truck.

"I tried calling him the other day," I said. "His wife answered and acted odd."

"Actually, she isn't Bob's wife. He never divorced his previous wife. He had hit all these check-cashing places, borrowing something like twenty thousand dollars."

I telephoned Investigator Jim Gilliland, who had interviewed Stringer a few days ago. "He said he and his son had jumped into the restaurant business, had bought one from the IRS for back taxes," he said. "He had lost weight and was looking good."

He said Stringer talked about the meeting where Bowers gave Edgar Ray Killen the orders to kill "Goatee." "We talked a good two hours. We just shot that shit about all that old stuff."

"Did you notice anything?"

"He seemed fine and even asked me to drop by and visit on my next Harley trip to the Gulf Coast. It shocked me because he seemed to be okay."

Cecil Price's suspicious death, followed by a suicide.

This case wasn't good for the health.

The photographs of James Chaney, Andy Goodman, and Mickey Schwerner on the old FBI reward poster haunted me. I had put a digital photo of that poster on my computer desktop as a reminder to never forget them.

For years I had prayed for justice, but now—after so many setbacks—I had begun to wonder if it would ever come. The other day, I had stumbled across the verse, "I am the Lord, the God of all mankind. Is anything too hard for me?"

I hopped in my Honda and headed to Meridian, where I found a road that snaked past the Okatibee Baptist Church Cemetery. When I opened my car door, the winter blast cut through me. As I stepped up the hill I spotted his name, "James Earl Chaney."

Vandals had knocked his headstone over so many times that huge metal supports now protected it. I knelt, brushed away the leaves, and read the inscription: "There are those who are alive, yet will never live. There are those who are dead, yet will live forever. Great deeds inspire and encourage the living."

Before I left, I prayed for justice.

66

When FBI agents first showed up on the streets of Philadelphia in the summer of 1964, white citizens circled the wagons and refused to talk. Many black citizens knew what would happen if they did talk.

Two years later, Martin Luther King Jr. faced such a raw reaction when he and other civil rights activists arrived downtown that he called the town "the worst" he had ever seen, saying, "There is a complete reign of terror here."

And when the case finally did fade from the headlines, this small town stayed silent. In 1989, local officials welcomed the families of the slain civil rights workers, and native son Dick Molpus expressed his community's regret and sorrow for what had taken place. But those I spoke to in Philadelphia, then, were less than eager to discuss the case. A few told me they didn't want to talk about that "unpleasantness," as if gunning down three people carried the same social weight as being shunned by the bridge club.

By the 2000s, local sentiment had shifted. What was once unspeakable now became a topic of conversations, the community realizing that what had happened decades ago would never fade away. "Come hell or high water, it's time for an accounting," Editor Stanley Dearman wrote in an editorial in the *Neshoba Democrat*.

When local leaders gathered for a retreat at Lake Tiak-O'Khata in 2004, discussions centered on how to revive their sleepy town of 7,000. One talked about planting roses downtown. Another suggested creative ways to revive the economy. When Molpus arose to speak, he told them, "This place is dead, dead, dead."

He said Americans thought of Philadelphia as an inhospitable place because of the murders of these three young men. "There's no way we can get around this stain—unless it can be lifted."

When that stain is lifted, the town can be lifted, he said. The crowd stood and applauded.

In the wake of that speech, the University of Mississippi's William Winter Institute of Racial Reconciliation held a series of sessions where local citizens—white, black, and Native American—met together. They shared their hopes, their fears, their dreams, and their experiences in hopes of understanding one another better.

On May 26, 2004, this Philadelphia Coalition called for authorities to prosecute the Mississippi Burning case. "We state candidly and with deep regret that some of our own citizens, including local and state law enforcement officers, were involved in the planning and execution of these murders," the coalition declared at a press conference. "Now, forty years after the fact, the right of all citizens to vote, here and throughout the South, is commonplace and universally accepted, a far cry from the old days. But once upon a time, three young men died because they believed in this right for all citizens."

Two days later, Mississippi Attorney General Jim Hood told me his office had shared its files with US Attorney Dunn Lampton and Assistant US Attorney Jack Lacy to review. Now, this was good news.

When I reached Lacy, he bubbled with enthusiasm about getting to help with the Mississippi Burning case. He said one of the main complaints of Lee Martin, the prosecutor leading the attorney general's charge, was the lack of a live witness.

I told Lacy there was indeed someone that authorities could call to testify. His name was Mike Hatcher, a former Klansman who testified in the 1967 federal trial that Edgar Ray Killen had shared an implicating statement a day after the three civil rights workers disappeared. Hatcher had refused to talk with me, but I knew Lacy would have a much better shot of succeeding.

This revelation stunned Lacy. "Holy shit. A live witness!"

On the fortieth anniversary of the deaths of James Chaney, Andy Goodman, and Mickey Schwerner, more than 1,800 people gathered in Neshoba County, Mississippi, to honor their lives. The Philadelphia City Council, the Neshoba County Board of Supervisors, and the Community Development Partnership all passed resolutions calling for justice in the murders.

As I gazed at the crowd, I wondered what Edgar Ray Killen would think. The town that had once protected these killers now wanted to see them prosecuted.

I marveled at what was unfolding on the dais. Mississippi governor Haley Barbour, who had once headed the Republican National Committee, was talking to Congressman John Lewis, the legendary figure from the civil rights movement.

When Barbour rose to speak, he talked of terrorists hitting our homeland long before the 9/11 attack, comparing them to those trying to steal America's freedom today. "History has taught us that sin and evil must be punished."

Lewis had been willing to stand up against that evil. He had been beaten as a Freedom Rider and in the march across the Edmund Pettus Bridge in Selma. He talked of the killings of his brothers, Chaney, Goodman, and Schwerner. "Some of us gave time, some of us a little blood. These three citizens of the world gave all they had."

Molpus praised them as "American patriots"—words that resonated in this close-knit community, which had sent more soldiers to war per capita than many places in America. For forty years, he said, "our state judicial system has allowed murderers to roam our land. Night riders, church burners, beaters, and killers deserve no protection from sure justice."

He appealed to his hometown's soul, calling on people to share what they knew before it was too late. "Until justice is done, we are all at least complicit in those deaths. Now is the time to liberate those dark secrets."

A service followed at the Mount Zion United Methodist Church, honoring the families of the slain civil rights workers. Dave Dennis reminisced about his fiery eulogy at Chaney's funeral, where he talked about the "living dead that we have right among our midst," voicing his belief that these killers would never be punished. Now, forty years later, he said he hoped that "something will be done."

As the last rays of light slanted across the church's steeple, Goodman's mother, Carolyn, and other families placed wreaths on a memorial to her son and the two others slain. After the service, she whispered to me, "It's never too late for justice."

67

In the wake of the fortieth ceremony, momentum began to build again, thanks to two catalysts. What initially seemed innocuous would breathe life back into the case.

The first came on September 14, 2004, when Carolyn Goodman returned to Mississippi. The death of her son, Andy, had been one of a string of tragedies in her life, including childhood molestation, a teenage abortion, her father's suicide, and two husbands' deaths. She could have been angry or bitter. Instead she poured her life into helping others. She became a clinical psychologist, treating troubled single mothers and others in New York City.

The Philadelphia Coalition had invited her that September for a conversation over a potluck dinner. Her son David accompanied her.

There was another guest as well, Mississippi attorney general Jim Hood, the son of a prosecutor in north Mississippi. In 1976, his first cousin had been murdered, shot in the back, but a jury only convicted the killer of manslaughter. Hood ditched his plans to become a doctor, becoming a prosecutor instead.

Over dinner, Goodman told Hood about her son Andy. He had wanted to join Mississippi's Freedom Summer, and as a mother, she didn't want him to go. But she knew that if she didn't let him, it would go against all that she had stood for.

After his killing, the family buried him in Mount Judah Cemetery in Queens. She quoted from the words on his sculpted headstone, where hands reached toward each other. "He traveled a short while toward the sun and left the vivid air signed with his honor."

She talked of Mississippi, the place where her son took his last breath. "This is an important place for me to be. This is where my heart is."

Some wiped away tears.

"My son didn't die here. He's always been here, and he's always in your heart and always will be. All of you are a part of my heart."

David Goodman handed Hood a compilation of the telegrams that President Lyndon Johnson had sent their family, along with eulogies from the funeral. He told the attorney general, "Sometimes you try a case, even if you think you're going to lose, because it's important. This country, Mississippi, and Neshoba County want to see something done."

Hood clutched the telegrams, tears welling in his eyes. He said he hoped to make a decision by the end of October on whether to move forward with the case. He planned to consult with federal authorities and District Attorney Mark Duncan.

In the parking lot, Special Assistant Attorney General Lee Martin told me, "This is a matter of the head, not the heart. If this were a matter of the heart, we would have prosecuted this a long time ago." But Carolyn Goodman's words would leave a mark on the attorney general.

68

The second catalyst for prosecution came in an even less likely way. One day, I was thumbing through a publication put out by white supremacist Richard Barrett. Amid his racist cartoons and photographs of shirtless skinheads, there was his interview with Edgar Ray Killen. Barrett played the part of a commiserating character as he brought up the 1967 federal conspiracy trial. "You were put on trial, once, over trying to keep communists out of Mississippi."

Killen strolled down memory lane, recalling the Justice Department lawyer who headed the prosecution team. "Old John Doar kept staring at me, like he was trying to look right through me. I stared right back at him and sent him a signal that made him mad. He was really mad when he could not convict me."

Killen recalled the racist question he had his attorney ask. "During the trial, I wrote a note for my lawyer, Laurel Weir, to bring up about the plan by Negroes to rape white women that summer. He did, and the judge rebuked him for it, but the point got made."

Barrett asked if there was any chance he would change his beliefs "and turn against your own people, the way George Wallace did?"

"No, I sure will never do that. People come up to me, all the time, and hug my neck."

In his publication, Barrett identified photographs of James Chaney, Andy Goodman, and Mickey Schwerner as "Communists who invaded Mississippi in 1964." The white supremacist also put a diagonal slash through their images, forming the universal "no" symbol.

I telephoned Barrett, who defended the symbol and told me he was going to have a booth at the Mississippi State Fair to honor the preacher. "I talked with Killen, and he's willing to make an appearance on Saturday after the opening of the fair. Might even do it twice, he said. We kind of joked about it."

He suggested that while Killen was there, he could sign autographs and shake hands with the crowd. "He's got a lot of support. He's not taking it laying down."

After my interview ended, I discussed the matter with my editor, Debbie Skipper. *The Clarion-Ledger* generally ignored Barrett's racist pronouncements, but our boss, Executive Editor Ronnie Agnew, agreed this would be an important exception to cover Barrett's plan to honor the KKK leader at the state fair. If this was the cost when Mississippi officials refused to pursue charges, they should know it.

My story began:

> Visitors to next month's Mississippi State Fair may gawk at their reflections in the Fun House, witness the Mississippi State Championship Mule Pull or shake hands with the key suspect in the Klan's 1964 killings of three civil rights workers.

The story drew outrage. Protesters flooded the streets of Jackson. Their signs read, "Stop Racism," "Mississippi Is Still Burning" and, most succinctly, "Why?" Derrick Johnson, holding the same job Medgar Evers did as field secretary for the Mississippi NAACP, declared, "This needs to lead to an indictment." Within days, the protesters swelled to five hundred. They sang "Keep Your Eyes on the Prize" and yelled for prosecution.

When the furor reached a fever pitch, Killen's wife announced he was staying away from the state fair, and Barrett canceled his plans for the booth.

By this time, thousands had signed Hinds County sheriff Malcolm McMillin's counter-petition, calling for Killen's prosecution. After Barrett's cancellation, the sheriff called me: "We fixed his ass, didn't we? Son of a bitch, I got tired of it. This asshole doesn't speak for anybody."

If Killen ever does get indicted, the sheriff said, "I think he'll owe Mr. Barrett a debt of gratitude."

As the end of October crept closer, I telephoned Special Assistant Attorney General Lee Martin. I told him I was touching base because Attorney General Jim Hood had said he would make a decision by the end of the month.

"Damn boss," he replied. He told me he didn't have a problem with the timetable, just the fact that Hood had told me. These days, the case consumed 95 percent of Martin's time.

He told me Hood wanted a Neshoba County grand jury to decide on the case, one way or the other, and that they were weighing the evidence and the legal hurdles. "My concern is less legal and more practical. How convincing for a jury is a dead witness?"

I pointed out that Byron De La Beckwith had been convicted, in part, by the testimony of such dead witnesses, but Martin sounded far from convinced.

The October deadline passed with no grand jury. Weeks passed and then months. Nothing.

I pressed the sources I knew, but they were as clueless as me. Were authorities going to close the case, just as they had done each time it seemed the case might lurch forward?

69

On the evening of January 5, 2005, a longtime source telephoned, saying he had information about Edgar Ray Killen. I stepped outside into the darkness to meet him. When I heard a honk, I saw the outline of his car across from the Hinds County Courthouse.

When I opened the passenger's door, the dome light stayed off.

In the red glow from the traffic light, I could see his hands trembling. "I could get in trouble for talking with you."

I stayed silent, not sure what to say.

"The grand jury is going to meet in the morning in Neshoba County to consider charges. Jim Hood is supposed to be there before the grand jury gets started. You can get your story then."

That night, I wrote the story about the Neshoba County grand jury meeting on the Mississippi Burning case, asking *The Clarion-Ledger* editors to hold the story until I gave the okay. The next morning, I walked inside the Neshoba County Courthouse and spotted Attorney General Jim Hood.

His presence confirmed the story, and I walked outside and dialed my editors, who posted my story online. Then I telephoned the three civil rights workers' families to let them know what was happening and to get any comments they wanted to share.

Inside the courthouse, I watched the arrivals of suspects. There were Billy Wayne Posey, Jimmy Arledge, and Jimmie Snowden, who had each gone to federal prison for a few years for being a part of the mob that abducted and killed the three civil rights workers. There was Olen Burrage, who was quoted in FBI files as saying, "Hell, I have a dam that will hold a hundred of them." There was Pete Harris, the KKK investigator who had reportedly recruited Klansmen for that night's work. Burrage and Harris had both dodged prison.

On the second floor, the suspects appeared one by one in front of the Neshoba County grand jury. The most noticeably missing suspect? Edgar Ray Killen. This made it obvious that authorities had made him their key target because the Mississippi Supreme Court ruled some years back that appearing before a state grand jury gives that person immunity from prosecution.

Inside the grand jury room, prosecutors warned suspects to tell the truth or face possible indictment. It was a bold bluff that failed as suspects refused to talk or blamed poor memories. Burrage insisted he knew nothing about a bulldozer burying the trio's bodies that night on his property—a story that grand jurors found hard to swallow.

Afterward, the old men made their way down the stairs, complaining the whole time. Posey mouthed, "After forty years to come back and do something like this is ridiculous." And Arledge's attorney proclaimed, "This is a sad day for Mississippi. This is going to open up old wounds."

Upstairs in the grand jury room, prosecutors shared all the evidence they had against the suspects, much of it from the federal transcript. Statements from Cecil Price, Bob Stringer, and Ernest Gilbert were inadmissible as trial evidence because all of them had since died.

Prosecutors explained Mississippi's murder statute. Under the law, all those involved in scheming, planning, or carrying out a killing, even if they are not present, can be prosecuted for murder. For example, if a getaway driver drops off a bank robber and that bank robber kills someone, the driver can also be charged with murder.

After grand jurors deliberated, all but one of the eighteen voted to indict Killen. Only a dozen votes had been needed.

The grand jury indicted no one else. Posey dodged a murder charge by one vote, his distant cousin among those refusing to indict him.

As for the other suspects, some grand jurors felt more evidence was needed. Some felt the suspects who went to federal prison had already done their time. Some felt the only target that prosecutors cared about was Killen.

As the grand jurors made their way down the stairs, the smiles on their faces telegraphed that there had been an indictment.

Authorities arrested Killen that same day, and he spent the night in the Neshoba County Jail.

Stanley Dearman, the veteran journalist who had called for justice for so many years, cheered the news. "It feels like a weight has been lifted off the community. Some local people say, 'Why do they keep bringing this up? It's just bad for the county.' The damage we've done to the county is not because of the media or the people who wanted justice, but the people who conceived, engineered, and carried out this crime. They're the ones who deserve the credit for the notoriety."

The next morning, more than twenty reporters from across the country descended on the Neshoba County Courthouse. Several national reporters marveled at seeing charges brought in the Mississippi Burning case, including longtime journalist Paul Hendrickson. "Mississippi has brought its first-ever murder charges in a long-ago crime against three young men whose names are still mythical in America: Schwerner, Goodman, Chaney. It is a very late start, but it is a start all the same, a cause for uplift, it seems to me, for singing," he wrote in an op-ed for *The New York Times*. "What I have come to learn about Mississippi is that everything there is always changing. And in another way, nothing there ever changes at all."

Edgar Ray Killen entered the courtroom in an orange jumpsuit. When the judge asked the seventy-nine-year-old a few questions, he mumbled his answers. When the judge asked him for his plea to the three counts of murder in the deaths of James Chaney, Andrew Goodman, and Michael

Schwerner, Killen raised his voice, "Not guilty . . . Not guilty . . . Not guilty."

The judge ordered Killen held without bond and concluded that the preacher possessed enough assets to hire his own lawyer.

Before the arraignment ended, word came of a bomb threat. As we exited the courthouse, Killen's sixty-three-year-old brother, J.D., slugged a television cameraman and barked, "Get all of your shots now. We're going to make sure you're not around for his funeral. My brother's innocent."

70

Letters, emails, and telephone calls came in from as far away as China, some thoughtful and some angry. "Why don't you let this damn thing die?" one white Mississippian asked me. Another suggested in a letter to the editor that I should be "tarred and feathered and run out" of the state of Mississippi. White supremacists came to the fore, with one group of Klansmen requesting permission to demonstrate outside the courthouse in support of Edgar Ray Killen.

Journalist David Halberstam saw the prosecution as a reckoning. "What cruelty there is to murder American kids, to murder them on American soil just because they want to register people to vote. That's about as un-American as you can get. There's something about a nation that allows that to happen. A nation that allows that to happen is not a decent nation."

Killen hired Mitch Moran to represent him. The forty-three-year-old lawyer from the nearby town of Carthage told me, "When I saw an eighty-year-old man without his false teeth and his glasses at six thirty in the morning, laying on that concrete floor of the jail cell, I knew it wasn't right. A lot of people will say, 'Well, if he'd been convicted forty years ago, he'd still be there.' That's true, but forty years ago, he could have defended himself."

The judge freed Killen on $250,000 bond, and Moran howled that the justice system was meant to take the dangerous off the street. "This case is not going to serve any of that. Whether he did it or not, we need to put it in God's hands because that's going to happen soon enough."

Moran grew up in San Diego, where his father worked for NASA. He preferred working the land, but when hard times hit in the 1990s, he changed careers. Mississippi College School of Law looked attractive because it wasn't far from his deer hunting camp.

These days, he often represented minorities, many of them on drug charges. He, too, had been arrested on a drug charge—a charge he told me was bogus. "In this case, Killen is a minority. He's being singled out."

When it comes to racial matters, "everybody's prejudiced. If you're not, there's something wrong with you. I am a white Anglo-Saxon, half German-Irish. Proud of it. Don't want to be anything else."

He said politics kept Mississippi from prosecuting Killen before. "So now, forty years later, politics again: 'Hey, we can prosecute him at our advantage and get votes, make a name for ourselves, popularity, whatever.' Our justice system and the political arena are too close together."

Most defense lawyers barred their clients from talking to the press. Not Moran. So far Killen had done at least four TV interviews, and he believed they had helped humanize his client, hoping to counter the prosecution view he felt was filling the newspapers and television.

The lawyer shared his strategy for the trial, saying he would show that Sheriff Lawrence Rainey and Deputy Cecil Price had been the ones calling the shots, not his client. "They were mean motherfuckers—crooked, dirty cops. They're not going to take orders from my dumb-ass, I mean, my client."

He sought to portray his client as a coward. "Killen is not the type of person that can look you in the eye and shoot you. He's the pussy of the group. He's the guy in back of the pickup truck who says, 'Go get 'em, boys.'"

Driving home from *The Clarion-Ledger* on the evening of March 10, my pager buzzed. It was the office number of my boss, Debbie Skipper, followed by "911"—in other words, an emergency.

When I called back, she told me, "Edgar Ray Killen broke both of his legs."

"What?"

"I need for you to do a story."

I telephoned Mitch Moran, who said a tree had hit his client over the head. He said if the preacher's femur was broken, "he probably won't live."

The next day, I learned Killen hadn't broken one femur; he'd broken *both*. But the good news was that he would live. When I talked to Moran, he said doctors were inserting pins in both of his legs at the University of Mississippi Medical Center. "The surgery is expected to last four hours. They're just now starting on the second leg."

He explained that Killen had been cutting timber with his brother near Sebastopol, Mississippi. A tree he had cut fell onto a second one, and as he cut the supporting tree, the top tree fell, driving him into the ground. "He must be a hard-headed son of a bitch. He broke both of his legs standing."

The marshy soil had saved him, giving way when his legs hit, Moran said. "We are going to have a trial with twenty-three dead witnesses. The question is, will we also have a dead defendant?"

71

Edgar Ray Killen survived, mostly recovering from his wood-chopping incident, except now he was in a wheelchair. His lawyers tried to get his murder charges thrown out, tried to claim he was incompetent, and tried to postpone his murder trial. The judge rejected the defense's arguments, and the trial began June 13, 2005.

More than two hundred reporters, some from as far away as Sweden, swarmed the Neshoba County Courthouse, curious how the final chapter of the saga would end. CourtTV broadcast the trial live. Would the Klan leader who apparently orchestrated this event dodge conviction again? Or would a Neshoba County jury finally convict him?

Edgar Ray Killen arrived the morning of June 13 in a white Mercury Grand Marquis. When he emerged in his wheelchair, one white man yelled out his support, and J. J. Harper, imperial wizard of the American White Knights of the KKK in Georgia, greeted Killen with the offer of a favor, "Anything I can do." (The KKK leader had already made his views clear on his website: "Brother Killen is being charged with murdering a nigger and two Jews back in 1964. Personally, I'd ask, 'What's wrong with that?'")

As jury selection began, the large number of potential jurors were led to cramped quarters inside the courtroom. James Chaney's brother, Ben, sat behind the Klansmen gathered. Killen's family sat in front of Mickey Schwerner's widow, Rita Bender, and her husband, Bill.

Killen, who fancied himself as a jury investigator, sat at the defense table, taking meticulous notes. He didn't like what he saw. Black residents made up a third of potential jurors. If he had been tried for murder four decades earlier, his jury would undoubtedly have been all white and all male.

The six-foot-three, white-haired veteran judge Marcus Gordon commanded the courtroom with his calm, authoritative presence. Back when he was district attorney in 1974, he had successfully prosecuted Killen for threatening a woman. But their history was more complicated than that. Killen had presided over the funerals of both Gordon's parents. More recently, and more disturbingly, Killen's brother, J.D., had reportedly made threats against the judge. Gordon turned down the offer of a bodyguard, saying, "I've always been a two-fisted kind of guy. And if I take on a bodyguard, in a way, I'm saying that I'm no longer capable of taking care of myself."

The judge asked the pool of more than one hundred potential jurors if any had opinions so strong on the case that it would take evidence to remove them. Eleven potential jurors said yes, and he dismissed them.

When he asked the potential jurors if any were related to Killen, three raised their hands. The judge dismissed them. When he asked if any were related to the victims, no hands went up. District Attorney Mark Duncan stood up from the prosecution table, where he had been sitting with Attorney General Jim Hood and his assistant, Lee Martin. Despite the whirlwind of press attention, Duncan remained plainspoken and humble, telling reporters, "I'm anxious to get done with this and go back to being a small-town DA nobody ever heard of."

The middle-aged prosecutor, who had a reputation for being more talented on the golf course than he was in the courtroom, stepped toward potential jurors. He said he had heard some people justify the killings of the three young men, saying they were outsiders who "came down here looking for trouble."

He moved closer. "Tell me you'll treat them like they were from here and were our neighbors."

They agreed.

In contrast, defense lawyers extracted promises from those in the jury pool that they would presume that Killen was innocent and that they would treat him no differently than anyone else on trial.

For two days, lawyers individually questioned potential jurors. Prosecutors tried to pry out prejudice, using answers they had given in jury questionnaires. The defense did its best to rehabilitate those that prosecutors questioned. After both sides executed their strikes, a jury made up of nine white members and three black members emerged. They included two teachers, a librarian, a bus driver, an auto plant worker, a chicken plant worker, a registered nurse, and an engineer. Almost half of them had been born after the killings took place.

Jurors included some who questioned the politics of bringing the case, some who worried it might make Neshoba County look bad, and some who wondered why the trial didn't take place forty years ago. When Killen emerged from the jury selection, he flashed an "okay" sign to his family. Defense lawyer James McIntyre, who was assisting Moran, crowed victory. "It's going to be a hung jury. Mark my word," he said. McIntyre had helped Sheriff Lawrence Rainey win an acquittal in 1967, and he believed Killen would walk free, too.

On June 15, 2005, the dozen jurors and five alternates took their seats in the courtroom. Judge Gordon addressed them. He urged them to give both Killen and the state a fair trial, letting "the chips fall where they may." In the end, he explained that "what we are doing and what we have done will be recorded in the history of Neshoba County."

In his opening arguments, Attorney General Jim Hood spoke about that history. While many white Mississippians in the summer of 1964 viewed the incoming civil rights workers as "invaders" or even "communists," Hood talked about how these young people were pursuing the noble tasks of registering voters, educating children, and improving nutrition.

He detailed the evidence against Killen, identifying the preacher as a White Knights organizer known as a Kleagle, who helped start the KKK in Meridian and swore in many Klansmen. Killen, he said, had led a Klan meeting where it was announced that Imperial Wizard Sam Bowers gave the orders to kill Mickey Schwerner. Hinting that prosecutors would use the federal trial transcript, he said some witnesses would "speak from the grave."

Rather than argue Killen's involvement, the defense fingered Neshoba County's sheriff Lawrence Rainey as the real organizer of the killings. To prove that point, Moran read from the FBI statement by Horace Doyle Barnette, who said the sheriff warned Klansmen that he would kill anyone who talked, "even if it was my brother."

Moran said Killen may have passed Imperial Wizard Sam Bowers's message to fellow Klansmen about the need to "eliminate" Schwerner and later told them that the jailed civil rights workers needed their "butts torn up," but that didn't make him guilty. Moran said law enforcement carried out the killings, and "Edgar Ray Killen was just a bystander in an organization a lot of other people were in. The Klan is not on trial in this case."

72

The next morning, Rita Bender stepped forward. Four decades before, she had come to Neshoba County, hoping to find out the truth about what happened to her then husband, Mickey. Now she had returned, hoping to find justice.

She looked out across the courtroom, where families and friends of the three slain civil rights workers filled the front rows, including James Chaney's only child, Angela Lewis, born just days before Klansmen executed her father. Bettie Dahmer, daughter of slain NAACP leader Vernon Dahmer, showed her support. So did members of the Philadelphia Coalition.

I glanced at the defense table, noticing Edgar Ray Killen was missing. No one mentioned why, but it seemed odd that he wouldn't be present.

District Attorney Mark Duncan asked Bender about Mickey Schwerner. She brightened. The two married in June 1962. He was twenty-two, and she was twenty. "We came to Mississippi to work in the civil rights movement."

They arrived in January 1964 and began "working on voter registration," she said. "There were very few African-American voters in the state of Mississippi at the time."

They also started a community center in Meridian, where young people could play Ping-Pong, read books, and talk, she said. "It was a safe place to be."

Roscoe Jones, who sat in the audience, was among those young people who spent time at the center. Mickey Schwerner trained him in nonviolent protests, and police arrested him and other teens after they sat at a "white" lunch counter.

Bender said their work was far from popular in the community, and she spoke of the constant threats they received. "There were calls in which they used vile language, or calls saying that my husband was dead, or I better watch out because he was going to be killed."

In June 1964, the couple trained for Freedom Summer along with James "J.E." Chaney in Oxford, Ohio. While there, they heard about the burning of Mount Zion Methodist Church, which they had visited in Mississippi. Members had voted to start a Freedom School, which went on to inspire the Head Start program.

Her voice broke with emotion as she spoke about learning the news that the church had been burned down and members beaten. She said Mickey and J.E. decided to return to Mississippi and talk to the church members. They "both felt they had a responsibility to the people who put themselves at risk. You don't abandon people you put at risk."

At about three or four in the morning of June 20, "Mickey got up, got dressed, kissed me good-bye, and left."

Tears welled in her eyes. "That's the very last time I saw him."

He left in the station wagon with Chaney, a Freedom Summer volunteer named Andy Goodman, and others. She stayed in Oxford, Ohio, to train more volunteers.

The next day, her husband drove with Chaney and Goodman to investigate the fire at the church. After midnight, the call came from a fellow civil rights worker that the three men had never reported back from their trip to Neshoba County.

Two days later, while waiting at the Cincinnati airport, she saw Fannie Lou Hamer, who would capture national attention later that year when she challenged the all-white Mississippi delegation at the Democratic National

Convention. As the two women began to speak to each other, reporters interrupted, telling them that the FBI had found the burned-out station wagon.

Bender told the jury, "It really hit me for the first time that they were dead. There was really no realistic possibility that they were still alive."

Hamer wrapped her huge arms around her. "The two of us had our faces together," she recalled, choking up at the memory. "Our tears were mingling with each other."

Moisture streaked the face of a female juror, and some in the crowd wiped away tears.

In many murder trials, defense lawyers avoid questioning family members, realizing their words might backfire. James McIntyre, however, couldn't resist.

The red-faced Texas native, who had written some of Governor Ross Barnett's major speeches, had called Killen's prosecution a "persecution." Now the lawyer complained about Bender's testimony. "I've been sitting over there for some 45 minutes. . . ."

I found his complaint ironic. Bender had been waiting for forty-something years.

He chided her interest in "civil rights," hoping to connect with some-one on the jury who might bristle at the phrase. Then he asked, "Do you know Mr. Edgar Ray Killen?"

"No, I don't."

"Have you ever met and talked with him?"

"The first time I saw him in person was in this courtroom a few days ago."

McIntyre pressed her. "You have no personal knowledge whatsoever in this case, do you?"

"I have a lot of personal knowledge in this case," she shot back.

"Of his involvement in the case?"

"I don't have any knowledge, one way or the other."

"Could you tell me then why the state of Mississippi called you to testify?"

Before she could answer, prosecutors objected, and the judge agreed.

McIntyre sat down, a smug smile filling his face. His grandstanding move might have worked decades ago when segregation was the law in Mississippi. Instead, his ploy to spin this place back in time made her seem more sympathetic to the jury.

When the court recessed, I learned why Killen was missing. Earlier that morning, he had complained about shortness of breath, and emergency medical technicians had discovered his systolic blood pressure had shot past 200. Moran told me his client had been taking blood pressure medicine, which made the high number more frightening. Ambulance workers sped Killen to the hospital, and Judge Gordon ended the trial for the day.

73

The next morning, a nurse sat near Edgar Ray Killen in the courtroom. The trial somehow lurched forward. Prosecutors spent much of the second day of testimony trying to implicate Killen through a series of witnesses, both dead and living. Authorities had long worried how jurors might react to a case that relied on the testimony of dead witnesses. In the Byron De La Beckwith trial, prosecutors did such an impressive job of casting people to play the dead witnesses that Myrlie Evers declared that one of them deserved an Oscar.

But in Killen's trial, prosecutors took few steps to make the witnesses come alive, playing many of the parts themselves. Adding to the problem was that those portraying the witnesses spent much of their time flipping pages because prosecutors used only portions of the federal court testimony and hadn't created a script for themselves and the witnesses to use.

That testimony included Ernest Kirkland, who met the three civil rights workers at the burned-down church at about 1 p.m.; Mississippi Highway Patrolman Earl Poe, who helped transport them to the Philadelphia jail that afternoon; and Minnie Lee Herring, the jailer's wife, who recalled them being in jail from about 4 p.m. until 10:30 p.m., when

Deputy Cecil Price released them with the line, "See how quick you all can get out of Neshoba County."

But more critical to the case was the testimony of the late Meridian policeman Wallace Miller, who grew up with Killen and was distantly related. In early 1964, he said, Killen approached him about a "strong organization and asked me if I was interested in joining to help keep the colored people from integrating our schools, and I told him I was definitely interested." That night, he said Killen came to his home and swore him into the White Knights of the KKK, telling him it was "a very patriotic, political organization and it was a Christian organization and . . . that better men and better businessmen and better citizens, officers, doctors, lawyers, and peace officers belonged to it."

In May 1964, the White Knights gathered for a meeting, and some members "wanted to go whip Schwerner," Miller said. "Mr. Killen told us to leave him alone, that another unit was going to take care of him, that his elimination had been approved."

"Did he say by whom it had been approved?" the prosecutor asked.

"By the imperial wizard."

Just after the three civil rights workers disappeared (before they were publicly known to be dead), Miller said Killen came to his home and shared all the details of how the KKK had killed them. Fellow Klansmen had burned the Mount Zion Church to lure Schwerner and the civil rights workers there. Deputy Cecil Price had jailed the three men and then released them the night of June 21, 1964. Miller said, "Mr. Killen told me that they had been shot, that they were dead, and that they were buried in a dam about fifteen feet deep."

Miller acknowledged that the FBI paid him $2,400 over a two-year period. That money, he said, reimbursed him for travel and expenses, posing as a Klansman while he was working as an informant for the FBI. In December 1964, the White Knights, suspecting he was sharing information, banished him.

Under cross-examination, the defense lawyer had asked Miller about his KKK oath. "There was nothing in that oath swearing you to commit any act of intimidation, violence of any nature, isn't that correct?"

"There was nothing committing us to do that at all."

In addition to reviewing Miller's past testimony, prosecutors called his widow, Nell Miller, to the witness stand. She testified that her husband grew up with Killen, that the preacher performed their wedding ceremony, and that he had visited their home on three occasions. "He always thought Wallace made a good glass of iced tea."

When the two men talked, "they usually sat in the kitchen," she said, "but on one occasion, they sat in the back bedroom."

Attorney General Jim Hood tried to pin her down on a year, rather than ask her if this happened after the three civil rights workers disappeared. But she struggled to come up with a year.

Regaining her footing, she had no trouble recalling the horror her family went through after her husband testified in the 1967 federal trial. The Klan burned their grocery store to the ground, and she said death threats came against him and their family. "They threatened my children."

She finished her brief testimony, but the lack of clarity on dates meant the points that prosecutors had hoped to make became lost in the mists of time.

After her testimony, former FBI agent Dean Lytle described finding the burned-out Ford Fairlane in the Bogue Chitto Creek swamp on June 23, 1964. He identified his photographs, showing the blaze was so hot, it consumed the seats. "All that was left was the metal springs."

Defense lawyer James McIntyre asked him if he was testifying from memory or from notes. "From memory," Lytle replied.

McIntyre asked how he could recall so much detail forty years after the fact.

"It was a memorable time," he replied, "and I was a young memorable man at the time."

"You understand that the FBI paid some witnesses?"

"I understand that, but I was not directly involved."

The defense scored on this point, albeit the question was somewhat misleading. The FBI indeed paid informants for information, but they did not pay witnesses to testify.

"Would you disagree with me that the FBI paid out over two hundred thousand dollars in that 1967 case?" McIntyre asked.

Lytle replied that he didn't know the numbers.

"Is this normal policy for the FBI to go out and pay money for witnesses?" McIntyre asked. "Have you ever heard of that before or since?"

"I don't know. I heard about the reward that was being offered, and that was my first experience with it."

"Do you think payment to a witness would influence his testimony?"

Prosecutors objected, and the judge sustained their objection.

"Who was in charge of the money?" McIntyre asked.

"I expect it was Mr. Hoover," Lytle replied.

Laughter could be heard in the courtroom.

Seeking to repair the damage to the prosecution's case, Duncan asked about the atmosphere then in Neshoba County, and Lytle shared the story of how he and eight other agents left the Neshoba County Courthouse late one night. As they descended into the darkness, they met a mob that packed the square, hurtling insults at them. Making their way past the mob, they drove together in a convoy.

Duncan asked if that attitude made it difficult for the FBI to obtain information about the three missing young men.

"Oh, yes," Lytle replied. "We talked to people who said they weren't going to talk to us because if they got involved they could be the next person. . . ."

Through Rita Bender, prosecutors had brought Mickey Schwerner and the civil rights movement to life. Now they hoped to connect jurors with Freedom Summer volunteer Andy Goodman by calling his mother, Carolyn, to the witness stand. She told them, "I will be ninety years old in October."

After quizzing her about her education, Attorney General Jim Hood asked where her son, Andy, went to college.

She was unable to recall that it was Queens College, where she had spoken to graduating students just days earlier. This was the first sign that her questioning was not going to go well.

Then Hood asked her what year her son had traveled to Oxford, Ohio.

She couldn't recall that it was 1964, saying she struggled with numbers. But she did recall that Andy went to Mississippi because "a group of young people were going to register black people to vote. . . . He told us that's what he wanted to do. We thought that was important, and we gave him permission to go."

Hood handed her a piece of paper.

"This is Andy's handwriting," she told him.

"What's the date on that?"

"June 21, 1964. It's a copy of the postcard. He sent this to us."

She read the words, the last her son ever wrote. "Dear Mom and Dad, I have arrived safely in Meridian, Mississippi. This is a wonderful town, and the weather is fine. I wish you were here. The people in this city are wonderful, and our reception was very good. All my love, Andy."

When she finished, she sighed, the words hurtling her back in time.

"Dr. Goodman, how were you notified that Andy was missing in Mississippi?"

She exhaled in frustration. "Wish I could remember some of these things."

"Was it very long after he got here that you were notified that he wasn't around?"

She thought again and then put her head in her hands. She finally rose back up with a smile. "I'm sorry, you know."

Her head sunk down. Her fading memory, combined with her stress and a lack of witness preparation, distracted from what could have been a moving moment.

"Were you ever notified that the vehicle he was traveling in had been found?" he asked.

"Somebody called us. I think it might even have been the president at the time. That was President Johnson, who was president at the time. And the vehicle was found in a swamp."

She massaged her temple. "These things are all hazy in my mind. You'll have to forgive me."

"Did you ever come down to Mississippi?" Hood asked.

Lawyers typically tell other lawyers to never ask a question that they don't know the answer to. I knew the answer to that one—that she didn't set foot in Mississippi until 1989, the twenty-fifth anniversary of the killings. What was Hood doing up there?

Her hazy memory made her stumble on the answer. "The things I remember are so choppy—the red soil. I remember he was buried here. It was all so horrible."

He handed her a picture. "Do you recognize the person in this photograph?"

She choked up. "I certainly do. It's my son. It's Andy."

"Do you recall about when that photograph was taken?"

"I think it was taken right before he went to Mississippi."

She bowed her head and raised her intertwined fingers, as if in prayer. There were no more questions.

Prosecutors moved to the scene of the crime, calling retired FBI agent Jay Cochran Jr. to the witness stand. The mechanical engineer turned FBI lab examiner received the call to go to Mississippi after the men's disappearance. He examined the burned-out station wagon before helping out with other duties in the case.

On July 31, 1964, Cochran said FBI inspector Joe Sullivan shared the tip, which he had received from Mr. X, that bodies had been buried more than a dozen feet down in a new dam on the Old Jolly Farm, owned by Olen Burrage. Some agents drove around, finding plenty of dams, but none that were new. Finally, agents went up in a helicopter, and the new dam "stuck out like an orange shirt," Cochran recalled.

On the morning of August 4, 1964, FBI agents delivered a subpoena, and Cochran accompanied the bulldozer, dragline, and operators the FBI had hired. The digging started at 9 a.m., and by 2:50 p.m. on that blistering day, agents began to whiff the odor of decaying flesh, calling for a halt to the dragline. With blowflies swarming and vultures circling overhead, agents used shovels and then their hands, pawing away the dirt until they glimpsed a man's boots and then the outline of his body.

After two hours of careful digging, they made their way to his back pocket, Cochran said. "We were able to remove a billfold, which contained the Selective Service card of Michael Schwerner."

Agents soon discovered the bodies of Andy Goodman and James Chaney, and they worked well into the darkness. Cochran said the coroner arrived—with none other than Deputy Cecil Price. They transported the bodies at 11:15 p.m. to Jackson's University of Mississippi Medical Center for autopsies. Later that night, television cameras captured the ironic image of Price helping carry those bodies into the medical center.

Defense lawyer Mitch Moran objected to pictures of the three young men's bodies found in the dam as "prejudicial," but Judge Marcus Gordon concluded otherwise. "The jury may consider this as the issue of motive and plan, especially as evidence of concealment of the crime."

Under cross-examination, Cochran said his duties during the Mississippi Burning case excluded interviewing witnesses.

Asked anyway about the FBI paying money to witnesses, Cochran said he had no direct knowledge of that.

"Did you find any evidence that would link Mr. Killen to the crime?" Moran asked.

"No, I did not."

74

To give more behind-the-scenes details of the White Knights of the KKK and the role that Killen played, prosecutors read the testimony of the late Klansman turned FBI informant Delmar Dennis, who said Killen told White Knights members in spring 1964 that "we were here to do business." That business, Killen explained, included burning crosses, beatings, and eliminations.

When Klansmen suggested eliminating Schwerner, whom they called "an atheist and a communist," Dennis said Killen told Klansmen the project had already "been made a part of their program, and it would be taken care of."

Under cross-examination, Dennis acknowledged that he received $15,000 for expenses and travel from the FBI over the three-year period he worked as an informant talking to Klansmen. He said he knew who the Klansmen were because they discussed Klan business with him.

"The Federal Bureau of Investigation discussed Klan business with you, didn't they?" the defense lawyer asked.

"Yes, sir, they did."

"You didn't conclude from their discussions that they were members of the Klan, did you?"

"I did not."

The defense lawyer retorted, "You just concluded . . . whatever was convenient to you to be concluded."

"No, sir," Dennis responded. "The Bureau of Investigation didn't give me the [Klan] handshake, nor did they know what was going on in the local klavern in Neshoba County."

Before Dennis's testimony ended, a snafu interrupted the trial. Prosecutors had failed to gather proof of the witnesses' deaths through death certificates.

Judge Gordon became incensed. "Mr. Hood, I don't understand where all you have been. It's very elementary the process that you must go through to prove an unavailable witness."

He then detailed that process: "First, you must prove there was a trial and that that witness testified on the circumstances to show his interest and motive in the case. Then you must show that that testimony was recorded, and it was preserved, that the witness was cross-examined and subject to examination. Then you must show, after you get beyond that, the relevancy of that testimony and that he is unavailable. You've not shown that."

Exasperated, the judge allowed prosecutors to obtain faxes while they awaited overnight shipping of documents. But it was clear that any more mistakes could torpedo the case against Killen.

The next witness to implicate Killen was alive, but he carried plenty of baggage—which became obvious as soon as he entered the courtroom. Mike Winstead wore a bright yellow jumpsuit that read, "MDOC [Mississippi Department of Corrections] Convict."

The forty-eight-year-old inmate was in prison for rape and sexual battery. He had already served twelve years and two months behind bars. He had another two years and four months to go.

Despite his criminal history, he seemed credible, sharing the story of growing up in Neshoba County near Killen. On one Sunday, probably in late 1967 when he was ten, he heard of Killen's arrival at the church he and his family attended. To him, the preacher was as big a celebrity as those he saw on TV's *Gunsmoke.* "It was just like someone saying Matt Dillon had walked in."

That afternoon, Killen visited his grandfather's house. "My grandfather asked him if he had anything to do with those boys being killed, and he told my grandfather, 'Yes, and he was proud of it.'"

"Did you receive anything for having come forward with that information?" Hood asked.

"No, sir," Winstead replied.

"Have you asked for anything in coming forward with that information?"

"No, sir."

Hood asked if he had received any special treatment, a better room or bunk or anything else.

"I'm sitting in an isolated cell right now with nothing but me and flies, if you call that special treatment."

Scattered laughs could be heard, and Judge Gordon called for order.

Under cross-examination, Moran tried to punch holes in the inmate's story. He asked if Killen walked or drove there.

Winstead said he drove.

"What kind of car was he in?"

"I don't remember that."

"How long was he there?"

"I couldn't say. I can't remember back that good."

Moran questioned why he would remember words spoken so long ago.

When Killen "mentioned somebody being killed, it caught my attention," Winstead said. "A statement like that would kind of stick in a kid's mind."

"That's true. What motivated you to come forward?"

He said he came forward after he heard about Killen possibly signing autographs at the Mississippi State Fair. "The fact is I've got a son that's over in Iraq fighting for the same thing that these boys were killed for," he said. "I don't think what was done was right."

• • •

Prosecutors next read the testimony of a dead witness who had been a member of the killing party. More than any other witness, James Jordan put Killen front and center of the Klan operation to kill Chaney, Goodman, and Schwerner.

In his testimony, Jordan described joining the White Knights in spring 1964. On the first day of summer, June 21, 1964, he was at the Longhorn Drive-In in Meridian, where his wife worked. He said Killen approached him and said he had a job he needed some help with in Neshoba County,

"Did he say what kind of job it was?" the prosecutor asked.

"He said that two or three of those civil rights workers were locked up, and they need their rear ends tore up."

Jordan said Killen indicated Schwerner, whom Klansmen had spied on before, was one of them. "We started calling them on the telephone, trying to line up some more men to go with us."

Fearing too big a crowd at the drive-in, they shifted their operation to Akin Mobile Homes. Jordan said Killen shared that two or three men were on the way and asked if he knew a couple more, "that we needed about six or seven men."

Jordan said he picked up Klansman Wayne Roberts. On the way back, he said they tried to buy the rubber gloves Killen requested, purchasing cloth gloves instead. When they returned, Killen told the group that "they had three of the civil rights workers locked up, and we had to hurry and get there and were to pick them up and tear their butts up."

After the Klansmen arrived in Philadelphia, he said Killen "came from around the corner, told us that he would take us by and show us the jail and then we would be told where to wait until they were released." Jordan said Killen then took them by the jail and showed them a spot to wait behind an old warehouse.

After this, Jordan and other Klansmen dropped Killen off at a funeral home. "He said that he had to go there because if anything happened, he would be the first one questioned."

Klansmen caught the three civil rights workers, killed them, and buried them in an earthen dam. About twenty minutes later, Jordan said he heard a bulldozer crank up. Then he gathered up the gloves from Klansmen and disposed of them.

Not long after this, he lost his job, and he said FBI agents approached him about cooperation. He said they gave him $3,000 so that he could buy a car and move his family away. He continued to receive about $100 a week for a year until he was able to get a new job, and the FBI continued to supplement his $175-a-week salary at the NASA missile base in Picayune.

Under cross-examination, Jordan admitted he had been convicted of using a car without the owner's consent, bad checks, petty larceny, and grand larceny. "I was never arrested for any major crime."

Jordan's 1967 testimony made clear that he had received about $8,000 total from the federal government over the past three years. That help included receiving $100 the month before for his trip to the trial.

"Do you expect to continue to receive help from time to time from the federal government?" the defense lawyer asked.

"No, sir, I do not expect to receive anything from them."

"Do you think this will be your last hundred dollars?"

"I believe I've got my plane ticket back."

Mike Hatcher, who served as assistant police chief at the Meridian Police Department, became the next witness to implicate Killen. The sixty-eight-year-old retired officer wore a white shirt, a dark tie, and a gray jacket that matched his hair.

These days, he "turns nuts and bolts on cars," but more than a half century earlier, he fibbed about his age so that he could leave the farm in Kemper County and join the navy. Several years later, he returned to Mississippi and began his dual career as a cop and a mechanic. In spring 1964, fellow officer Wallace Miller invited him to a "citizens' meeting" that turned out to be a KKK gathering, where he was sworn in by a man wearing dark brown cowboy boots—Preacher Killen.

As summer approached, Hatcher and several other carloads followed the preacher to a KKK meeting at an old gym in Neshoba County, where Killen spoke to about seventy-five Klansmen. "He talked some about 'Goatee,'" Hatcher testified. "I knew who he was talking about."

"Who was he talking about?"

"Michael Schwerner."

Hatcher said Killen warned "about outsiders coming in and causing trouble, and something needed to be done about it."

A day after the three civil rights workers disappeared, Hatcher said Killen met him after 4:00 p.m. at the Meridian City Court. He said they went outside, where Killen described how Klansmen killed the men and buried their bodies in the middle of a pond dam off Mississippi Highway 21. "We got rid of those civil rights workers. You won't have no more trouble out of Goatee."

He said Killen shared that the civil rights workers' station wagon had been burned, worrying that authorities would find it. Killen also shared that two workers showed up early at the dam site, found blood, and had to be sworn to secrecy.

Hatcher said Killen handed him a pistol to pass on—a pistol he wound up removing the firing pin from and tossing away. He said the killings put him in a difficult position as a police officer. "I didn't know the Klan would do anything like that."

That fall, the officer ran into Killen at the Mississippi-Alabama State Fair, where he said the KKK leader revealed the FBI was checking his phone calls from June 21. Killen shared that he wasn't worried because he drove down to Meridian that night "to get that bunch together," but he hoped nobody saw him in Meridian because he was "supposed to be at the funeral home," where he later made an appearance, signed the register book, and made sure he talked to plenty of people.

Soon after, Hatcher began cooperating with the FBI. Asked why he didn't tell the FBI sooner, since agents were offering a huge reward for the location of the bodies, he replied, "The way I was raised, you don't tell on people."

After this ordeal, he said he decided to become the best police officer he could, graduating from the FBI Academy. "At that time, I was in the Klan. I learned a lesson. I regret it. I feel I've come a long way, as everybody has."

Under cross-examination, Moran tried to distance his client from the murders. He asked Hatcher if a lot of Klansmen would have the same knowledge that Killen had.

"I can't answer that," Hatcher replied.

Prosecutors objected, and the judge sustained the objection.

"Have you ever seen Edgar Killen give Sheriff Rainey orders?" Moran asked.

"No, sir."

"Have you ever seen Edgar Killen give anybody orders?"

"I haven't seen him give orders. I've heard him talk about things."

"You've never seen him give anybody orders?"

"No, sir."

"The only thing you know is he came to you and said, 'We got rid of the civil rights workers.'"

Hatcher replied that other Klansmen substantiated the details of Killen's statement, including Wayne Roberts, who killed Schwerner and Goodman.

"So, he [Killen] just told you what happened, not that he did it?"

"He never said, 'I.' He said, 'We.'"

"He never stated that he planned it."

"No, sir."

The next morning, prosecutors wrapped up their case by returning to those who'd been living with the pain of these events the longest. Using a wooden cane to guide her way, eighty-two-year-old Fannie Lee Chaney took small, unsteady steps to the witness stand. There was nothing unsteady, however, about her memory.

While her children and grandchildren watched from the front row and others in the audience sat spellbound, she detailed the devastation her family experienced. She spoke of her oldest son, James Earl, whom she and the family called "J.E.," and the time he spent with Mickey and Rita Schwerner. On the Saturday before he disappeared, J.E. came with Mickey and a new volunteer named Andy. "[J.E.] come back, and me and him sit up and talk until about two or three o'clock," she said. "Then we went to sleep."

The next morning, she made him breakfast, and he left to go to the

COFO office. Her youngest son, Ben, sat on the porch, upset because he wanted to go, too.

"J.E. promised, 'You wait until I get back. I'll take you with me. You'll see.' And he never come back. Mmm-hmm."

That Sunday night, a preacher came up about eight and told her, "We've been trying to track the boys, and we ain't found 'em yet." He said he and others were heading to Neshoba County, and she told him she wanted to join them.

"No, you stay here 'cause if he calls, you'll be home."

She removed her glasses and wiped her eyes.

She remembered seeing the burned-out station wagon on TV days later and also getting calls from Washington, reports of finding bodies. One wound up being a horse's grave. Then there were two bodies found, both with khaki pants.

"I told them it wasn't none of James, that he didn't wear that."

"Were you threatened?"

"Oh, yeah, I was getting phone calls," she said, adding that one time gunfire came screaming toward her house. "If it had been any closer, I would have been dead."

"Why did you have to move from Mississippi?"

"I couldn't get a job no more. They were threatened me and my little son, Ben, so bad. They said they were going to put dynamite under the house and blow us to bits."

When Hood showed her the photograph from the FBI's famous reward poster, she said, "I got that picture hanging up in my house. That's my oldest son, James Chaney."

Sadness swept across her face, and she pressed her lips together. There was nothing more to say.

75

The prosecution made it to the finish line, but not without stumbling. I wondered what jurors would make of the testimony of the dead witnesses. If they rejected these witnesses, Edgar Ray Killen would likely walk free again.

The defense fought back by giving him an alibi, not just for that evening, but for the entire day of June 21, 1964. His seventy-one-year-old sister, Dorothy Dearing, and his seventy-four-year-old brother, Oscar, testified that Killen was home that day with their parents because it was Father's Day. Oscar Killen swore he saw his brother that morning at nine.

Wait a minute. Wasn't this a Sunday morning? Wouldn't Killen have been preaching?

Oscar Killen said the family began eating lunch "at eleven o'clock and ate till we left" at about 4 or 5 p.m. He said a good friend of the family, Alex Rich, died, and that he went to the funeral home. "I'm sure I went up there, but, you know, that's forty-something years ago."

"Did your brother, Edgar Ray Killen, go to the funeral home, also?" defense lawyer James McIntyre asked.

Starting to answer, "I think so," Oscar Killen switched to, "Yes, sir."

"You saw him there?"

"I seen him there. I didn't stay long, but I was there for a while."

I didn't stay long, but I was there for a while. Which one?

"About what time was it y'all met at the funeral home?"

"I imagine it was seven or eight o'clock."

"Do you remember how long you stayed there?"

"No, sir, I don't. I don't hang around too long. I go and get out."

"Do you remember if you left first or your brother left first?"

"I left first."

Under cross-examination, District Attorney Mark Duncan asked, "Mr. Killen, did you know that Edgar Ray was in the Klan?"

"No, sir, I didn't even know that. I've heard more talk that your daddy and granddaddy was in the Klan more than I have him."

The audience seemed stunned and so did the jurors.

Oscar Killen continued. "Sure have. I'm honest."

He cut his eyes toward the lawyers, now grandstanding. "I swore on the Bible, gentlemen. That's the way I've heard it all these years."

The district attorney asked, "So, you didn't know if Edgar Ray was in it or not?"

"I still don't know if he was in it. Until he tells me, I won't believe it."

He shot a grin at the prosecutors. "Most all the stuff y'all have is paid stuff."

After he stepped down from the witness stand, Judge Marcus Gordon told the jury to ignore the extra statements from Oscar Killen.

Duncan's face grew red, angry at what he regarded as a falsehood against his family. The district attorney had long believed in prosecuting this case. Now he was fighting mad.

Defense lawyers switched from alibi witnesses for Edgar Ray Killen to those who could praise his character. They turned to Reverend James Kermit Sharp, who seemed every bit a preacher with his blue-gray suit, his gray hair, and his never-ceasing smile. He described Killen as a friend, neighbor, high school classmate, and fellow Baptist preacher. He regarded Killen's character as "very good."

Attorney General Jim Hood stepped forward to cross-examine Sharp.

Throughout the prosecution's case, Hood seemed hesitant at times, some-times repeating questions to witnesses. Now, facing a preacher in front of a Bible Belt jury, the attorney general regained his footing, asking Sharp about the Klan's beliefs. "They say that the Bible preaches about you shouldn't intermingle the races. Do you know where those scriptures are?"

"Not offhand," Sharp replied.

"Do you believe that as a Baptist?"

Sharp hesitated. The defense objected, and the judge ruled he didn't have to answer. But Hood's point was made.

"The men that were responsible for the murders of these young men, they should pay for what they did, shouldn't they?" he asked.

"All sin will answer in payment of some kind."

The theological response led Hood to respond in kind. "We're subject to Caesar's laws as long as we're on this earth, aren't we?"

"Right."

"So, is it fair to say that those who committed this crime should be held responsible by the state of Mississippi, shouldn't they?"

"I suppose so."

Defense lawyer Mitch Moran tried to introduce into evidence the state-ment from Horace Doyle Barnette to the FBI. He believed the statement would help prove the defense theory that Sheriff Lawrence Rainey was behind the operation and make Killen no more than a bystander.

Hood objected to the statement going into evidence, and the judge agreed. I cringed. This was the biggest mistake I had seen the prosecution make yet.

The Barnette statement did implicate the sheriff, but it implicated Killen far more. In addition to describing how Killen recruited Klansmen to attack the civil rights workers, Barnette said Killen told him that Klans-men had a place to bury the bodies and someone to run the bulldozer to cover them up. No other testimony—living or dead—could reveal such detailed knowledge of Killen's role that bloody night.

76

The trial resumed Monday, June 20, a day after a service at the Mount Zion Methodist Church honored James Chaney, Andy Goodman, Mickey Schwerner, and their families. Just as prosecutors had a surprise witness, now defense lawyers called their own surprise witness.

Wearing a drab green button-up shirt, David Winstead bore a resemblance to his younger brother, Mike, who had testified that he overheard Edgar Ray Killen talk about being involved in the trio's killings.

David Winstead had seen his brother testify on CourtTV and contacted Killen's lawyers to contradict that testimony. "He's lying."

He explained that he and his siblings weren't allowed to sit around and listen to adults talking inside the home. "We were never inside anyway on a Sunday afternoon."

Except that his brother, Mike, said he overheard Killen talking to his grandfather outside the home.

Defense lawyer Mitch Moran asked if his brother had ever before confided what Killen had said.

"No."

"Have you ever seen Edgar Ray Killen at your grandfather's house on a Sunday?"

"No."

"Would you believe your brother under oath?"

"No."

Under cross-examination, District Attorney Mark Duncan questioned Winstead about his relationship with Killen.

"Most of his life I've known him and his brothers. I've rode horses on their place and stuff like that a lot."

"How far did you live from him?"

"Probably eight or nine miles."

"Would you call yourself friends with him?"

"Why, yeah."

"The fact is you weren't present for that conversation that your brother overheard between Mr. Killen and your grandfather, were you?"

"No, and I doubt he was there."

"So, you wouldn't know what was said between your grandfather and Mr. Killen, would you?"

"No."

The witness finished and left the courtroom. Killen continued to scribble on his legal pad.

The next defense witness who vouched for Killen was a two-term mayor of Philadelphia. Harlan Majure told jurors that on the evening of June 21, 1964, he was in McClain-Hays Funeral Home because of the death of his young niece. He estimated he left as the funeral home shut down about 9 p.m. or so. But before that happened, he saw Edgar Ray Killen and spoke with him.

Majure told jurors he had known Killen for forty-five or fifty years.

"Have you formed an opinion of his character?" defense lawyer James McIntyre asked.

"Yes, sir."

"And what is it?"

"It's good."

This stunned me. A few years back, when I had interviewed Majure, he had called Killen "a compulsive liar."

Under cross-examination, the district attorney asked Majure if he had any idea what Killen was doing prior to coming to the funeral home.

"No, sir."

"So, if he had been to Meridian that day, you wouldn't know about it?"

"No, sir."

"I believe you also testified that in your opinion, he had a good reputation, is that right?"

"Yes, sir."

"Did you know he was in the Ku Klux Klan?"

"No, sir."

"Suppose he was in the Ku Klux Klan. Would that change your opinion about him?"

"No, sir," he said, stretching his hands toward the audience, "because I know some things about the Ku Klux Klan that a lot of people here don't know."

"Do you know they're a violent organization?"

"Not necessarily so. They did a lot of good, too."

"Did you know they carried out murders and burnings and beatings and things like that?"

"I don't know."

Defense lawyer James McIntyre objected, saying, "The Klan is not on trial."

The judge said since Majure didn't know, the objection was overruled.

The district attorney asked Majure to suppose the KKK did carry out such acts. "Would you call them a peaceful organization?"

"I'd have to know more about it than I know right now. As far as I know, it's a peaceful organization."

The district attorney became agitated. "C'mon, Mr. Majure. You've lived here all your life. You've read books, seen movies, read newspapers, and heard stories. You know they're not a peaceful organization."

Majure volunteered to tell a story, but the judge cut him off. A self-satisfied smirk settled on Majure's face, unaware that he had probably hurt Killen more than he helped him.

• • •

Finding possible contradictions in Mike Hatcher's testimony, the defense called him back to the witness stand. Defense lawyer Mitch Moran pointed out differences between his lengthy testimony the other day and his brief 1967 testimony in which he said Killen "told me that the three had been taken care of and the bodies were buried south of Philadelphia beyond the fairgrounds in an earthen dam and that they had burned the car."

Hatcher, now wearing a white shirt and a bolo tie, said he testified to as little as he could in 1967. "I didn't want to be killed."

"So, you're saying that the answer you gave in 1967 is not correct and that you lied?" Moran asked.

"No, sir, I did not lie. I only gave the amount of information to a certain extent, and as I said, the conditions back then and all is the reason for that."

"Is it not also true that in the 1967 trial, that you stated that Edgar Killen told you he had nothing to do with it?"

Hatcher acknowledged he could have. In the 1967 trial, defense lawyer Laurel Weir asked, "Brother Hatcher, Reverend Killen told you that he was at the funeral home and didn't have nothing to do with it, didn't he?"

"Yes, sir," Hatcher replied then.

He explained that his response in 1967 had been partly correct and his testimony here had been totally correct.

Under cross-examination, Attorney General Jim Hood handed Hatcher his May 4, 1967, statement to the FBI. Hatcher read what he quoted Killen as saying in the statement: "We got rid of the civil rights workers."

"Is that what you told the FBI?" Hood asked.

"Yes, sir. When he told me he got rid of the civil rights workers, he also told me Michael Schwerner's last words were, 'I understand how you feel, sir.'"

He said Killen did talk about being at the funeral home for an alibi, but that Killen never said he had nothing to do with it.

When Hood finished, Moran rose again to question him about who was at the murder scene. "You also know that Edgar Killen was not there, do you not?"

"I can't say that. No, sir, I don't know that."

"Have you ever heard any evidence that he was there that night?"

"No, sir, not anything direct at the scene."

"You had no evidence that Edgar Killen planned or orchestrated that crime?"

"Sir, at that time I was in the Klan. I regret it. I learned a lesson. I feel I've come a long way since then, as everybody has. It was common knowledge . . . among Klan members about who ran the Klan at that time. Preacher Killen was the main one under Mr. Bowers."

When Killen had discussed the killing with him, Hatcher said, "There was nothing I could do about it unless I wanted to leave where I was born and raised, get my name changed and all that. I was aware of the FBI's plan. I never said anything, because of the threats then and the people that I knew was in the Klan and what could happen."

"Was the testimony that you gave Friday, is that correct, or was the testimony in 1967 correct?"

"Partially 1967 correct, and honest to God's truth, Friday correct," Hatcher replied, raising his right hand.

"You did not lie in 1967?"

"I wouldn't say necessarily I lied."

Moran interrupted. "That's a yes-or-no answer. Did you lie in 1967?"

"I guess you could say I lied, but there was a reason."

"So, you lied under oath. Is that correct?"

"Like I said, I guess you could say I lied."

The defense had just coaxed the most important live witness for the prosecution into saying, "I lied." How was the jury going to take that?

77

After lunch, closing statements began. Attorney General Jim Hood took center stage, addressing arguments against the case's prosecution as much as the evidence itself. He reassured jurors that pursuing this prosecution was hardly good politics. "I was never able to watch the movie, *Mississippi Burning*, because I didn't want to deal with the emotions to know that people just down the road from where I grew up didn't do the right thing."

He apologized to jurors for not being able to show them who pulled the trigger—a detail contained in the Horace Doyle Barnette statement he kept out of evidence. "Many think it's too late to look back at the skeletons of our past," Hood said, "but these skeletons have names, and they have faces."

He held up photographs of James Chaney, Andy Goodman, and Mickey Schwerner. "Their spirits are still here today."

He compared Edgar Ray Killen to a drug dealer who gets children to sell drugs. "He did it all, and like a coward, he went and hid in the funeral home."

He reminded jurors of Mike Hatcher quoting Killen as saying, "We got rid of those civil rights workers."

He told jurors, "That's a confession. That's an admission by the defendant."

He told them that even if they believed this was a beating that went awry, Killen was still guilty—of manslaughter.

Concerned some of the jurors might decide against conviction, Hood took on the air of a pulpit-pounding preacher, saying the good people of Neshoba County had been misled by this so-called minister, who convinced them "the Bible sanctioned the division of the races," but ignored this command from God: "Thou shall not kill."

These actions "were not sanctioned by God—they were sanctioned by that man right there."

He pointed at the KKK leader, who mouthed back the words, "You son of a bitch."

Hood continued: "That was a mob that murdered those young men down there that night. And that coward is still sitting in that courtroom right there."

He talked about the venom visible in the testimony of the defendant's brother, before guiding jurors' attention to the defense table. "That venom is sitting right there seething behind those glasses. That coward wants to hide behind this thing and put the pressure on you. He wants one of you to be weak and not do your duty to find him guilty of this crime."

He held up Killen's 1964 photograph, transporting jurors back to the time when he was a young KKK leader. "This is the man right here that had that venom."

He pointed at the preacher. "There he sits, wanting your sympathy, wanting your sympathy to get involved. He doesn't want you to know that he left these young boys in a grave, no funeral, no casket, dumped in there like a dog."

He called on jurors to "do your duty, honor this country, honor Neshoba County, and honor these victims and find this man right here, Edgar Ray Killen, guilty of murder."

The words of defense attorney James McIntyre had helped convince a jury to acquit Neshoba County sheriff Lawrence Rainey on federal conspiracy charges. Could McIntyre convince another jury to acquit?

He shook his head as he spoke about Killen being in a wheelchair.

"What is justice and fair play coming to now?" he asked. "What is it coming to with all the crime on the streets? Is this case justice and fair play? No, I suggest that it's not."

He told jurors there was no proof against Killen. "Did any of these witnesses say he was at the scene and pulled the trigger? No, the only thing that comes close is he had a big mouth, and he was talking all the time. That's the only thing he's guilty of."

He questioned why Killen was being singled out. "How can you hold one man accountable for a group of people? Where are the rest of the defendants in this case? There are seven people of them still alive. Where are they? You know why?"

He leaned toward jurors and whispered, "He's a preacher. They want to get the preacher."

He urged them to acquit Killen, calling the charges "nothing more than a political indictment. That's all it is."

Seeking to deflect his client's guilt, he blamed the press. "This is not a case to solve a crime. This is a case to pull back the curtains for the TV cameras."

He pointed toward the victims' families and others present in the courtroom, saying they would all be gone after the trial is over. "What is that going to do for us?" he asked. "We're going to have to live with this trial."

He waved his arm around the courtroom. "This is nothing but a show. They're trying to put the state of Mississippi on trial."

When it comes to race relations in Mississippi, "we're doing wonderful here today," he said. "Why go back and open an old wound that healed forty-one years ago?"

Defense lawyer Mitch Moran took the floor next. He attacked the age of the case, saying that the passage of time had made justice impossible. "Two wrongs don't make a right. It was wrong what happened to those civil rights workers in 1964, and it would be wrong today to deprive Edgar Killen of a fair trial."

He insisted that prosecutors had failed to prove their murder case.

He said just because Killen belonged to the KKK and just because he had knowledge of the crime didn't mean he was guilty of the crime. "I state to you that Edgar Killen was a man with a four-door car and gasoline, and he drove everybody around. He wasn't even there that night. The state admits to you that Edgar Killen was not there that night. He did not participate in the killings."

Moran questioned why Killen was the only one on trial when a number of others were involved, then he reviewed the evidence in the case. He zeroed in on the testimony of Mike Winstead, the convicted rapist. "He could be telling the truth, but he's still not credible," Moran said.

What surprised me in listening to the inmate's testimony, however, was how credible he seemed. Jurors never heard this, but I knew he had passed a lie detector test.

The defense lawyer criticized Mike Hatcher, saying "that man sat in a [KKK] meeting, and listened, and made a statement under oath that he heard 'em plan the elimination of Michael Schwerner. Did he, a police officer sworn to protect the citizens of the state of Mississippi, come forward? He could have stopped it. He's the man with the badge and then stands in this courthouse and talks about his duties and responsibilities of being a professional law enforcement person. That certainly is not credible."

Moran asked the jury to hold the state to its burden of proof. "You can't convict an eighty-year-old man on a forty-year-old crime of capital murder by a convict and a so-called police officer who admits to lying under oath."

District Attorney Mark Duncan tried his best to connect with jurors as a fellow native of Neshoba County. People in the community, he said, have long heard about the 1964 murders of Mickey Schwerner, J. E. Chaney, and Andy Goodman, but what they have not heard are the stories of these young men, who "devoted themselves to helping others." They helped build a community center, where people could meet, where children could come and read books. They helped people register to vote.

"That's something that no one would ever dream of denying anyone today, but it was something back then that was so despised that it cost them their lives," Duncan said. "They paid for it with their lives while Edgar Ray Killen, on the other hand, has been able to enjoy the last forty-one years of his life."

Killen was the main instigator, he said, "and no one else. He was the man who led these murders. He is the man who set the plan in motion. He is the man who recruited the people to carry out the plan. He is the man who directed those men into what to do. And then he didn't have . . . the gumption to carry out his own dirty work. He went and hid down at the funeral home to try and establish himself an alibi. . . . The evidence that Edgar Ray Killen is responsible for these murders is just absolutely overwhelming."

Then he turned to the jurors and their role in deciding what Neshoba County stood for today. Duncan noted that the anniversary of the murders would be tomorrow.

"For forty-one years, it's been Edgar Ray Killen and his friends who have written the history of Neshoba County. You can either change the history that Edgar Ray Killen and the Klan wrote for us, or you can confirm it," he said. "Is a Neshoba County jury going to tell the rest of the world that we are not going to let Edgar Ray Killen get away with murder anymore? Not one day longer."

78

At 5:30 p.m., jurors returned to the courtroom after more than two hours of deliberations. Circuit judge Marcus Gordon quizzed them about their progress. The jury's forewoman responded that they were evenly divided—six jurors to six—and I saw stunned faces among the family members and their supporters.

The jurors left, and I joined the bevy of reporters chasing lawyers and others for comments. Outside the courthouse, James McIntyre told me his client had won. When other reporters edged closer, he softened his words. "So far it's a victory. We're just delighted the jury is listening to our side of the story."

Attorney General Jim Hood discounted the split, saying that it was likely not a split between conviction and acquittal but about the severity of the charges. During deliberations, the jury had sent out a question about manslaughter, wanting to know if another underlying charge (presumably assault) could be substituted for kidnapping. Judge Gordon had said no.

"Maybe a good night's rest will let them reach a decision," Hood said. He believed "the evidence is there. The question is, is this jury going to hold him accountable? Is the time lapse enough to forgive a person of murder? That's where we started and where we'll end up."

Ben Chaney praised the work of the prosecutors. "They've done a good job in representing James, Andy, and Mickey." He followed that compliment with a shrug. "It's going to be difficult for the jury to come back with what I want—a verdict of guilty of murder in the first degree."

Back in my motel room, I telephoned Assistant US Attorney Jack Lacy and shared what had happened with jurors. I could understand their question. There had been plenty of testimony about Killen telling Klansmen to "tear up the butts" of the jailed civil rights workers, but there had been little testimony about their abduction.

Our discussion moved on to the 6–6 split in the jury. "I presume that split is on murder versus manslaughter," I told Lacy.

"That's what I thought, too, until you told me the jury's question."

"Now what do you think?"

"It could be 'guilty' versus 'not guilty.'"

"If that's the case, Jack, we could have a hung jury."

"Yes, we could."

Before the night ended, I talked with Dick Molpus, who had kept his distance from the trial. He told me the last thing he wanted to do was to give a juror an excuse to vote in favor of Killen.

"So, what's going to happen, Jerry?"

"I don't know. With a six–six vote, this jury could easily deadlock."

"What if they do?"

"Killen would go free again."

79

When I arrived the next morning, June 21, 2005, I saw Edgar Ray Killen smiling as he spoke with friends and family. He announced that he was going to walk free.

I noticed he was breathing oxygen from a tank, the first time I had seen him with it. Perhaps he was more nervous than he was letting on.

Family members of the slain men milled about, wondering what the 6–6 vote had meant. Rita Bender remained cool, content to let the jury keep deliberating. I had seen her swing through many emotions since we began talking in 1989. The very fact of a trial was a big win, and now she was ready to see it through.

Just after 11 a.m. a bailiff announced that the jury was returning to the courtroom. Judge Marcus Gordon told those gathered that this was "probably the most high-profile case in the history of this state, and hopefully we'll not have another occasion such as this."

The judge called in the jurors, who gathered in a semicircle in front of him. He asked the forewoman, Shirley Vaughn, a fifty-six-year-old office manager, "Has the jury unanimously agreed to a verdict?"

"Yes, we have."

"Have you unanimously agreed to a verdict on all three counts of the indictment?"

"Yes, we have."

"May I see the verdict?"

A bailiff took the verdict form from her and handed it to the judge, who read it. Killen let out a deep sigh.

The judge handed the form to Neshoba County Circuit Clerk Patti Duncan Lee, who read it aloud, "We, the jury, find the defendant, Edgar Ray Killen, as to Count One, guilty of manslaughter. We, the jury, find the defendant, Edgar Ray Killen, as to Count Two, guilty of manslaughter. We, the jury, find the defendant, Edgar Ray Killen, as to Count Three, guilty of manslaughter."

Killen emerged from the courthouse in a yellow jail jumpsuit. As deputies rolled his wheelchair into the scorching heat, he was even hotter, swatting at journalists' cameras and microphones. He continued his defiance at the Neshoba County jail, where an African-American jailer posed a standard question about suicide.

"I'll kill you," Killen shot back, "before I kill myself."

When the prosecution team emerged, Attorney General Jim Hood declared there was now "justice for all in Mississippi."

Rita Bender hoped the verdict would prompt Mississippi to more deeply examine its role in the terror campaign against African-Americans. "I hope this case is just a beginning and not an end. I hope this conviction helps to shed light on what has happened."

She and Ben Chaney expressed disappointment at the manslaughter verdict instead of murder, but they both thanked Neshoba County. Chaney said, "White folks walked up to me and told me that things are changing here, not as fast as they should be, but they're changing. I really believe there's hope."

He noted that seven men involved in his brother's killing were still alive and walking the streets. He expressed support for a cold cases unit in the Justice Department that would address unpunished crimes from that era.

He spoke with his mother after the verdict and said she was happy to know that the jurors believed her son's life had value. "No one," Ben noted, "would have known about James Chaney if he had been by himself."

When I reached Carolyn Goodman, she was sitting in her chair inside her Upper West Side home. She recalled her late husband, Robert, saying after their son's death, "I don't know if I'll live to see it, but justice will come."

Now, after all these years, she said she knew he was right.

More than sixteen years after *Mississippi Burning* debuted on the big screen, District Attorney Mark Duncan declared the verdict means Neshoba County would no longer "be known by a Hollywood movie."

He had delivered the most passionate closing argument. Now, speaking to me outside the courthouse, he parsed the jury's decision. "It's not a perfect verdict, but you have to understand it was not a perfect case."

He pointed out that three of the four main witnesses who testified for the prosecution were dead. But what he didn't mention were the details that jurors never heard. Prosecutors objected to Horace Doyle Barnette's confession going into evidence, and they never tried to admit Killen's taped threat, where he said he could get law enforcement officers to turn people over to him for violent purposes. In a case full of errors and problems, it seemed like a miracle Killen had been convicted at all.

After talking with Duncan, I interviewed the jurors themselves to find out what happened behind closed doors. Some believed Killen was guilty of orchestrating the trio's slayings. Others believed he was simply guilty of having a big mouth.

An hour or so into deliberations, they voted for the first time. Six believed Killen had been guilty of murder. Six others believed the state of Mississippi had failed to prove its case, some unwilling to accept the testimony of dead witnesses.

When jurors returned the next morning, they took another vote, now split 7–5 in favor of a murder conviction. One juror suggested, "If you're going to whip somebody, you don't need rubber gloves."

Some pushed for conviction, but others insisted there wasn't enough evidence to prove murder. "If your brother was on trial," one juror asked, "wouldn't you want him tried by the same standard?"

The debate continued, and juror Warren Paprocki spoke up. The fifty-five-year-old former aircraft electrician for the Marines, originally from California, had lived in Mississippi since 1991. He told fellow jurors that "it would be a hell of a deal" if they deadlocked, and Killen walked away because they couldn't agree on which charge to convict him.

One juror reminded them of the manslaughter charge—an option that didn't require proof of premeditation or an intent to kill. "Everybody was like, 'Yeah, we can go for that,'" Paprocki recalled.

Jurors voted unanimously to convict Killen of manslaughter but were hardly happy. "I heard a number of very emotional statements from some of the white jurors," Paprocki recalled. "They had tears in their eyes, saying that if they could just have better evidence in the case that they would have convicted him of murder in a minute."

I read Horace Doyle Barnette's confession to him. After hearing it, he became angry, telling me that if jurors had been given this confession, they would have convicted Killen of murder.

80

Mississippi Highway Patrol officers stood guard in front of the audience as the sentencing for Edgar Ray Killen began. Under the state's manslaughter law, the judge could sentence Killen to as little as one year on each count. The maximum was twenty years—something few locals believed the judge would give.

Killen sat at the defense table. This time, instead of wearing a dark blue suit, he wore a yellow jail jumpsuit.

Judge Marcus Gordon told the courtroom filled with families and reporters, "Those of you who have never been a judge do not understand the problems that a sentencing judge has. I've been a judge for twenty-six years, and it's one of the most difficult things I do."

He defended the jurors who heard the case, saying they followed the law and evidence to the best of their ability. "I watched CourtTV the other day, and I saw where Neshoba County, the jury, and even Mississippi was demeaned because the verdict was manslaughter and not that of murder. That was wrong."

He went about discussing the potential sentences Killen could receive. Because he was eighty and recovering from a serious injury, "there are those of you in the courtroom who would say that a sentence of ten years is a life sentence. There are those of you in the courtroom, no doubt, who are of the opinion that Edgar Ray Killen should be sentenced to serve sixty years."

Although Killen was convicted of manslaughter, the judge called this "a homicide case, where three persons were killed." The only distinction he saw was in punishment. "If there had been only one person killed, and Edgar Ray Killen was sentenced to serve twenty years in 1964, I don't think there would be one person who would say that that was an excessive sentence. But now today, forty years later, when Mr. Killen is eighty years old and we would consider the fact that three persons were killed, is sixty years an excessive sentence?"

The judge said Mississippi statutes do not give more severe sentencing to the young or more lenient sentencing to the old. "The law does not recognize a distinction of age."

The defense lawyers wheeled Killen before the judge, who slipped off his glasses before he spoke. "I take no pleasure at all in pronouncing sentence. The three gentlemen who were killed—each life has value, and each life is equally as valuable as the other life, and I have taken that into consideration. There are three lives involved in this case, and the three lives should absolutely be respected and treated equally.

"Therefore, Edgar Ray Killen, in Count One, it is the sentence of this court that you serve twenty years in the custody of the Mississippi Department of Corrections. In Count Two, it is the sentence of this court that you serve twenty years in the custody of the Mississippi Department of Corrections, with this sentence to run consecutive to the sentence pronounced on you in Count One. In Count Three, it is the sentence of this court that you serve twenty years in the custody of the Mississippi Department of Corrections, with this sentence to run consecutive to the sentences pronounced upon you in Counts One and Two."

The decision meant Killen had just been sentenced to sixty years in prison and that he wouldn't be eligible for parole until 2025—the same year he would turn one hundred.

Killen showed no reaction. The judge asked his lawyers if they had any comment.

"None, your honor," James McIntyre replied.

As the sheriff wheeled Killen out of the courtroom, Rita Bender and her husband, Bill, embraced. An endless smile filled her face.

For the victims' families, the bittersweet verdict had given way to the joy of justice. "This is a great day for Mississippi," Ben Chaney told reporters. "Thank God that today we saw Preacher Killen in a prison uniform taken from the courthouse to the jailhouse."

81

The sense of joy was short-lived, however. On the morning of August 12, 2005, I walked into the Neshoba County Courthouse for Edgar Ray Killen's appeal bond hearing. Gone were the reporters from around the globe. Gone were the families whose loved ones had been slain. In their place I saw a sea of Killen supporters. He brightened, smiling and waving to them.

Seven friends of his testified that he posed no flight risk and no danger to the community. Defense lawyer James McIntyre told the Associated Press that the only ones Killen would menace "are people north of the Mason-Dixon line," a statement that hardly reassured the victims' families, many of whom lived in the North.

Sitting in his wheelchair, Killen propped up his right arm with his left to take the oath. He testified he had lost use of his right hand and had to eat with his left. He told the judge he was in constant pain and confined to the wheelchair. He said the only time he left it was to sleep.

Killen praised his doctors but had nothing nice to say about the medical personnel at the Central Mississippi Correctional Facility. "They checked me through the line like a cattle auction. I'm very unhappy."

He told the judge the cot he rests on has injured the pins in his leg. "I can barely sleep. I still don't understand how I could lie in severe pain for twenty-four hours, and no one even bring me an aspirin. I'm not a drug addict." He didn't even have a pillow at first, Killen said. "I know the court is not going to like this, but I bribed a black convict, and he got me one out of the trash can."

District Attorney Mark Duncan disputed Killen's contention that he was harmless. The prosecutor shared a letter from Rita Bender, who wrote that if Killen were released on bond, "he will continue to spread his venom and hatred. He will claim to have cheated the state of its ability to punish his vile acts. He will continue by this to intimidate and threaten, and to encourage others to act in brutish disregard of the rights of the citizenry."

Trial testimony showed that Killen "is a dangerous and wicked man," she wrote. "Three young men were robbed of their lives. Their only 'crime' was to assert that all citizens have the right to vote in a democracy."

His two convictions and his conduct during the trial "demonstrated that he continues to be a threat," giving an "okay" in full view of the jury after the panel was picked, she wrote. "I believe that he meant to intimidate the potential jurors into believing he had stacked the jury."

Duncan told the judge that Killen has threatened people and incited violence for years. The district attorney cited the KKK leader's 1975 conviction and quoted from his threat, captured on tape: "That son of a bitch will be dead by eight o'clock. . . . I like revenge."

The district attorney said until Killen's conviction, he had been free for the past four decades. "It's time for him to start serving the sentence."

In the end, Judge Gordon concluded he had little choice but to grant an appeal bond to Killen. "Bail is a matter of right."

He explained that Mississippi law says that unless a person is convicted of a charge that carries a life or death sentence, that person is entitled to bond. He also cited Killen's medical condition and the state's failure to prove that Killen posed a flight risk or danger to the community.

The district attorney asked the judge for a stay, saying the prosecution planned to appeal to the Mississippi Supreme Court.

Gordon replied no. He pointed out that the trial transcript was almost complete and that the justices should be able to take up the appeal within a year.

When the hearing ended, family and friends crowded the preacher. They slapped backs and shook hands, congratulating the convicted killer, as if he had won "Man of the Year."

Duncan looked dazed. He finally muttered, "His day will come."

In the 90-degree heat, the preacher emerged from jail, his friends posting his $600,000 bond. Wearing his white cowboy hat, he refused to speak with reporters as he left with his wife in their white car.

The couple pulled away, a stunning sight in the wake of such an incredible victory. How in the world did this happen?

82

Attorney General Jim Hood's office dashed to the Mississippi Supreme Court in hopes of getting Killen's appeal bond thrown out. The main reason cited was a bombshell. Hood's office revealed that it had uncovered evidence that Killen's brother, J.D., was willing to pay three thousand dollars to kill Judge Marcus Gordon if he did not let Killen out of prison on an appeal bond. According to documents, J.D. said he "had a mule that needed to be shot, and he asked the confidential informants if they would be the one to put the nails on him to make him stay." J.D. reportedly pointed out that "the mule was old, and he knew where the mule sits on his back porch." Hood argued that this revelation showed Killen was a threat after all, someone who should not be allowed bail.

Photographers who covered the trial, Kyle Carter and Suzi Altman, told me that J.D. Killen had threatened them, too. "He came right up in my face, and we had to have a cop come between us," Carter said.

Altman told me that when she drove by Edgar Ray Killen's house in her Volkswagen, his brother, J.D., "was standing on the porch with a shotgun." She later heard him say, "If that bitch in the Bug comes back out here again, I'm going to take a shot at her."

When I shared the latest with my wife, Karen, she asked, "How do you know he won't take a shot at you?"

She was far from pleased with Killen's release. I told her I doubted he would come our way.

"I'm not worried about him. I'm worried about his family."

She grabbed my arm. "I'm worried about our family."

I saw tears well up in her eyes and wondered what I could say. We had come so far, and now it seemed that all these years of work were for naught. Killen was free again.

Years earlier, we had purchased a life insurance policy, just in case something happened to me. I brought up the policy now, scrambling in the moment, thinking this might reassure her that our family would be taken care of.

She shook her head. "You don't understand."

I gazed into her eyes, hoping to calm her fears. She stared back, crossing her arms. "Just promise me this will be over soon."

"Promise," I told her, hoping there was some way I could keep this vow.

Days later, white supremacist Richard Barrett called me, crowing that Edgar Ray Killen would never see a jail cell. I was worried he was right. At best, the Mississippi Supreme Court would hear Killen's appeal in a year. But even with that optimistic time frame, delays were inevitable. Given Killen's age, he might die a free man before he ever went to prison.

Barrett told me he was planning a "Killen Appreciation Day" on September 18, 2005, on the lawn of the Neshoba County Courthouse. "There are still many people who think, and perhaps rightly so, sometimes vigilante justice is needed when ordinary government doesn't do its job—in this case keeping Schwerner, Goodman, and Chaney out of Mississippi."

The more Barrett talked, the angrier I became. Celebrating the KKK killer after his conviction? It was all too much.

But before Killen Appreciation Day could take place, Rita Bender forwarded me an email from a woman with a tip: "I just received a call from an individual of impeccable reputation who informed me that he had just witnessed a sight that caused his stomach to sink. The individual was at the Conoco gas station on Highway 16 in Philadelphia getting gas when Edgar Ray Killen drove, yes, drove, up in a truck. He got out, unassisted, and proceeded to fill his numerous gas cans. The individual is willing to give this information to whoever necessary, whenever necessary. Again, he is very reliable."

I emailed the woman, and she telephoned, sharing the number of Connie Dwayne Hampton, chief deputy for the Winston County Sheriff's Department. I called him, and he confirmed the story about Killen filling the gas cans.

"It was kind of a surprise, seeing everything I'd seen with his condition when he was portrayed as down and decrepit and couldn't get around because of a tree accident," he said. "To see him in motion like that with no problem, it was a surprise."

I knew this revelation was a story for the newspaper. I also knew this revelation held the power of possibly putting Killen back behind bars, where I believed he belonged. I wrote up the story as quickly as I could on Friday, and it ran the next morning.

I was working at *The Clarion-Ledger* office the next day with other reporters. We were still writing about Hurricane Katrina, which had torn up the Mississippi coast and New Orleans. The telephone rang, and I answered.

I recognized the deep voice as Judge Marcus Gordon.

"My wife just read me your story this morning."

"Yes, sir."

"How credible is this man?"

"I don't know, Judge, but if he's a chief deputy, I assume he's credible."

"If that's verified, I'm going to ask the Supreme Court to remand this for further hearing."

He asked me how to get in touch with the deputy, and I shared the deputy's number.

Judge Gordon set a hearing date, and the defense lawyers were furious. "Killen cannot walk, and I'll have a doctor who can testify to that," his lawyer, Mitch Moran, told me. "I don't even like Killen, but I don't like people to change the law."

As a country, he said, "we have to follow the law and the Constitution. We prosecute assholes and terrible people every day."

On September 9, District Attorney Mark Duncan asked the judge to revoke Edgar Ray Killen's bond, saying it appeared that he had "misrepresented his physical condition to the court."

Chief Deputy Connie Dwayne Hampton testified that he saw Killen get out of his truck and pump gas. Several deputies testified they witnessed Killen driving all over Neshoba County, from Union to Philadelphia to the House community. One deputy said he shook Killen's right hand—the same one the preacher had testified he couldn't use.

A physical therapist testified Killen had asked for treatment for his knee. He had not, however, asked for therapy on his right arm.

Judge Gordon questioned Killen's miraculous improvement. "I feel fraud has been committed on this court."

The judge also voiced anger toward Killen Appreciation Day. Killen agreeing to appear at "a day set aside to commemorate someone who had been convicted of three violent crimes seems to me that's grounds to deny bond," he said. "This trial involved the death of three persons who died in a cruel, heinous, and atrocious manner. They were murdered."

The judge revoked Killen's $600,000 bond, a ruling that sent the KKK leader back to prison for good.

Killen's family and friends fumed, while the rest of the courtroom now felt a rush of relief. Scanning the scene, my eyes caught FBI agent Jim Ingram. Had it really been sixteen years since I stood in the movie theater, listening to Ingram and the others talk about the KKK's killings of James Chaney, Andy Goodman, and Mickey Schwerner?

At the time I had no idea how that encounter would alter my life, ushering me into the limbo of lives stolen, brave and decent people whose killers had sauntered away. Now those killers—Medgar Evers's assassin, the imperial wizard who masterminded the KKK attack on Vernon Dahmer and his family, the Klansman who bombed the Birmingham church that killed four girls, and the Klan leader who orchestrated the execution of three civil rights workers—had begun to pay for their barbarity.

As I left the courthouse that day, Killen's lawyer, James McIntyre, walked up beside me. He glared at me, still steaming from the judge's decision. "You won again."

"No, Mr. McIntyre," I said, "you've got it wrong."

He looked puzzled.

"Justice won."

Epilogue

The KKK gunned down three young men on a dark, dusty road in Mississippi in the summer of '64. Klansmen buried their bodies fifteen feet down in hopes they would never be found. The bodies were uncovered, but justice wasn't—not for years, for decades. A quarter-century later, I had no idea that a fictional movie about the case would send me on a road to discovery. I had no idea that digging into *Mississippi Burning* would lead to a resolution of the case, a full forty-one years after the killings. Nor could I have known that it would lead to a broader unearthing of injustices across Mississippi, across the South, and across the nation.

The four Klansmen I wrote about who went to prison—Byron De La Beckwith, Sam Bowers, Bobby Cherry, and Edgar Ray Killen—spent the rest of their lives behind bars. But they were far from the only killers I looked into. Far more Civil Rights Era cold cases ended with no convictions, with more than one hundred twenty families watching in sorrow as the cases of their loved ones never saw a courtroom. I failed far more often than I succeeded in the cases I worked on. The killings of Emmett Till, Lamar Smith, Mack Charles Parker, Paul Guihard, Louis Allen, the Rev. James Reeb, Oneal Moore, Ben Brown, and Wharlest Jackson all went unpunished.

But other reporters and authorities carried on, many succeeding through remarkable work. Despite my failings, a Klansman involved in the 1964 beatings and killings of two African-American teenagers, Henry Hezekiah Dee and Charles Eddie Moore, went to prison in 2007. So did nineteen other men, including four who killed a one-armed sharecropper named Rainey Pool. His crime? Wandering up to an all-white bar not far from his home in Midnight, Mississippi. In 2010, former Alabama state trooper James Bonard Fowler finally spent time behind bars for killing Jimmie Lee Jackson, whose slaying inspired civil rights workers to march from Selma to Montgomery, Alabama.

I have long thought of the work that journalists and authorities have undertaken as a pursuit of justice. But the more time I've spent on these cases, the more I've come to believe that they are just as much a pursuit of memory.

Through their reign of terror, the Klan sought to send a warped message throughout the nation—about who holds power, about who must live in fear, about who gets to set the final record. Their world was one where a man like Sam Bowers could be remembered as a small-town pinball salesman rather than a mass murderer. Their world was one where African-Americans could be called "enemies" in their own nation, the country their ancestors had helped build, shape, and improve for centuries.

The work of reinvestigating the KKK's crimes in Mississippi has long been the work of correcting the record, of reclaiming memory from Klansmen and their sympathizers in the halls of power. In the cases where I've succeeded and those where I've failed, my aim has been to ensure that the truth was what wound up on the record. Only then could justice be done. Only then could the Klan's false narrative be righted. Only then could hate be shown for what it was.

In the years following these convictions, a wave of hate has risen up again. When Dylann Roof searched the Internet for "black on White crime," he found the website of the Council of Conservative Citizens, the descendant of the white Citizens' Council in Mississippi. Just as "Black Monday" changed the man who went on to murder Medgar Evers, Roof declared he was never the same after finding the Council website. The ninth-grade dropout embraced a racist narrative, which led him to kill. On a steamy spring night in 2015, he strolled into the Emanuel African Methodist Episcopal Church in Charleston, and he fired off bullet after bullet from his Glock, killing nine churchgoers mid-prayer. "I have to do it," he shouted. "You rape our women and you're taking over our country. And you have to go."

Wasn't this the same gospel that the KKK had preached against minorities since it began? Wasn't this the same message that generations of white politicians had delivered to Mississippi voters over the course of the state's history? And wasn't this the message that many Americans still bought? Somebody is taking over our country—and we have to take it back.

Since that bloodbath in Charleston, domestic terrorism and white nationalism have only spread. Hate crimes have reached record levels in the US, with shootings at synagogues in Pittsburgh, Pennsylvania, and Poway, California, and the burning of a mosque in Victoria, Texas. White nationalists, who once spewed their hate online, now chant Nazi slogans in the streets, saying, "You will not replace us."

When I talk with Myrlie Evers now, she shudders at the rise in hate. "My days are numbered. I've lived my life," she said, "but I look at my children. I look at my grandchildren. What kind of fools are we? Are we going to destroy this world with hate before this generation comes up? I do ask for healing for all of us, including those whose souls are ill with hatred and bitterness," she said. "At times like this, when I feel I cannot pray, my prayer becomes one word, 'Help.' That is all I can do."

Despite those fears, she feels hope. Hope there will be an uprising for what is right. Hope there will be an uprising for justice.

"When will that be?" she asked. "I have no idea, but I know that truth rules."

Truth rules. This has been a guiding principle of mine throughout my career. Truth rules, while hate thrives on obfuscation, murkiness, and fear.

I've been told time and again to let the past be. But I have long found that a true account of a painful past does more good than murky optimism. In our current fight against a new wave of white supremacists, a clear memory is important.

We must remember the past waves of white supremacy and the myths they spread. We must remember the many innocent African-Americans and activists the Klan killed. We must remember what civil rights activists like Medgar Evers fought for—American values as simple as equality and the right to vote. And we must remember what they fought through— the intimidation and violence, the death threats eventually made real. We must remember, to point our compass toward justice. We must remember, and then act.

Acknowledgments

The courage and persistence of the following families made these prosecutions possible: Medgar Evers, Vernon Dahmer Sr., Addie Collins, Denise McNair, Cynthia Wesley, Carole Robertson, James Chaney, Andrew Goodman, and Michael Schwerner. And families, such as those of Charles Eddie Moore and Henry Hezekiah Dee, made sure other prosecutions took place. Authorities heard their cries and won convictions against all odds. (A list of those involved in these prosecutions can be found at the end of these acknowledgments.)

In addition, I extend my thanks to my fellow journalists, some of whom have played a critical role in resurrecting unsolved murder cases from the Civil Rights Era, as well as others who have shed light on these killings, including David Ridgen, Stanley Nelson, John Fleming, Harry Phillips, Keith Beauchamp, Mike Hoover, Hank Klibanoff and his students at Emory University, Ben Greenberg, Chip Brantley, Andrew Beck Grace, Connor Towne O'Neill, Stephanie Saul, Donna Ladd, Kate Medley, Allen G. Breed, Holbrook Mohr, Joe Shapiro, and many others.

I would be remiss if I didn't thank Robert Rosenfeld with The Center for Investigative Reporting, who headed the Civil Rights Cold Cases Project that I was honored to serve on with some of the most talented journalists I know. Thanks also go to many who pushed for justice in these cases, including Alvin Sykes, the architect of the Emmett Till Unsolved Civil Rights Crime Act.

Thanks also go to the LSU Cold Case Project, Syracuse University's Cold Case Justice Initiative, and Northeastern University's Civil Rights and Restorative Justice Project, which have collected about 170,000 FBI files on these crimes, witness statements, and other evidence. A new law, championed by U.S. Senator Doug Jones and a high school class, will open even more files.

I certainly have to thank those who taught me journalism, writing, and so much more at (Texarkana) Texas High School, Harding University, and The Ohio State University. I owe even more gratitude to the many talented journalists I worked with at *The Clarion-Ledger* for three decades. They have taught me so much.

I want to thank all the journalists whose work has inspired me, including Bob Woodward and Carl Bernstein, whose book, *All the President's Men*, taught me how to do investigative reporting. Thanks, too, to all the researchers, librarians, and archivists, especially at the Mississippi Department of Archives and History, who assisted in this work, as well as the fellow reporters, experts, lawyers, sources, and others who provided valuable information and advice.

Thanks to my terrific book agent David Black, who sold my book and has since navigated its path. Thanks to everyone at Simon & Schuster, for so many of them have worked so hard to make this book a reality. I must especially thank publisher Jonathan Karp, who believed in my book and bought it; and my editor Jonathan Cox, who took my raw material and helped me transform it into a memoir. I can't thank him enough for his five years of patience, guidance, and wisdom. And my gratitude goes as well to Emily Simonson and Sean Manning, who helped me get the book across the finish line.

A special thanks as well goes to my editor at *The Clarion-Ledger* for more than a quarter-century, Debbie Skipper, who now guides the Mississippi Center for Investigative Reporting. Whatever success I've achieved is largely due to her.

And thanks to Ian Isaacs for turning this dream of a powerful investigative reporting nonprofit into a reality.

Thanks to my partner in writing screenplays, Mike Roden, who has been kind enough to read every incarnation of this book (along with Debbie Skipper), and to Charles and Brenda Eagles, who provided valuable edits to the manuscript. Thanks to Yale Canfield and everyone else at Skyway for their incredible support. Thanks to Kim Johnson and her mother, Sarah Hudson, for their love and prayers during the last stretch of this journey.

And my deepest gratitude goes to my family. I thank my children, Katherine and Sam, for their love and support, despite a sometimes scary childhood. And thanks to Karen as well. Although we aren't married anymore, I am grateful for her support. Thanks to my mom, who had me reading three newspapers a day by the time I was seven, and to my dad, the best man I've ever known. Thanks, too, to the rest of my family and all my friends who have supported me. They have made this journey a joy.

Thanks, most of all, to the One, who has strengthened and guided me. It is a matter of faith with me, but I believe his hand has helped bring about these convictions.

• • •

As promised, here is a list of the prosecution teams in each of the convictions since 1977:

1977:
State of Alabama v. Robert Chambliss
1963 bombing of a Birmingham, Alabama, church that killed Addie Collins, Denise McNair, Cynthia Wesley, and Carole Robertson. Tried only for McNair's murder.
Murder Conviction. Life Sentence.

Prosecutors:	Investigators/Agents:
Bill Baxley	Jack Shows
John Yung	John East
George Beck	Tom Ward
	Bob Eddy

1994:
State of Mississippi v. Byron De La Beckwith
1963 murder of Medgar Evers in Jackson, Mississippi.
Murder Conviction. Life Sentence.

Prosecutors:	Investigators/Agents:	Trial consultants:
Bobby DeLaughter	Charlie Crisco	Andrew Sheldon
Ed Peters	Benny Bennett	Pete Rowland
	Doc Thaggard	Lawrence Wrightsman
		Kirk Elifson

1998:
State of Mississippi v. Sam Bowers
1966 murder of Vernon Dahmer Sr. near Hattiesburg, Mississippi.
Murder Conviction. Life Sentence.

Prosecutors:	Investigators/Agents:	Trial consultants:
Robert Helfrich	Jim Gilliland	Andrew Sheldon
Lee Martin	Bill East	DeAnn Gibson
Lindsay Carter	Jim Ingram	Sinrich
Mike Moore		

1999:

State v. James Caston, Charles E. Caston, Hal Crimm, and Joe Oliver Watson
1970 murder of Rainey Pool near Louise, Mississippi.
Manslaughter Convictions. All but Watson received twenty years in prison;
Watson, who testified against the others, received two.

Prosecutors:
James Powell
Ted Batson

2001:

State of Alabama v. Thomas Blanton
1963 killings of Addie Collins, Denise McNair, Cynthia Wesley, and Carole
Robertson.
Four Murder Convictions. Four Life Sentences.

Prosecutors:	Investigators/Agents:	Trial consultants:
Doug Jones (then U.S. attorney)	Bill Fleming	Andrew Sheldon
	Ben Herren	Beth Bonora
Robert Posey	Bob Eddy	Kirk Elifson
Jeff Wallace		Norma Silverstein
		Steve Paterson

2002:

The Commonwealth of Pennsylvania v. Robert Messersmith and Greg Neff
1969 murder of Lillie Belle Allen in Race Riots in York, Pennsylvania.
Second-degree Murder Convictions. Messersmith received nine to nineteen years
in prison. Neff received four-and-a-half to ten years.

Prosecutors:	Investigators/Agents:
Tom Kelley	Rodney George
Tim Barton	John Daryman
Stanley Rebert	Keith Stone

2002:

The Commonwealth of Pennsylvania v. Stephen D. Freeland and Leon Wright
1969 murder of Henry Schaad in Race Riots in York, Pennsylvania.
Second-Degree Murder Convictions. Freeland received nine to nineteen years in
prison. Wright received four-and-a-half to ten years.

Prosecutors:	Investigators/Agents:
Bill Graff	Rodney George
Tim Barton	John Daryman
Stanley Rebert	Keith Stone

2002:

State of Alabama v. Bobby Frank Cherry
1963 murders of Addie Collins, Denise McNair, Cynthia Wesley, and Carole Robertson.
Four Murder Convictions. Four Life Sentences.

Prosecutors:	Investigators/Agents:	Trial consultants:
Doug Jones	Bill Fleming	Andrew Sheldon
Robert Posey	Ben Herren	Beth Bonora
Don Cochran	Bob Eddy	
Jeff Wallace		

2003:

United States v. Ernest Avants
1966 murder of Ben Chester White.
Murder Conviction. Life Sentence.

Prosecutors:	Investigators/Agents:	Trial consultants:	Paralegal:
Paige Fitzgerald	Kevin Rust	Andrew Sheldon	Yefat Levy
Jack Lacy		David Cannon	
		DeAnn Sinrich	

2005:

State of Mississippi v. Edgar Ray Killen
1964 killings of James Chaney, Andrew Goodman, and Michael Schwerner.
Three Manslaughter Convictions. Sixty Years.

Prosecutors:	Investigators/Agents:	Trial consultants:
Mark Duncan	Jim Gilliland	Andrew Sheldon
Lee Martin	Tony Shelbourn	Beth Bonora
Jim Hood	Bill East	

2007:

United States v. James Ford Seale
1964 killings of Henry Hezekiah Dee and Charles Eddie Moore near the
Mississippi River.
Two Kidnapping Convictions, One Conspiracy Conviction. Three Life Sentences.

Prosecutors:	Investigators/Agents:	Trial consultants:	Paralegal:
Paige Fitzgerald	Jim Ingram	Andrew Sheldon	Connie Lee
Dunn Lampton	William Stokes	David Cannon	
Eric Gibson		DeAnn Sinrich	
Angela Givens			

2010:

State of Alabama v. James Bonard Fowler
1965 killing of Jimmie Lee Jackson in Marion, Alabama.
Misdemeanor Manslaughter Conviction. Six Months.

Prosecutors:	Investigators:	FBI agent:
Michael W. Jackson	Larry Colston	Johnny Tubbs
John Oxford	Clyde Carter	
Vanetta Perkins		
James Ransom		
Jimmy Thomas		
John Waddell		

　　　　Prosecutors, investigators, and others involved in these cases, as well as journalists, helped me assemble this list. It does not include all the authorities who had the courage to pursue these cases during the Civil Rights Era. There is no question FBI Director J. Edgar Hoover did all he could to fight the civil rights movement. It is also true that many FBI agents risked their lives investigating these cases, and their work made up the backbone of a large portion of these reinvestigations and reprosecutions. Nor does this list include the prosecutors, FBI agents, investigators, and others who worked hard to bring these cases to court, only to lose the race against time.

A Notes on Sources

Most of the reporting and the quotations contained in this book are derived from my many years of reporting on these cases for *The Clarion-Ledger* in Jackson, Mississippi, as well as the reporting of my colleagues at the newspaper. With regard to various hearings and trials I have covered, I have relied on our reporting as well as transcripts and my notes. In addition to that, I have looked at the work of others who covered these cases. Where I have quoted from their work, I have credited them in the text or in the notes.

Throughout this journey, I have relied on many books written about these cases, these characters, and this history. Here are books that proved most valuable.

Notes

PART I

5 senator Jim Eastland: His June 23, 1964, conversation with then-President Lyndon B. Johnson was recorded by the White House and can be listened to at this website: https://millercenter.org/the-presidency/secret-white-house-tapes /conversation-james-eastland-june-23-1964.

5 could be in Cuba: *Racial Reckoning: Prosecuting America's Civil Rights Murders* by Renee C. Romano (Cambridge, Massachusetts: Harvard University Press, 2014), p. 3.

5 days before: "Gov. Johnson Nixes Violence But Hits North's Browbeating," *The Delta Democrat-Times*, August 13, 1964, p. 1.

5 extra pockets: Author interview, Erle Johnston Jr.

11 Original Knights: author interview, E. L. McDaniel; also see Michael Newton, *The FBI and the KKK: A Critical History* (Jefferson, NC: McFarland, 2009), p. 104.

12 "When the first waves of blacks": Don Whitehead, *Attack on Terror: The FBI Against the Ku Klux Klan in Mississippi* (New York: Funk & Wagnalls, 1970), pp. 6–7.

12 "When the black waves": Ibid., p. 8.

13 "I believe": Nick Kotz, *Judgment Days: Lyndon Baines Johnson, Martin Luther King Jr., and the Laws That Changed America* (Boston: Houghton Mifflin Company, 2005), p. 360.

13 "the worst": Florence Mars, *Witness in Philadelphia* (Baton Rouge, LA: Louisiana State University Press, 1989), p. 210.

19 In the mid-1960s, Binder: For detailed information on Al Binder's transformation, read Jack Nelson, *Terror in the Night: The Klan's Campaign Against the Jews* (New York: Simon & Schuster, 1993), pp. 95–102.

27 Mickey Schwerner stepped: Nick Kotz, *Judgment Days: Lyndon Baines Johnson, Martin Luther King Jr. and Laws That Changed America* (New York: Houghton Mifflin, 2005), p. 158; seemingly twisted by hate: William Bradford Huie, *Three Lives for Mississippi* (New York: WCC Books, 1965), photograph inside of Ernest Kirkland shows the rubble and twisted tin roof left after the June 16, 1964, fire at Mount Zion Methodist Church.

27 Few weeks before: Author interviews, Rita Bender and Schwerner family; June 24, 1964, FBI to Special Agent in Charge of the New Orleans office from Assistant Agent in Charge Sylvester.

27 a blue baseball cap: June 30, 1964, interview with Mount Zion Methodist Church member Ernest Kirkland by Special Agents Richard B. Vivian and Declan J. Hughes, BU file 157-2346; Wrangler jeans: August 12, 1964, FBI report by Special Agents Jay Cochran Jr. and Anthony O'Tousa; While attending: author interview, Stephen Schwerner.

27 His new wife: Author interview, Rita Schwerner Bender.

27 Today Chaney: June 1964 airtel to FBI director from the Special Agent in Charge, New Orleans, in the MIBURN (Mississippi Burning) investigation, giving details about each of the three missing civil rights workers, James Chaney, Michael Schwerner, and Andrew Goodman.

28 At age sixteen: Seth Cagin and Philip Dray, *We Are Not Afraid: The Story of Goodman, Schwerner, and Chaney and the Civil Rights Campaign of Mississippi* (New York: Macmillan, 1988), pp. 167–68; so busy: author interview, Angela Lewis, daughter of James Chaney.

28 Like Schwerner: Author interviews, Carolyn Goodman and David Goodman.

28 dabbled in theater: Author interviews, Ralph Engelman and Ruth Grunzweig Roth, Andy Goodman's former girlfriend; majoring in anthropology: July 2, 1964, FBI report, interview with Robert and Carolyn Goodman by Special Agents Francis P. Henry and James J. Rogers; writing papers: Joshua Zeitz, "1964—The Year the Sixties Began," *American Heritage*, May 2006; In 1963: author interview, Ralph Engelman; Goodman told: author interview, Carolyn Goodman.

34 R. L. Bolden: In an interview, Bolden admitted to me that he worked for Day Detectives, but he denied being Mr. X or working for the Sovereignty Commission. Pete Stoner and other activists told me that the activities of Agent X detailed in the commission reports were identical to the known activities of Bolden, who gave Stoner a ride home from Freedom Summer training in Ohio.

38 Justice Department revealed: Michael Newton, *The Ku Klux Klan in Mississippi: A History* (Jefferson, NC: McFarland, 2010), p. 146.

38   Hoover balked: Ibid.

41   What didn't make: A list of those who worked on the 1963 campaign of
      Paul Johnson Jr., including KKK leader Edgar Ray Killen, is contained in the
      former governor's papers at the University of Southern Mississippi. In a 1970
      interview with the President Lyndon B. Johnson Library, Paul Johnson Jr.
      said many of those involved in the 1964 killings of three civil rights workers
      worked on his campaign.

41   successful gubernatorial campaign: Author interviews, E.L. McDaniel and
      other sources.

PART II

50   "Mississippi is a better state": Carl Rowan, June 8, 1978, *Democrat and
      Chronicle* (Rochester, New York), "Supreme Court yielded to anti-press
      piques."

50   "I assure you": Michael Vinson Williams, *Medgar Evers: Mississippi Martyr*
      (Fayetteville: University of Arkansas Press, 2011), p. 76.

50   Evers believed: Medgar Evers, as told to Francis H. Mitchell, "Why I Live in
      Mississippi," *Ebony*, November 19, 1958, pp. 65–70.

51   death threats: "Testament of a Murdered Man," CBS Special Report, June 12,
      1963; he told: "Medgar Evers, Whose Assassination Reverberated Through
      the Civil Rights Movement," *New York Times*, July 2, 2016.

53   "The NAACP, under the direction of its leadership": *Washington Post*, Febru-
      ary 1, 1994.

53   "tears of joy": Byron De La Beckwith discussed this in a bond hearing fol-
      lowing his 1990 arrest. Bobby DeLaughter detailed this testimony in *Never
      Too Late: A Prosecutor's Story of Justice in the Medgar Evers Case* (New York:
      Scribner, 2001), p. 215.

53   Gordon Lackey: Michael Newton, *The FBI and the KKK: A Critical History*
      (Jefferson, NC: McFarland, 2009), p. 98; Jackson police: author interview,
      then–Jackson police detective Fred Sanders.

53   In 1967: Newton, *The FBI and the KKK*, p. 98.

62   Days later: Author interview, Charles Evers; Maryanne Vollers first discussed
      this in her book, *Ghosts of Mississippi*.

71   labor organizer: John H. M. Laslett, *Sunshine Was Never Enough: Los An-
      geles Workers, 1880–2010* (Oakland: University of California Press, 2012),
      pp. 185–86.

76   rubbed his hands: Author interview, John Hammack, who was working at
      The Clarion-Ledger at the time and witnessed this.

79   "possible perjured witness": Ti-Hua Chang, a producer for ABC's *Primetime
      Live*, first alerted me to this letter, contained in the Bill Minor papers at Mis-
      sissippi State University.

87 Up until recent years: Ronald Smothers, "Town Distances Itself from Suspect in Evers Case," *New York Times*, December 21, 1990.

94 circulation higher: James Coates, *Armed and Dangerous: The Rise of the Survivalist Right* (New York: Hill & Wang, 1987), pp. 195–96; *Spotlight* promoted: Linda P. Campbell, "Liberty Lobby in the Spotlight with Duke, Buchanan in Race," *Chicago Tribune*, January 12, 1992.

95 "I didn't kill": From WLBT-TV journalist Ed Bryson's May 1, 1990, interview with Byron De La Beckwith, which later appeared in ABC's *Prime Time Live* broadcast.

109 "Can I ask": Edgar Ray Killen's grand jury testimony is contained in the book by Bobby DeLaughter, *Never Too Late: A Prosecutor's Story of Justice in the Medgar Evers Case* (New York: Scribner, 2001), pp. 166–68.

110 Hollis Creswell walked in: Hollis Creswell's grand jury testimony is contained in the 1990 Hinds County Circuit Court file, *State of Mississippi v. Byron De La Beckwith*.

111 his former partner: James Holley's grand jury testimony is contained in the 1990 Hinds County Circuit Court file, *State of Mississippi v. Byron De La Beckwith*.

122 Beckwith later told: September 13, 1973, FBI memo, from informant JN 1122-PSI.

122 1966 FBI document: July 21, 1966, A. Rosen to DeLoach memo.

126 he didn't mention: "Measells Heads Citizens Council," December 23, 1955, *The Clarion-Ledger*. (Article lists Roy Noble Lee as serving on the executive committee for the white Citizens' Council in Forest, Mississippi.)

128 kept his distance: Author interview, Byron De La "Delay Jr." Beckwith VII.

PART III

155 the Justice Department: Gordon A. Martin Jr., *Count Them One by One: Black Mississippians Fighting for the Right to Vote* (Jackson: University Press of Mississippi, 2010), p. 211.

156 January 9: Don Whitehead, *Attack on Terror: The FBI Against the KKK in Mississippi* (New York: Funk & Wagnalls, 1970), p. 235.

159 the first rays of light: Testimony of retired FBI agents Loren Brooks and James Awe, 1998 Sam Bowers trial.

159 Mirroring the work: Author interview, Jim Ingram; many of them: Jack Nelson, *Terror in the Night: The Klan's Campaign Against the Jews* (New York: Simon & Schuster, 1993), p. 29; They tried to lift: testimony of former FBI agent Loren Brooks, 1998 Sam Bowers trial.

159 When agents searched: Testimony of retired FBI agents Loren Brooks and James Awe, 1998 Sam Bowers trial.

159 Moore and his agents: Author interview, Jim Ingram; put a rattlesnake: author

interview, Deke DeLoach, then deputy director for the FBI in Washington, D.C.

160 Eleven days: Fredric Dannen, "The G-Man and the Hit Man," *New Yorker*, December 16, 1996.

160 Scarpa shoved Byrd: Author interview, Chet Dillard, a prosecutor then in Jones County who talked to Byrd in the hospital. The White Knights believed the one who carried out Byrd's beating was Jack Watkins and wound up beating him.

160 On March 28: "A Byte Out of History: The Case of the 1966 KKK Firebombing," FBI.gov; Weeks after: Fredric Dannen, "The G-Man and the Hit Man," *New Yorker*, December 16, 1996.

160 insisted his confession: "Pitts puts finger on Sessum, other Klansmen," *Hattiesburg American*, March 14, 1968.

162 Less than a month: House Un-American Activities Committee hearing on Samuel H. Bowers Jr., February 1, 1966.

164 His more prominent grandfather: Mississippi Department of Archives and History interviews with Sam Bowers, 1983–1984.

164 About a decade: Charles Marsh, *God's Long Summer: Stories of Faith and Civil Rights* (Princeton, NJ: Princeton University Press, 1997), pp. 54–55; author interview, Charles Marsh.

168 a Bavarian man: Wilmer Watts Backstrom and Yvonne Bevins, "The Family Origins of Vernon F. Dahmer, Mississippi Civil Rights Activist," Renegade South, https://renegadesouth.wordpress.com/2009/12/06/the-family-origins -of-vernon-dahmer-civil-rights-activist/.

168 When a white mob: Ibid.

181 ruled that: *Travis Buckley v. State of Mississippi*, 223 So. 2d 524 (1969).

186 lynched three: Alex Heard, *Eyes of Willie Magee: A Tragedy of Race, Sex, and Secrets in the Jim Crow South* (New York: Harper Perennial, 2010), p. 40, also "Mississippi Mob Lynches a Slayer," *New York Times*, October 18, 1942; fourteen years old: "Negro Lynched in Mississippi," *Abilene Reporter-News,* October 18, 1942; p. 49; defense lawyer: "The Hattiesburg Acquittals," *St. Louis Post-Dispatch*, April 25, 1943, p. 18.

189 In the summer of 1964: "State of Siege," American RadioWorks, American Public Media, http://americanradioworks.publicradio.org/features/mississippi /e1.html.

189 Duke could afford: David M. Halbfinger, "Prison Term for David Duke," *New York Times*, March 13, 2003.

202 Back in 1967: "KKK'er Says His Comrades Wounded Him," *Delta Democrat-Times*, July 21, 1967.

210 Fannie Lou Hamer: Taylor Branch, *Pillar of Fire: America in the King Years 1963–1965* (New York: Simon & Schuster, 1998), p. 219.

PART IV

224 Before that: "Six Dead After Church Bombing," *Washington Post,* September 16, 1963; A police officer: Jon Reed, "Virgil Ware and Johnny Robinson: Families Want History to Remember Teen Boys, Too," al.com, September 14, 2013; A white teenager: Virgil Ware, biography.com; The officer: Johnny Robinson, biography.com.

225 agents to write: Howell Raines, "The Birmingham Bombing," *New York Times Magazine,* July 24, 1983.

228 Back in 1997: T. K. Thorne, *Last Chance for Justice: How Relentless Investigators Uncovered New Evidence Convicting the Birmingham Church Bombers* (N.p.: Chicago Review, 2018).

247 The shutdown stemmed: Dana Beyerle, "Moore Makes Cutbacks Official," *Tuscaloosa News,* April 20, 2002.

PART V

264 "When I walk": Author interview, Carolyn Dearman.

291 "nigger-Communist invasion": Don Whitehead, *Attack on Terror: The FBI Against the Ku Klux Klan in Mississippi* (New York: Funk & Wagnalls, 1970), pp. 4–6.

291 their first contact: Whitehead, *Attack on Terror,* pp. 7–8.

301 Mr. X: Maynard King was obviously Mr. X, but how did he find out where the bodies were buried? Retired *Neshoba Democrat* editor Stanley Dearman believed the one who informed King was reputed Klansman Pete Jordan (pronounced JER-dun) because Jordan was close with King. Retired FBI agent Joe Sullivan said then–FBI agent John Proctor dealt directly with the source who supplied the location of the dam where the trio were buried. Family members told me that Jordan became friends later with Proctor, but the family denied that Jordan told where the bodies were buried. I found no documents or other evidence that suggested either King or Jordan received any part of the $30,000 reward—a reward that agents began to promise suspects after the FBI already knew where the bodies were.

305 Joe Sullivan: The Rotary Club of New York website: http://nyrotaryhistory.org /Joe_Sullivan/Joe_Sullivan.html; Tom Clancy: "On the Case: Iron County," University of Wisconsin-Madison website, "All Ways Forward," https://www .allwaysforward.org/feature/thank-you-iron-county/.

307 November 8: David Stout, "Lawrence Rainey, 79, a Rights-Era Suspect," *The New York Times,* November 13, 2002, p. 10.

313 There is a complete: Liz Willen, "Next generation of activists confronts Mississippi's violent past on Freedom Summer anniversary," Hechinger Report, June 20, 2014.

317 Carolyn Goodman: Author interviews, Carolyn Goodman and David Goodman.

329 had already made: Howard Ball, *Justice in Mississippi: The Murder Trial of Edgar Ray Killen* (Lawrence: University Press of Kansas, 2006), p. 106.

330 The six-foot-three: Billy Watkins, "Judge for Killen Case Seen as Efficient, Organized, Respectful," *Clarion-Ledger*, June 13, 2005.

331 He urged them: Harriet Ryan, CourtTV, "Defense: Killen a 'Bystander' in the Klan," CNN, June 16, 2005.

335 red-faced Texas native: Ball, *Justice in Mississippi*, p. 139.

367 He announced: *Neshoba: The Price of Freedom*, a 2010 documentary by Micki Dickoff and Tony Pagano.

373 James McIntyre: Emily Wagster Pettus, Associated Press, "MDOC Commissioner Epps Says No Problems with Killen in Prison," July 8, 2005.

Selected Bibliography

Anderson, Devery S. *Emmett Till: The Murder That Shocked the World and Propelled the Civil Rights Movement*. Jackson: University Press of Mississippi, 2015.

Arsenault, Raymond. *Freedom Riders: 1961 and the Struggle for Racial Justice*. Oxford: Oxford University Press, 2011.

Asch, Chris Myers. *The Senator and the Sharecropper: The Freedom Struggles of James O. Eastland and Fannie Lou Hamer*. Chapel Hill: The University of North Carolina Press, 2008.

Ball, Howard. *Justice in Mississippi: The Murder Trial of Edgar Ray Killen*. Lawrence: University Press of Kansas, 2006.

Beito, David T., and Linda Royster Beito. *Black Maverick: T. R. M. Howard's Fight for Civil Rights and Economic Power*. Urbana: University of Illinois Press, 2009.

Branch, Taylor. *Parting the Waters: America in the King Years 1954–63*. New York: Simon & Schuster, 1988.

Branch, Taylor. *Pillar of Fire: America in the King Years 1963–65*. New York: Simon & Schuster, 1998.

Brooks, Maegan Parker. *A Voice That Could Stir an Army: Fannie Lou Hamer and the Rhetoric of the Black Freedom Movement*. Jackson: University Press of Mississippi, 2014.

Bullard, Sara, executive editor. "Free at Last: A History of the Civil Rights Movement and Those Who Died in the Struggle," *Teaching Tolerance* magazine, 1989.

Cagin, Seth, and Philip Dray. *We Are Not Afraid: The Story of Goodman, Schwerner, and Chaney and the Civil Rights Campaign of Mississippi*. New York: Macmillan Publishing Co., 1988.

Carson, Claiborne, and David J. Garrow, Gerald Gill, Vincent Harding, Darlene Clark Hine, editors. *The Eyes on the Prize Civil Rights Reader: Documents, Speeches, and Firsthand Accounts From the Black Freedom Struggle.* New York: Penguin, 1991.

Chalmers, David M. *Hooded Americanism: The History of the Ku Klux Klan.* New York: New Viewpoints, 1965.

Coates, James. *Armed and Dangerous: The Rise of the Survivalist Right.* New York: Hill and Wang, 1987.

Cobb, James C. *The Most Southern Place on Earth: The Mississippi Delta and the Roots of Regional Identity.* New York: Oxford University Press, 1992.

Dannen, Fredric. "The G-Man and the Hit Man," *The New Yorker,* December 16, 1996.

Dattel, Gene. *Cotton and Race in the Making of America: The Human Costs of Economic Power.* Lanham, Maryland: Ivan R. Dee, 2009.

DeLaughter, Bobby. *Never Too Late: A Prosecutor's Story of Justice in the Medgar Evers Case.* New York: Scribner, 2001.

Dittmer, John. *Local People: The Struggle for Civil Rights in Mississippi.* Urbana: University of Illinois Press, 1994.

Doyle, William. *An American Insurrection: The Battle of Oxford, Mississippi, 1962.* New York: Doubleday, 2001.

Eagles, Charles W. *The Price of Defiance: James Meredith and the Integration of Ole Miss.* Chapel Hill: The University of North Carolina Press, 2009.

Etheridge, Eric. *Breach of Peace: Portraits of the 1961 Mississippi Freedom Riders.* 2008.

Evers, Myrlie with William Peters. *For Us, the Living.* New York: Doubleday, 1967.

Farmer, James. *Lay Bare the Heart: An Autobiography of the Civil Rights Movement.* New York: Arbor House, 1985.

Garrow, David. *Bearing the Cross: Martin Luther King, Jr., and the Southern Christian Leadership Conference.* New York: Vintage Books, 1986.

Goudsouzian, Aram. *Down to the Crossroads: Civil Rights, Black Power, and the Meredith March Against Fear.* New York: Farrar, Straus and Giroux, 2014.

Halberstam, David. *The Children.* New York: Random House, 1998.

Hampton, Henry, and Steve Fayer. *Voices of Freedom: An Oral History of the Civil Rights Movement from the 1950s through the 1980s.* New York: Bantam, 1991.

Heard, Alex. *Eyes of Willie Magee: A Tragedy of Race, Sex, and Secrets in the Jim Crow South.* New York: Harper Perennial, 2010.

Hendrickson, Paul. *Sons of Mississippi: A Story of Race and Its Legacy.* New York: Knopf, 2003.

Hogan, Wesley C. *Many Minds, One Heart: SNCC's Dream for a New America.* Chapel Hill: The University of North Carolina Press, 2007.

Holsaert, Faith S., Martha Prescod Norman Noonan, Judy Richardson, Betty

Garman Robinson, Jean Smith Young and Dorothy M. Zellner. *Hands on the Freedom Plow: Personal Accounts by Women in SNCC*, Urbana: University of Illinois, 2010.

Houck, Davis, and Matthew A. Grindy. *Emmett Till and the Mississippi Press.* Jackson: University Press of Mississippi, 2008.

Huie, William Bradford. *Three Lives for Mississippi.* New York: WCC Books, 1965.

Johnston, Erle. *Mississippi's Defiant Years 1953–1973: An Interpretive Documentary with Personal Experiences.* Forest, MS: Lake Harbor Publishers, 1990.

Jones, Doug, with Greg Truman. *Bending Toward Justice: The Birmingham Church Bombing that Changed the Course of Civil Rights.* New York: St. Martin's Press, 2019.

Kotz, Nick. *Judgment Days: Lyndon Baines Johnson, Martin Luther King Jr. and the Laws That Changed America.* Boston: Houghton Mifflin Company, 2005.

Laslett, John H. M. *Sunshine Was Never Enough: Los Angeles Workers, 1880–2010.* Oakland: University of California Press, 2012.

Lewis, John with Michael D'Orso. *Walking with the Wind: A Memoir of the Movement.* Harvest: San Diego, 1998.

Loewen, James W., and Charles Sallis. *Mississippi: Conflict & Change.* New York: Pantheon Books, 1974.

Manis, Andrew M. *A Fire You Can't Put Out: The Civil Rights Life of Birmingham's Reverend Fred Shuttlesworth.* Tuscaloosa: University of Alabama Press, 1999.

Mars, Florence. *Witness in Philadelphia.* Baton Rouge: Louisiana State University Press, 1989.

Marsh, Charles. *God's Long Summer: Stories of Faith and Civil Rights.* Princeton, NJ: Princeton University Press, 1997.

Martin, Gordon A., Jr. *Count Them One by One: Black Mississippians Fighting for the Right to Vote.* Jackson: University Press of Mississippi, 2010.

Martinez, Elizabeth, editor. *Letters from Mississippi: Reports from Civil Rights Volunteers and Poetry of the 1964 Freedom Summer.* Brookline, Massachusetts: Zephyr Press, 2002.

Mason, Gilbert R., with James Patterson Smith. *Beaches, Blood, and Ballots: A Black Doctor's Civil Rights Struggle.* Jackson: University Press of Mississippi, 2000.

Massengill, Reed. *Portrait of a Racist: The Man Who Killed Medgar Evers?* New York: St. Martin's Press, 1994.

McWhorter, Diane. *Carry Me Home: Birmingham, Alabama, The Climactic Battle of the Civil Rights Revolution.* New York: Simon & Schuster, 2001.

Mills, Kay. *This Little Light of Mine: The Life of Fannie Lou Hamer.* New York: A Dutton Book, 1993.

Minor, Bill. *Eyes on Mississippi: A Fifty-Year Chronicle of Change.* Jackson, MS: J. Pritchard Morris Books, 2001.

Mitchell, Francis H. "Why I Live in Mississippi," *Ebony*, November 19, 1958.

Moody, Anne. *Coming of Age in Mississippi.* New York: Bantam Dell, 1968.

Nelson, Jack. *Terror in the Night: The Klan's Campaign Against the Jews.* New York: Simon & Schuster, 1993.

Nelson, Stanley. *Devils Walking: Klan Murders along the Mississippi in the 1960s.* Baton Rouge: Louisiana State University Press, 2016.

Newton, Michael. *The FBI and the KKK: A Critical History.* Jefferson, NC: McFarland & Company, Inc., 2009.

Newton, Michael. *The Ku Klux Klan in Mississippi: A History.* Jefferson, NC: McFarland & Company, Inc., 2010.

Newton, Michael. *Unsolved Civil Rights Murder Cases, 1934–1970.* Jefferson, NC: McFarland & Company, Inc., 2016.

Nossiter, Adam. *Of Long Memory: Mississippi and the Murder of Medgar Evers.* Reading, MA: Addison-Wesley Publishing Company, 1994.

Olson, Lynne. *Freedom's Daughters: The Unsung Heroines of the Civil Rights Movement From 1830 to 1970.* New York: Touchstone, 2001.

Payne, Charles. *I've Got the Light of Freedom: The Organizing Tradition and the Mississippi Freedom Struggle.* Berkeley: University of California, 1995.

Raines, Howell. "The Birmingham Bombing," *The New York Times Magazine,* July 24, 1983.

Ransby, Barbara. *Ella Baker and the Black Freedom Movement: A Radical Democratic Vision.* Chapel Hill: The University of North Carolina Press, 2003.

Ridgeway, James. *Blood in the Face: The Ku Klux Klan, Aryan Nations, Nazi Skinheads, and the Rise of a New White Culture.* New York: Thunder's Mouth Press, 1990.

Roberts, Gene, and Hank Klibanoff. *The Race Beat: The Press, the Civil Rights Struggle, and the Awakening of a Nation.* New York: Alfred A. Knopf, 2006.

Rolph, Stephanie R. *Resisting Equality: The Citizens' Council, 1954-1989.* Baton Rouge: Louisiana State University Press, 2018.

Silver, James W. *Mississippi: The Closed Society.* Jackson: University Press of Mississippi, 2012.

Tell, Dave. *Remembering Emmett Till.* Chicago: The University of Chicago Press, 2019.

Thorne, T. K. *Last Chance for Justice: How Relentless Investigators Uncovered New Evidence Convicting the Birmingham Church Bombers.* Chicago: Lawrence Hill Books, 2013.

Till-Mobley, Mamie, and Christopher Benson. *Death of Innocence: The Story of the Hate Crime That Changed America.* New York: Random House, 2003.

Vollers, Maryanne. *Ghosts of Mississippi: The Murder of Medgar Evers, the Trials of Byron De La Beckwith, and the Haunting of the New South.* Boston: Little, Brown and Company, 1995.

Watson, Bruce. *Freedom Summer: The Savage Season That Made Mississippi Burn and Made America a Democracy.* New York: Viking, 2010.

Whitehead, Don. *Attack on Terror: The FBI Against the Ku Klux Klan in Mississippi.* New York: Funk & Wagnalls, 1970.

Whitfield, Stephen. *A Death in the Delta: The Story of Emmett Till.* Baltimore: The Johns Hopkins University Press, 1991.

Wideman, John Edgar. *Writing to Save a Life: The Louis Till File.* New York: Scribner, 2016.

Wilkerson, Isabel. *The Warmth of Other Suns: The Epic Story of America's Great Migration.* New York: Vintage, 2010.

Williams, Michael Vinson. *Medgar Evers: Mississippi Martyr.* Fayetteville: The University of Arkansas Press, 2011.

Zeskind, Leonard. *Blood and Politics: The History of the White Nationalist Movement From the Margins to the Mainstream.* New York: Farrar, Straus & Giroux, 2009.

Index

About the Author

JERRY MITCHELL's stories of investigative reporting have helped put four Klansmen and a serial killer behind bars. His stories have also exposed injustices and corruption, prompting investigations, state reforms, and the firings of boards and officials. He is a Pulitzer Prize finalist, a longtime member of Investigative Reporters & Editors, and a winner of more than thirty other national awards, including a $500,000 MacArthur "genius" grant. His memoir for Simon & Schuster, *Race Against Time*, tells the story of his pursuit of unsolved murder cases from the Civil Rights Era, leading to convictions in some of the nation's most notorious murders. After working for three decades for the statewide *Clarion-Ledger*, he left in 2019 and founded the Mississippi Center for Investigative Reporting, a nonprofit that exposes corruption and injustices, investigates malfeasance, empowers citizens, and raises up the next generation of investigative reporters.